Series Authors

Rev. Richard N. Fragomeni, Ph.D.
Maureen Gallagher, Ph.D.
Jeannine Goggin, M.P.S.
Michael P. Horan, Ph.D.

Scripture Co-editor and Consultant

Maria Pascuzzi, SSL, S.T.D.

Resource Consultants

Janaan Manternach, D.Min.
Carl J. Pfeifer, D.Min.

The Committee has agreed that the following statement now applies in reference to these student texts: "The Ad Hoc Committee to Oversee the Use of the Catechism, United States Conference of Catholic Bishops, has found this catechetical text, copyright 2004, to be in conformity with the *Catechism of the Catholic Church.*"

SILVER BURDETT GINN RELIGION
A SCOTT FORESMAN IMPRINT
PARSIPPANY, NJ

Multicultural Consultant
Angela Erevia, M.C.D.P., M.R.E.

Contributing Writer
Janie Gustafson, Ph.D.

Contributing Authors
Catholic Schools in America: Robert Kealey, Ph.D.
Family Time: Steve and Kathy Beirne
Feasts and Seasons: Marianne Lenihan
Our Catholic Heritage: Pat Enright
Unit Organizers and Reviews: Joyce Crider
We Care: Richard Reichert, M.A.

Advisory Board
William C. Allegri, M.A., Patricia M. Feeley, S.S.J., M.A., Edmund F. Gordon, Patricia A. Hoffmann, Rev. Daniel Kelly, Cris V. Villapando, D.Min.

Consultants
Margaret J. Borders, M.R.S., Kelly O'Lague Dulka, M.S.W., Diane Hardick, M.A., Debra Schurko, Linda S. Tonelli, M.Ed., Joy Villotti-Biedrzycki

Music Advisors
GIA Publications: Michael A. Cymbala, Alec Harris, Robert W. Piercy

Nihil Obstat
M. Kathleen Flanagan, S.C., Ph.D.
Ellen Joyce, S.C., Ph.D.
Censors Librorum

Imprimatur
✠Most Reverend Frank J. Rodimer
Bishop of Paterson
February 5, 2003

The *nihil obstat* and *imprimatur* are official declarations that a book or pamphlet is free of doctrinal and moral error. No implication is contained therein that those who have granted the *nihil obstat* and *imprimatur* agree with the contents, opinions, or statements expressed.

Acknowledgments
Excerpts from *The New American Bible* © 1970 by the Confraternity of Christian Doctrine, Washington, DC, including the revised *New Testament* © 1986 by the Confraternity of Christian Doctrine, Washington, DC, used with permission. All rights reserved.

All adaptations of Scripture are based on *The New American Bible* © 1970 and 1986.

Excerpts from the English translation of the *Rite of Baptism for Children* © 1969, International Committee on English in the Liturgy, Inc. (ICEL); excerpts from the English translation of the *Rite of Penance* © 1974, ICEL; excerpts from the English translation of *Eucharistic Prayers for Masses with Children* © 1975, ICEL; excerpts from the English translation of *The Roman Missal*, Second Edition © 1985, ICEL. All rights reserved.

Music selections copyrighted and/or administered by GIA Publications are used with permission of GIA Publications, Inc., 7404 So. Mason Avenue, Chicago, IL 60638-9927. Please refer to songs for specific copyright dates and information.

"Thumb Prayer" adapted from *Catechist* magazine. © Page McKean Zyromski, Contributing Editor.

In Appreciation: Blessed Kateri Church, Sparta, NJ; Blessed Sacrament Church, Newark, NJ; Church of the Assumption, Morristown, NJ; Our Lady of Mercy Church, Whippany, NJ; Our Lady of the Lake Church, Sparta, NJ; St. Ann's Church, Parsippany, NJ; St. Joseph's Church, Croton Falls, NY; St. Patrick's Church, Chatham, NJ; St. Peter the Apostle Church, Parsippany, NJ; St. Thomas More Church, Convent Station, NJ; OCP Publications, Portland, OR; GIA Publications, Inc., Chicago, IL; WLP Publications, Schiller Park, IL; Craig Baker, www.schooluniforms.com

ISBN 0-382-36501-1

5 6 7 8 9 10 – V003 – 11 10 09 08 07 06

Our Commitment Prayer

Name ______________________

Leader: God, our Creator, you take good care of everything that you have made.

All: **We will help care for the gifts of creation.**

Leader: God, our Father, the stories in the Bible tell us about Jesus' life and teachings.

All: **We will listen carefully to your holy word.**

Leader: Merciful God, you are always ready to forgive us. Your love for us is everlasting.

All: **We will be sorry when we choose to do wrong. We will ask for your forgiveness.**

Leader: Loving God, you sent your Son, Jesus, into the world to be our Savior.

All: **We will remember Jesus' life, death, and Resurrection each time we celebrate the Eucharist.**

Leader: God, you sent the Holy Spirit to help and guide the members of the Catholic Church.

All: **We will ask the Holy Spirit for the gifts we need to serve others.**

CONTENTS

UNIT 4 We Celebrate the Gift of Eucharist

UNIT 5 We Go in Peace

FEASTS AND SEASONS

OUR CATHOLIC HERITAGE

CELEBRATING CATHOLIC SCHOOLS

Blest Are We

2. For the poor, the meek and the lowly:
We are called, called to serve!
For the weak, the sick and the hungry:
We are called, called to serve!

3. For all those who yearn for freedom:
We are called, called to serve!
For the world, to be God's kingdom:
We are called, called to serve!

2. Por los pobres, los mansos y humildes:
¡Somos llamados para servir!
Por los enfermos, hambrientos, y débiles:
¡Somos llamados para servir!

3. Por los que sufren y quieren ser librados:
¡Somos llamados para servir!
Venga a nosotros el Reino de los Cielos:
¡Somos llamados para servir!

LET US PRAY

Sign of the Cross

In the name of the Father,
and of the Son,
and of the Holy Spirit.
Amen.

The Lord's Prayer

Our Father,
who art in heaven,
hallowed be thy name;
thy kingdom come;
thy will be done on earth
as it is in heaven.
Give us this day
our daily bread;
and forgive us
our trespasses
as we forgive those
who trespass against us;
and lead us not
into temptation,
but deliver us from evil.
Amen.

Hail Mary

Hail Mary, full of grace,
the Lord is with you.
Blessed are you among women,
and blessed is the fruit of your womb, Jesus.
Holy Mary, Mother of God,
pray for us sinners,
now, and at the hour of our death.
Amen.

Glory Be to the Father

Glory be to the Father,
and to the Son,
and to the Holy Spirit.
As it was in the beginning, is now,
and will be forever.
Amen.

Nicene Creed

We believe in one God,
the Father, the Almighty,
maker of heaven and earth,
of all that is seen and unseen.

We believe in one Lord, Jesus Christ,
the only Son of God,
eternally begotten of the Father,
God from God, Light from Light,
true God from true God,
begotten, not made, one in Being with the Father.
Through him all things were made.
For us men and for our salvation
he came down from heaven:

by the power of the Holy Spirit
he was born of the Virgin Mary,
and became man.

For our sake he was crucified under Pontius Pilate;
he suffered, died, and was buried.
On the third day he rose again
in fulfillment of the Scriptures;
he ascended into heaven
and is seated at the right hand of the Father.

He will come again in glory to judge
the living and the dead,
and his kingdom will have no end.

We believe in the Holy Spirit, the Lord, the giver of life,
who proceeds from the Father and the Son.
With the Father and the Son he is worshiped and glorified.
He has spoken through the Prophets.
We believe in one holy catholic and apostolic Church.
We acknowledge one baptism for the forgiveness of sins.
We look for the resurrection of the dead,
and the life of the world to come.

Amen.

Prayer to the Holy Spirit

Come, Holy Spirit,
fill the hearts of your faithful
and kindle in them
the fire of your love.
Send forth your Spirit,
and they shall be created;
and you will renew
the face of the earth.
Amen.

Morning Prayer

Loving God, bless the work we do.
Watch over us and guide us in
school and at home.
Help us realize that everything
we do gives praise to you.
We make this prayer in
Jesus' name.
Amen.

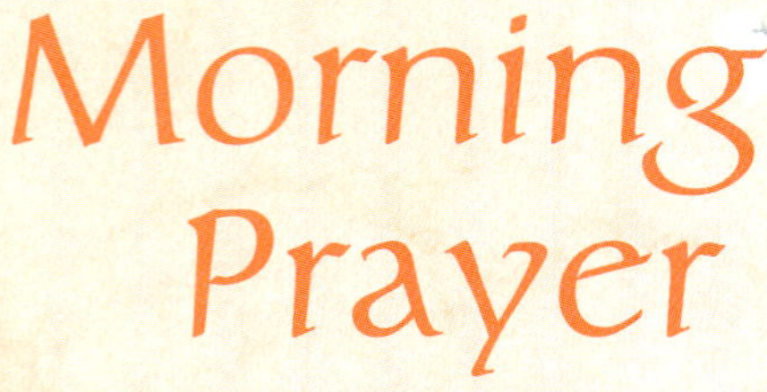

Evening Prayer

Parent:	May God bless you and keep you.
Child:	May he guide you in life.
Parent:	May he bless you this evening.
Child:	And keep us in his sight.
Parent:	May God be with you, (name).
Child:	And also with you.
Together:	In the name of the Father, and of the Son, and of the Holy Spirit. Amen.

Grace Before Meals

Bless us, O Lord, and these your gifts,
which we are about to receive
from your goodness,
through Christ our Lord.
Amen.

Grace After Meals

We give you thanks for all your gifts,
almighty God,
living and reigning
now and forever.
Amen.

Prayer to My Guardian Angel

Angel of God, my guardian dear,
to whom God's love commits me here.
Ever this day be at my side
to light and guard, to rule and guide.
Amen.

Prayer in Troubled Times

Lord,
protect your people always,
that they may be free from every evil
and serve you with all their hearts.
We ask this through Christ our Lord.
Amen.

UNIT 1

We Gather as Believers

Our parish church community comes together each week. We give praise and thanks to God and we celebrate our faith.

It is good to give thanks to the LORD,
to sing praise to your name, Most High.

Psalm 92:2

King David gave thanks to God through joyful song. We gather in church to sing our praise and thanks to God.

You Have Put On Christ

Music by Howard Hughes

1 Our Church Welcomes Us

O God, you have brought us here together. We give you thanks and praise.

Based on Eucharistic Prayer for Masses with Children I

Share

A community is a place where people make you feel welcome.

In a family community, people share life and love.

In a neighborhood, people live near each other.

In a classroom, people learn together.

What communities make you feel welcome?

1. I belong to the Tarian family.
2. I belong to O.L.M. Parish.

How is the Catholic Church a community?

A Warm Welcome

One day, Jesus met a man who collected taxes. His name was Levi. Jesus asked, "Levi, will you follow me?"

"Of course I will," Levi answered. He was happy to become a follower of Jesus.

That night, Levi invited Jesus and his friends to his home. Jesus was the guest of honor. Levi made Jesus and his friends feel very welcome!

Based on Luke 5:27–29

God's People

Levi invited Jesus and his friends to dinner. Levi made his guests feel very welcome. Our Church invites us to celebrate a special meal, too. Our church community welcomes us. The special meal we celebrate is the Mass. It celebrates God's love for us. We are God's People.

Activity Color the word. As you color, think about ways to make people feel welcome.

What is another way to describe God's People?

What God's People Are Like

One day Saint Paul explained what the Church is like. "Our Church community is like the human body," he said. "It is one, but it has many parts. God placed the parts, each of them, in the body."

Saint Paul explained that each part of the human body is important. The parts of the body need each other.

"So it is with the Church," Saint Paul continued.

The parts of the Church need each other. That is why the Church welcomes everyone.

Based on 1 Corinthians 12

Our Church Teaches

We call the Church the **Body of Christ**. A body has many parts. Jesus Christ is the head of the Body. We are the eyes, ears, arms, legs, hands, and feet. The body needs all its parts. The Church needs all its people.

Activity Circle the members of the Body of Christ. Complete the sentence.

I am part of the ____________________

______________________________________.

We Believe

We are God's People. With Christ as our head, we are the Church, the Body of Christ.

Faith Words

Body of Christ
The Catholic Church is the Body of Christ.

How do church members act?

Respond

Welcome, Neighbors!

Tommy and his family came to the United States to escape a war in their country. Soldiers had put them out of their home.

Father Louis and the people of St. John's parish decided to help. Father Louis let the family live in a house owned by the Church. Some families brought food and clothes. Others brought books and toys. A teacher in the parish is teaching Tommy's family to speak English. Father Louis helped Tommy's dad find a job.

? How do the people of St. John's parish show that they are God's People?

Activities

1. In the box, draw a picture of people who are caring for others.

2. Talk about ways to make other people feel welcome.

How can we celebrate being God's People?

Prayer Celebration

We Are God's People

We celebrate being God's People by praying together.

We welcome others by holding hands.

Leader: Sing with joy to God!
Be glad to serve the Lord.

All: **We are God's People.**

Leader: God made us.
He calls us together as one Church.

All: **We are God's People.**

Leader: Give thanks to God,
who is always good.
Be joyful, for his kindness
lasts forever.

All: **We are God's People,**
the Body of Christ.

Based on Psalm 100

2 We Belong to the Church

We are children of the light.
We are children of the day.

Based on 1 Thessalonians 5:5

Share

People have many ways to show they belong to a certain group.

Look at these pictures.
Match each sign of belonging with its group.
Then tell about a sign of belonging that you have.

SIGN

GROUP

CHOIR

LIBRARY READING CLUB

What signs of belonging do church members have?

Hear & Believe

The Sacraments

There are three sacraments of belonging. In **Baptism** we become new members of the Church. In **Confirmation** we receive strength to follow Jesus. In **Eucharist** we share a special meal with Jesus.

The Church uses many signs to celebrate Baptism.

1. The priest or deacon pours blessed water over the child or places the child in water. At the same time he says, "I baptize you in the name of the Father, and of the Son, and of the Holy Spirit."

2. The priest or deacon makes the Sign of the Cross on the child's forehead. He does this with blessed oil.

3. Next, the child receives white clothes. The priest or deacon says, "You have become new. You have put on Christ."

4. Then the child's godparents receive a lighted candle. The priest or deacon says, "Receive the light of Christ."

Faith Words

sacraments of initiation
There are three sacraments of initiation. In Baptism we become members of the Church. In Confirmation we receive strength to follow Jesus. In Eucharist we share a special meal with Jesus.

Signs of God's Love

A **sacrament** is a special celebration of the Church. The sacraments are signs that God is here with us now.

The three **sacraments of belonging, or initiation**, celebrate our new life with Jesus in the Church.

Activity What are the signs of Baptism? Write them here.

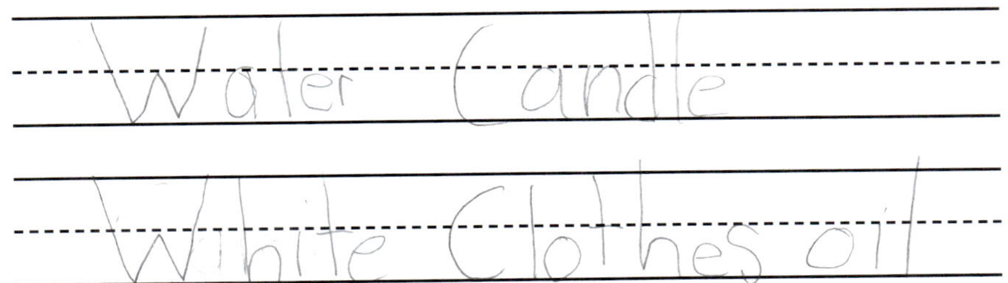

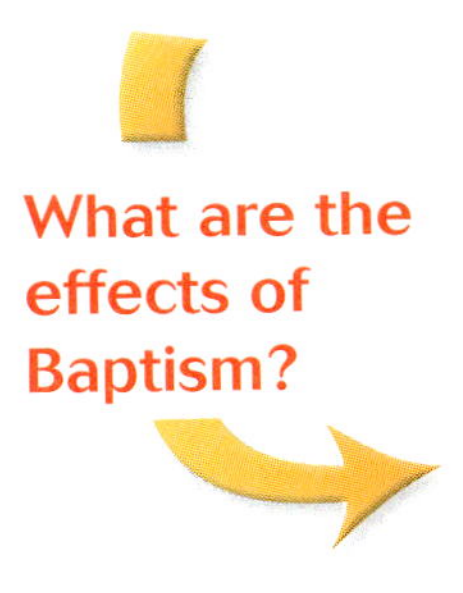

Hear & Believe

Children of God

One day a Roman soldier named Cornelius asked the Apostle Peter to tell him about Jesus. Because Cornelius was not Jewish, he had not heard the stories in the Bible. He did not know about God's wonderful creation. He had not heard how people first disobeyed God.

Peter taught Cornelius and his family about God's love and forgiveness. Jesus had come to save us from the original sin of disobedience. Jesus had come to save us from all sinfulness.

After Peter spoke, Cornelius asked to be baptized. That day he and his whole family became members of the Church. Peter said, "I see that God calls all people to be his children."

Based on Acts 10:1–49

Our Church Teaches

Soon after God created people, they sinned by disobeying God. This first sin is called **original sin**. Because we are born with original sin, it is harder for us to do what is right. Baptism takes away original sin and all other sins.

Through the sacrament of Baptism, we are filled with the Holy Spirit. We enter into new life in Jesus Christ. We are the children of God. We are members of the Church.

We Believe

Through the sacraments of initiation, God calls us to think and act as Jesus did.

Activity At Baptism, God calls us by name. Write on the candle the name you received at Baptism.

How can we show others we belong to the Church?

Respond

Bringing Light to Others

"What a great day!" thought Rita. "The new twins in our family, Samuel and Joshua, were baptized today. Someday, I will tell them all about the ceremony. I'll tell them about the beautiful Easter candle. It reminds us that Jesus is the Light of the World.

"I will tell them that their godfather, Uncle Al, lit two small candles from the Easter candle. The small candles remind us to keep the light of Jesus alive inside us. They remind us to bring Christ's light to others by our words and actions.

"Sam and Josh are already bringing light into my life!"

Activity

How can you bring God's light to others?
Draw or write your answer here.

How can we celebrate that we are God's children?

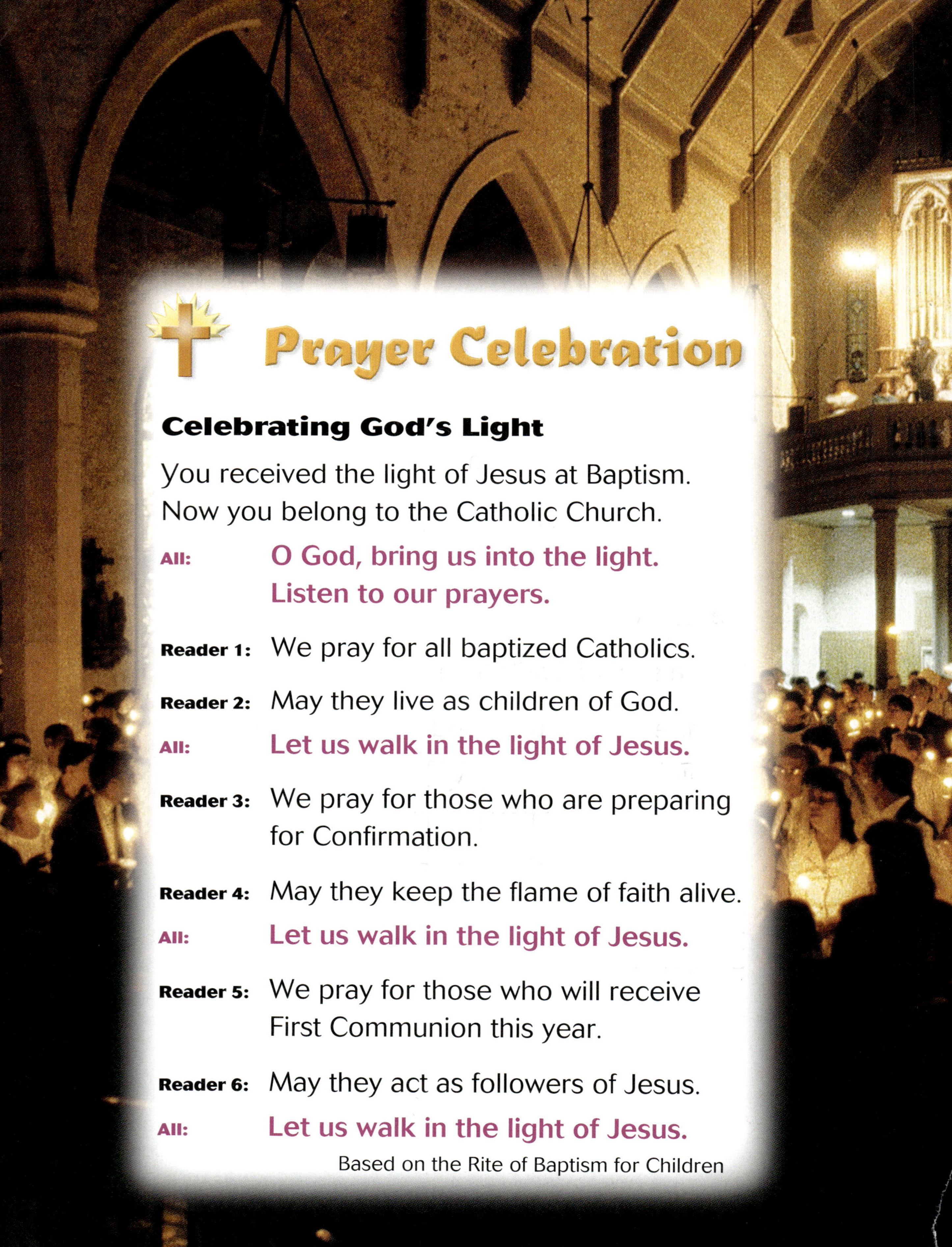

Prayer Celebration

Celebrating God's Light

You received the light of Jesus at Baptism. Now you belong to the Catholic Church.

All: **O God, bring us into the light. Listen to our prayers.**

Reader 1: We pray for all baptized Catholics.

Reader 2: May they live as children of God.

All: **Let us walk in the light of Jesus.**

Reader 3: We pray for those who are preparing for Confirmation.

Reader 4: May they keep the flame of faith alive.

All: **Let us walk in the light of Jesus.**

Reader 5: We pray for those who will receive First Communion this year.

Reader 6: May they act as followers of Jesus.

All: **Let us walk in the light of Jesus.**

Based on the Rite of Baptism for Children

3 Our Church Shows Us How to Live

Love one another. Then everyone will know that you are my followers.

Based on John 13:35

Share

Some people are heroes. They help others. They show us how to live.

Find the heroes in these pictures. Draw circles around them.

Who is your favorite real-life hero? Why?

Who are the Church's heroes?

Hear & Believe

The Real Hero

One day, Jesus told a story about a hero.

A man was traveling by himself. Robbers attacked him. They beat him and took his money. He was left lying in the road, badly hurt.

Soon a priest came by. He saw the man, but he just kept going.

Next, a man who worked in the Temple came along. He also passed by without helping.

Then, a third man came by, riding a donkey. He was from the country of Samaria. When he saw the hurt man on the road, he stopped at once. He washed the man's wounds and bandaged them. Then the man from Samaria put the hurt man on the donkey. He took him to an inn. There he paid the innkeeper to care for the man.

Based on Luke 10:29–35

Heroes of Our Church

The Church has many heroes who are like the good man from Samaria. The Church has Mary, the mother of Jesus, and the **saints**. From these church heroes we learn how to be **holy**. We learn how to be good followers of Jesus.

Activity Who is your favorite saint?

____

How does this saint help you to follow Jesus?

Faith Words

saint
A saint is a person who shows great love for other people and for God.

holy
To be holy means to be like God. Holy people act like Jesus.

How do we become good and holy?

Hear & Believe

The Rich Young Man

One day a rich young man asked Jesus, "Good teacher, what must I do to follow you?"

Jesus answered, "Live a good and holy life. Obey God's laws. Do not kill. Do not steal. Do not lie or cheat. Honor your father and your mother."

"I have done all this," the young man said. "What more do I need to do?"

Jesus looked with love at the man. "Go, sell what you have. Give the money to the poor. Then come, follow me."

The young man became sad. He did not want to do this. So he walked away and did not follow Jesus.

Based on Mark 10:17–22

Our Church Teaches

All people are made to be like God. Through Baptism we are called to live good and holy lives. We become good and holy by following the example of Jesus, Mary, and the saints.

Activity Look at the footprints. Color the footprints that contain good and holy actions. Place an X over those that are not good and holy actions.

> **We Believe**
>
> We grow in holiness by living in love. We grow in love for God and others through constant practice.

What other good and holy actions can you do?

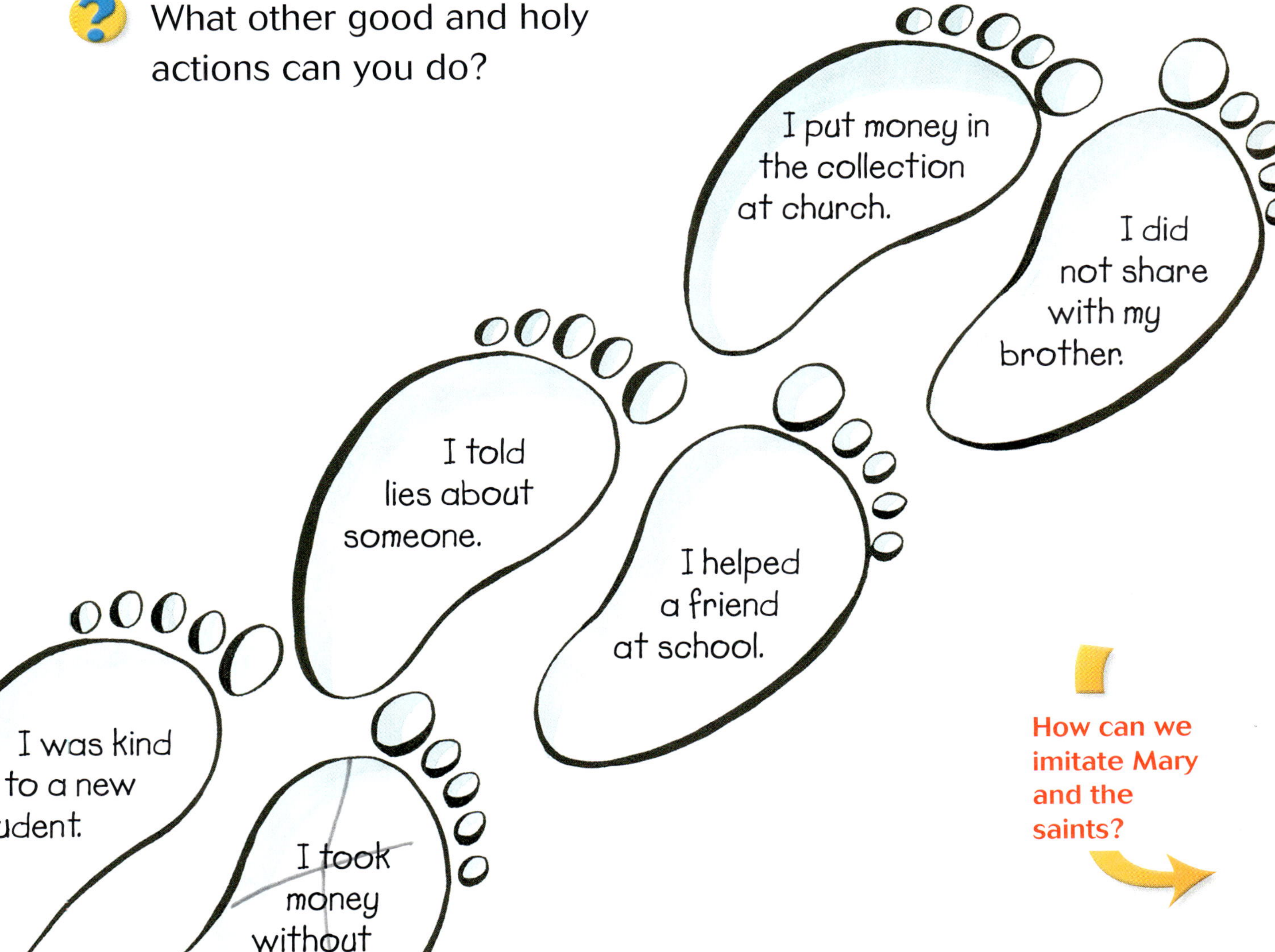

How can we imitate Mary and the saints?

Respond

Mary and the Saints

Mary and the saints teach us how to live as Christians.

Mary is the greatest saint of all. She was a good mother to Jesus. She teaches us to trust God and to care for others.

Saint Peter Claver cared for people nobody else cared about. He teaches us to reach out in love to everyone in need.

Saint Brigid sold her belongings and gave the money to poor people. She teaches us to share our blessings with others.

Saint Jerome loved to teach people how to read and understand the Bible. He teaches us to share the word of God with others.

The Church has many heroes like this.
They all teach us how to love God and follow Jesus.

Which saint is your favorite?
How can you follow this saint's example?

Activity

Draw a picture of someone you know who is a hero. Or draw a picture of yourself acting in a good and holy way.

What makes this person a real-life hero?

How can we ask holy people to pray for us?

Prayer Celebration

Litany of Saints and Heroes

A litany is a prayer that is said aloud.
A leader names different saints or other holy people.
After each name we ask the saint or person to pray for us.

Leader:	**All:**
Holy Mary, Mother of God,	**pray for us.**
Saint Peter Claver,	**pray for us.**
Saint Brigid,	**pray for us.**
Saint Jerome,	**pray for us.**
All who help the poor and the hungry,	**pray for us.**
All who care for the weak and the sick,	**pray for us.**
All holy men and women,	**pray for us.**

All: **Heavenly God, may we follow the example of your saints and other holy people. May we always try to help people in need. Amen.**

4 We Praise and thank God

Sing to the LORD a new song.

Psalm 149:1

Share

Celebrations are important times.
People come together to give thanks.
They say "thank you" for special people or gifts.

On the Fourth of July, we give thanks for freedom.

On birthdays we give thanks for life.

On Thanksgiving we give thanks for all our blessings.

On Christmas we give thanks for the birth of Jesus.

1. Write the name of a celebration you enjoyed.

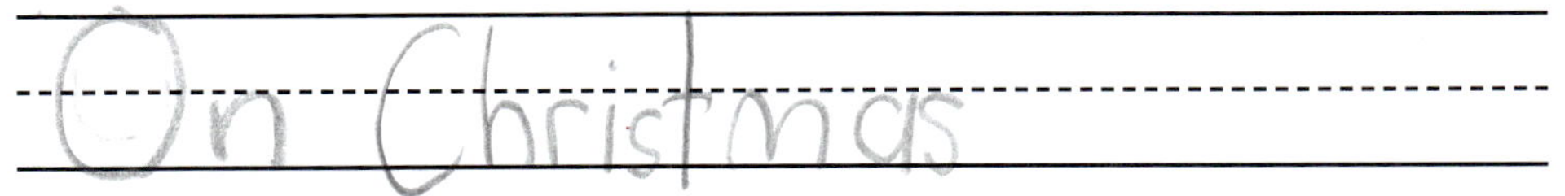

2. Write why you gave thanks.

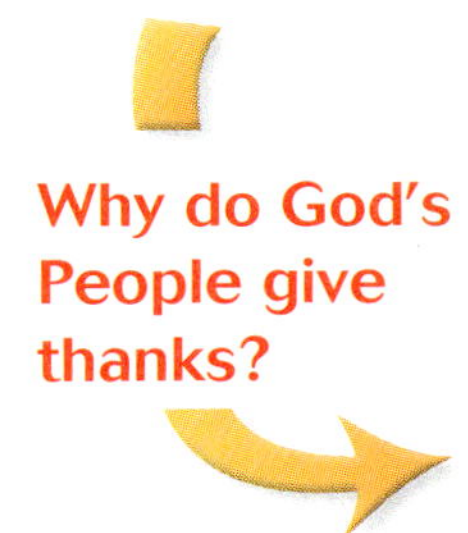

Hear & Believe

King David Gives Thanks

King David loved God. He liked to lead people in prayer. David especially liked to play the harp and sing. He sang about God's goodness. He thanked God for giving the people many gifts.

One day the priests carried into David's city the ark that held God's laws. David greeted the ark with joyful dancing. He ordered the musicians to play on their harps, lyres, and cymbals. Then David sang out,

"How good it is to give God thanks and glory!
I sing praise to your name, Most High.
Every morning you are kind to me.
You are with me all day and all night.
Your goodness fills me with gladness.
I rejoice because of the gifts you give me."

Based on 1 Chronicles 15 and Psalm 92:1–5

We Give Praise and Thanks

At Mass our parish community celebrates in prayer and in song. We **praise** God for his goodness. We also give God thanks.

Activity Use your own words to praise God.

____

____

____

Faith Words

praise

Praise is a joyful type of prayer. It celebrates God's goodness.

What is prayer?

Hear & Believe

The Songs of David

King David wrote many song-prayers called psalms. A psalm of praise is happy and joyful. David rejoices because God is good, kind, and loving.

Praise the Lord from the heavens;
Praise him all you angels.
Praise the Lord from the earth,
You mountains and all hills.

Based on Psalm 148:1–9

A psalm of thanks shows gratitude for something God has done.

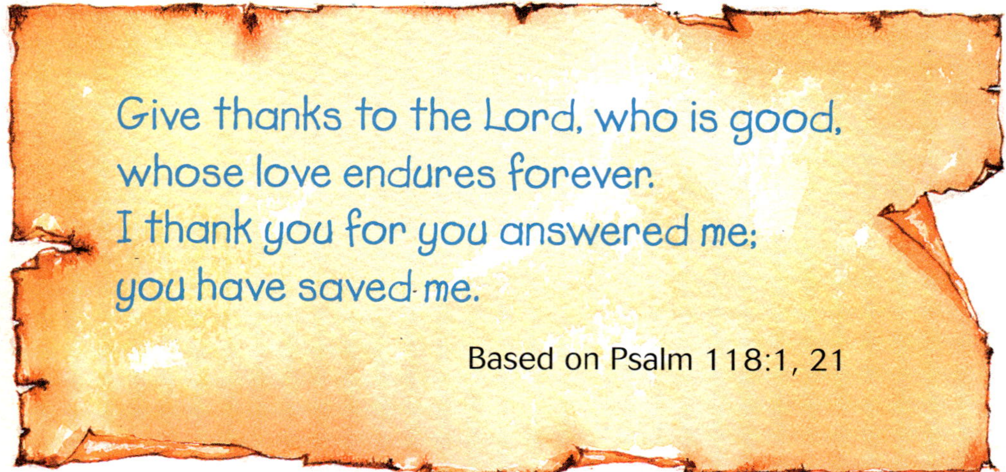

Give thanks to the Lord, who is good,
whose love endures forever.
I thank you for you answered me;
you have saved me.

Based on Psalm 118:1, 21

We can praise and thank God by singing the psalms of David.

Our Church Teaches

Prayer is talking to and listening to God. There are different types of prayer. Some prayers praise God. Some prayers give him thanks. We can pray silently or out loud. We can pray alone or with others. We can pray with words and with holy music.

Activity Think of something you are thankful for that begins with each letter in the word prayer. Write the words on the lines. The first one has been done for you.

Parents

Rabbit

Apple

Yellow

Eat

Red

We Believe

Singing and listening to holy music is one way to pray. The holy music helps us give thanks and praise to God.

Faith Words

prayer

Prayer is talking to and listening to God.

How can we praise and thank God?

Respond

Glory to God

In the first part of the Mass, we usually sing "Glory to God." This special song is called the Gloria. It is a prayer of praise and thanks. This is how it begins.

> Glory to God in the highest,
> and peace to his people on earth.
>
> Lord God, heavenly King,
> almighty God and Father,
>   we worship you, we give you thanks,
>   we praise you for your glory.
>
> The Order of Mass

Activities

1. Write your own prayer of thanks.

O God, I thank you for

loveing.

2. Write your own prayer of praise.

O God, I praise you for being

Being kind and forgiving.

You will use these prayers in the Prayer Celebration.

How can we praise and thank God with song?

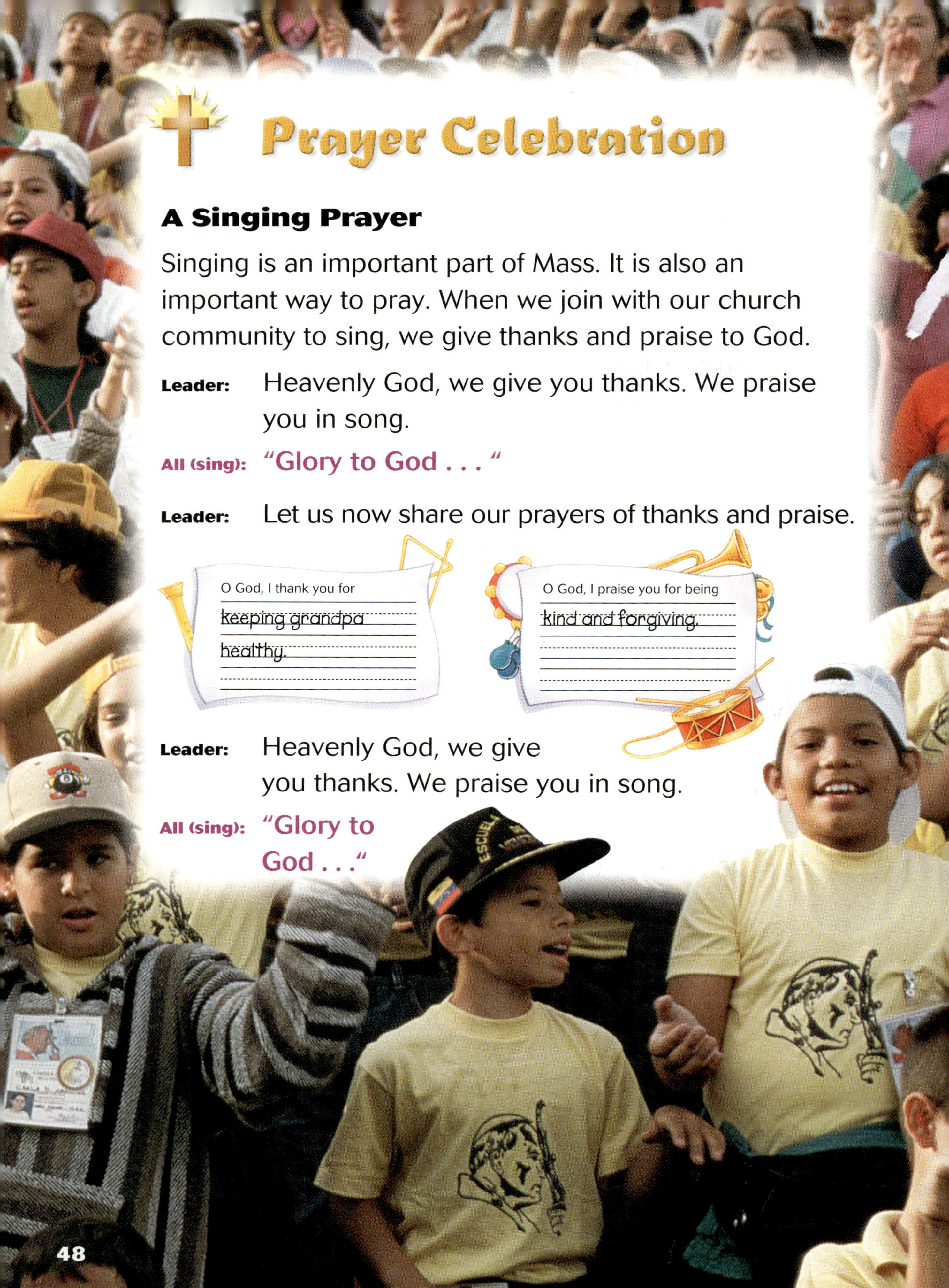

Prayer Celebration

A Singing Prayer

Singing is an important part of Mass. It is also an important way to pray. When we join with our church community to sing, we give thanks and praise to God.

Leader: Heavenly God, we give you thanks. We praise you in song.

All (sing): "Glory to God . . . "

Leader: Let us now share our prayers of thanks and praise.

O God, I thank you for keeping grandpa healthy.

O God, I praise you for being kind and forgiving.

Leader: Heavenly God, we give you thanks. We praise you in song.

All (sing): "Glory to God . . ."

The Gift

Zack thought, "My godmother's birthday is coming. I want to buy her a present, but I don't have any money."

Then Zack remembered what he learned in art class. He could make a pretty picture frame! So he asked his Mom for a photograph from the family album.

Then Zack drew a picture. It showed him with his godmother on the day he was baptized. Then he glued colored toothpicks into the shapes of four candles, one for each corner of the picture frame.

When Zack gave the picture to his godmother, he was proud. He said, "This gift did not cost any money. I made it for you myself."

"Great!" said Zack's godmother. "Money couldn't buy anything as wonderful as this. Thanks, Zack."

Sometimes the best gifts don't cost money. Why?

Think About It

Zack used something he had learned to make a gift. Read about learning and sharing below. Color the box blue if you agree. If you do not agree, color the box red.

Learning new things	Sharing what you learned
☐ **always costs money**	☐ **is not a good idea**
☐ **challenges you to make discoveries**	☐ **helps others to grow**

Learn About It

Saints are good and holy people. They use the things they have learned to help others. We follow their example when we share the things we learn.

Do Something About It

Maybe you have learned to do something special. Or you could start to learn something now.

Use a ✔ to show things you can already do.

- ☐ **give someone a big smile**
- ☐ **teach someone to play a game**
- ☐ **make a gift for someone**

Use a ✔ to show things you want to learn to do.

- ☐ **teach a pet to do tricks**
- ☐ **take photographs**
- ☐ **play a musical instrument**

UNIT 2

We Ask God's Forgiveness

God is always ready to forgive us when we sin. God calls us to be sorry for the wrongs we have done. He wants us to forgive others who have wronged us.

Rejoice with me because I have found my lost sheep.

Luke 15:6

God is like a shepherd who is happy to find his lost sheep. God rejoices when we are sorry for our sins.

Psalm 51: Be Merciful, O Lord

Psalm 51

Music by Marty Haugen

VERSE

1. Have mercy on me, God, in your kindness,
   in your compassion, blot out my offense.
   O wash me more and more from my guilt and my sorrow,
   and cleanse me from all of my sin.
   Refrain

2. My offenses, truly I know them,
   and my sins are always before me;
   against you alone have I sinned, O Lord,
   what is evil in your sight I have done.
   Refrain

3. Create in me a clean heart, O God,
   put your steadfast spirit in my soul.
   Cast me not away from your presence, O Lord,
   and take not your spirit from me.
   Refrain

4. Give back to me the joy of your salvation,
   let your willing spirit bear me up
   and I shall teach your way to the ones who have wandered,
   and bring them all home to your side.
   Refrain

5 We Can Choose What Is Good

Love the LORD, your God, and obey his word.

Based on Deuteronomy 30:20

Share

We make many choices every day. Some choices are easy, but some are hard. Some are right, but others are wrong.

Draw a happy face for each good choice below. Draw a sad face for each bad choice.

1. Tom does not share with his friends.

2. Juanita tells her dad the truth.

3. Wes obeys his mom and turns off the TV.

4. Mary takes a dollar that is not hers.

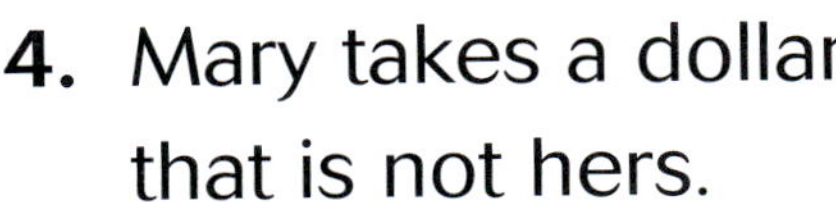

How do we know what is right and wrong?

Hear & Believe

The Forgiving Father

Once there was a man who had two sons. The younger son said, "I know you plan to give me money when I am older. May I have it now?" So his father gave him the money.

The boy moved far away. In no time at all, he had spent every cent! He was hungry and had no place to live. He wanted to go home.

The boy was sorry for the wrong choices he had made. He had wasted the money and hurt his father. The boy decided to ask his father to take him back.

While the boy was still far off from home, his father saw him and ran to greet him. "I'm sorry," the boy said, but his father had already forgiven him. The man hugged his son and gave him new clothes. Then he gave the boy a big "welcome home" party.

Based on Luke 15:11–24

Knowing Right from Wrong

The boy in the story knew he had done wrong. His **conscience** told him so. God gave everybody a conscience. Our conscience tells us the difference between what is right and wrong.

Faith Words

conscience

Our conscience helps us know right from wrong.

Activity What is right? What is wrong? Circle the correct word. Be able to explain why each action is right or wrong.

Jose hits a boy he does not like.	right	wrong
At the store, Linda takes a toy without paying.	right	wrong
Tyler helps his mother set the table.	right	wrong
Anne reads to her younger brother.	right	wrong

What can you do if you make a wrong choice?

Hear & Believe

Saul Changes His Life

Saul did not like the followers of Jesus. Saul made life hard for them. He arrested Jesus' followers and put them into prison.

One day, Saul heard the Risen Jesus' voice. "Why are you hurting me?" Jesus asked. Saul's conscience began to bother him. He saw that he was acting wrongly. He felt very sorry for harming the followers of Jesus.

"What should I do now?" Saul asked. "Start over," Jesus told him. "Stop acting in bad ways. Make good choices for your life."

On that day Saul decided to change his life. He even changed his name to Paul. Instead of hurting people, he helped them. He was baptized and became a good follower of Jesus. He began to tell everyone about Jesus Christ.

Based on Acts 9:1–20

Our Church Teaches

We **sin** when we freely choose to do bad things. When we sin, we hurt our friendship with God and with other people. God wants us to be sorry for our sins. God loves us very much, and he is always ready to forgive us.

Activity Complete the sentences using these words.

conscience	sin	free choice	good

Saul made a free choice to hurt the followers of Jesus.

Saul's conscience told him he had done wrong.

A sin is a wrong choice that hurts our friendship with God and other people.

God wants us to choose good and stay away from evil.

We Believe

God wants us to choose good and stay away from evil. But God lets us decide what to do. We call this **free choice**.

Faith Words

sin

We sin when we choose to hurt others and turn away from God.

How can we practice making good choices?

Respond

Making Good Choices

Mrs. Rabbit said, "Peter, you and your sisters may play outdoors. But stay away from Mr. McGregor's garden!"

Peter's sisters obeyed their mother, but Peter made a bad choice. He went into the garden and ate a lot of vegetables. Then Mr. McGregor saw Peter and began to chase him. Peter ran home as fast as he could.

Peter felt sick from eating so much. So Mrs. Rabbit gave him a hot drink and put him to bed. He missed having a nice supper with his mom and his sisters.

? What bad choice did Peter make?

Activity

We can practice making good choices every day. Unscramble the letters to complete the sentence for each picture.

t h g i f

Joey chooses not to

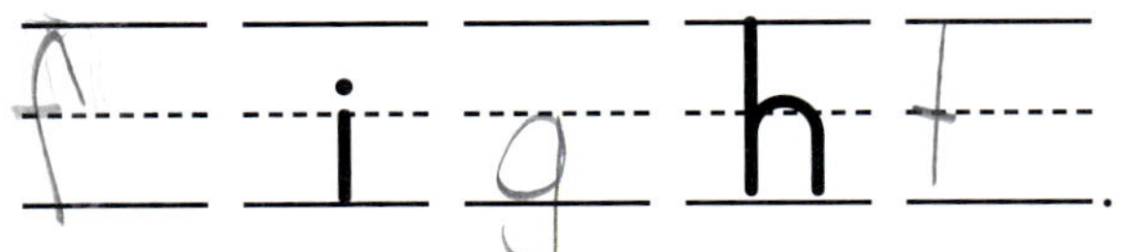

r h a s e

Tonya is happy to

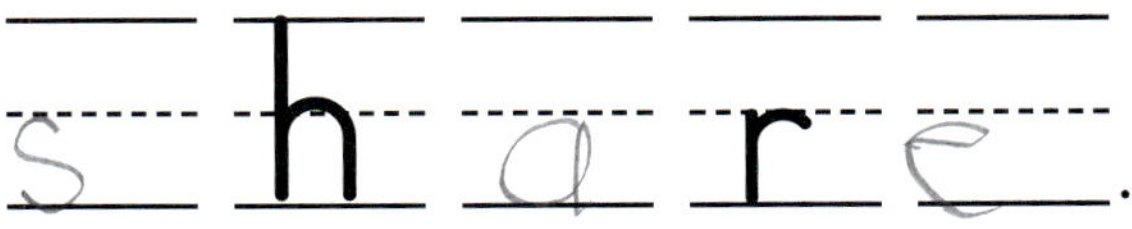

t r t u h

Lily decides to tell the

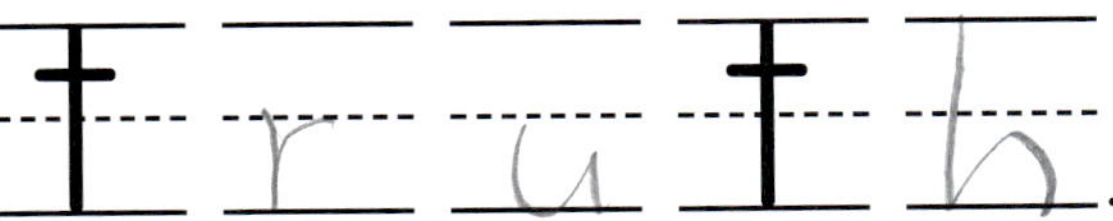

Talk about making good choices. When is it hard to make a good choice?

How can we celebrate the gift of free choice?

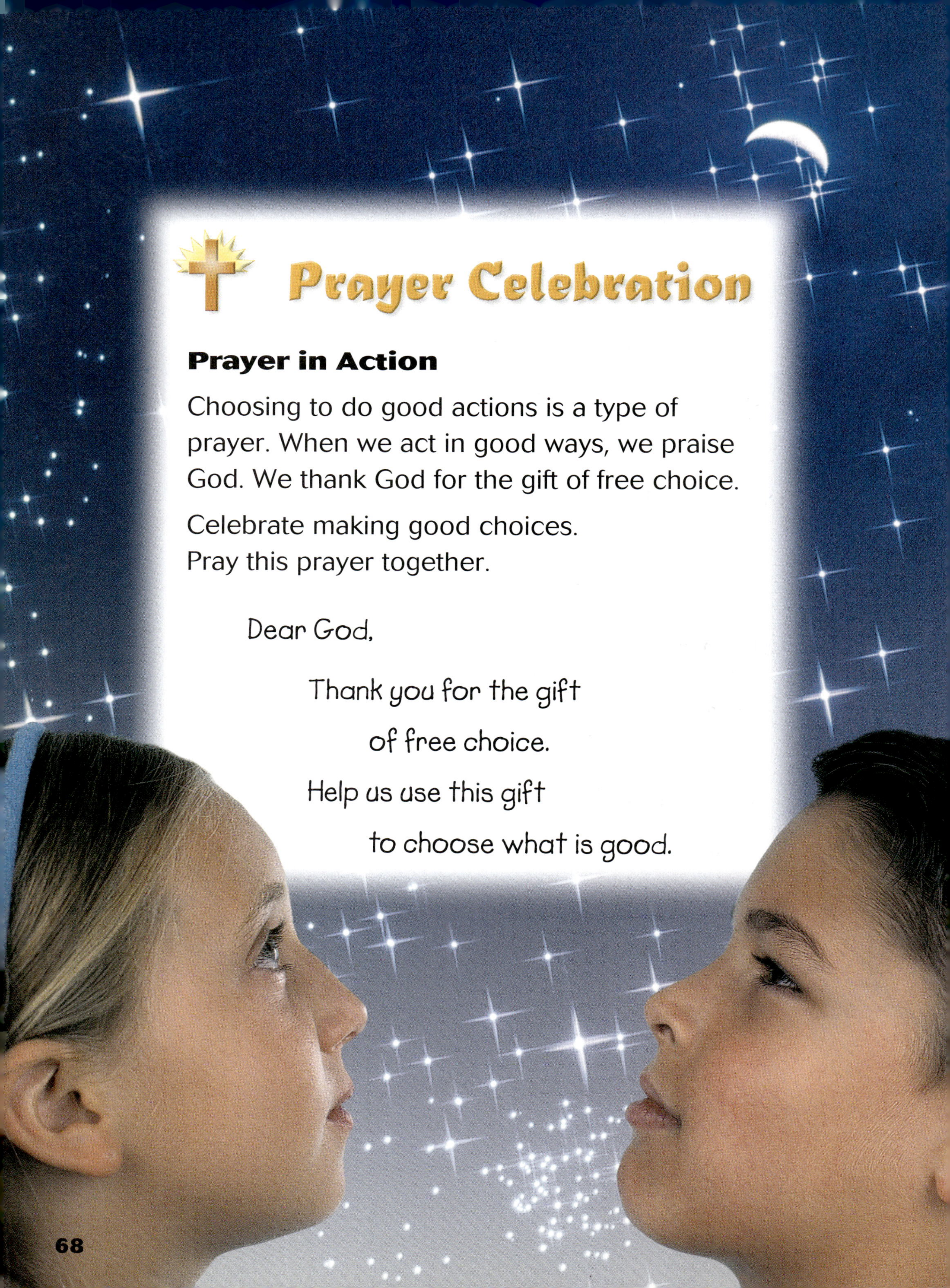

Prayer Celebration

Prayer in Action

Choosing to do good actions is a type of prayer. When we act in good ways, we praise God. We thank God for the gift of free choice.

Celebrate making good choices.
Pray this prayer together.

Dear God,

Thank you for the gift
of free choice.
Help us use this gift
to choose what is good.

6 We Celebrate God's Forgiveness

Based on Psalm 86:5

Share

Sometimes we say or do things that hurt other people. We can lose their friendship.

Put the pictures in order. In the boxes write 1, 2, 3, and 4 to tell a story about losing a friend and then making up.

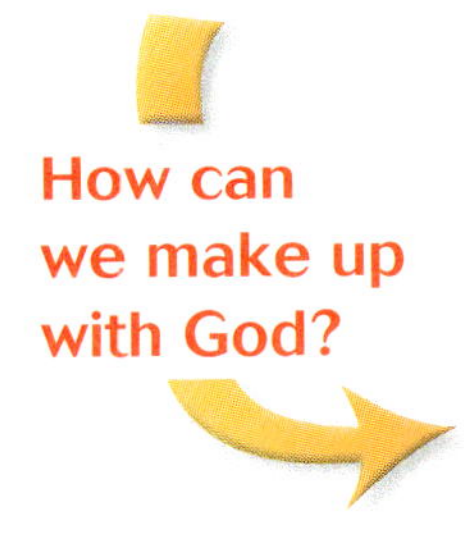

How can we make up with God?

Making Up

The sacrament of **Reconciliation**, or Penance, celebrates the gift of God's forgiveness. Here is what happens in the sacrament.

Welcome Father Lee greets Pat in the reconciliation room. They read from the Bible. They hear how God loves us and is always ready to forgive us.

Confession Pat talks about, or **confesses**, her sins. Father Lee helps her find ways to do better. He asks her to say a prayer or do a kind act to make up for what she has done wrong. This prayer or action is called a **penance**.

Prayer of Sorrow Pat says a prayer of sorrow, called the Act of Contrition. She tells God she is sorry and will try not to sin again.

Absolution Father Lee prays for Pat and asks God to forgive her. He gives Pat **absolution** in the name of the Father, Son, and Holy Spirit. Absolution is the forgiveness of God, given through the priest in this sacrament. Then Father Lee gives thanks and says, "Go in peace." Pat answers, "Amen."

A Sacrament of Healing

When we have sinned, we need to say we are sorry. We need forgiveness. The sacrament of Reconciliation celebrates God's forgiveness. God invites us to be at peace again.

Activity What should we remember about each part of the sacrament of Reconciliation?

Faith Words

Reconciliation

Reconciliation is a sacrament of healing that celebrates God's love and forgiveness.

absolution

Absolution is the forgiveness of God in the name of the Father, Son, and Holy Spirit.

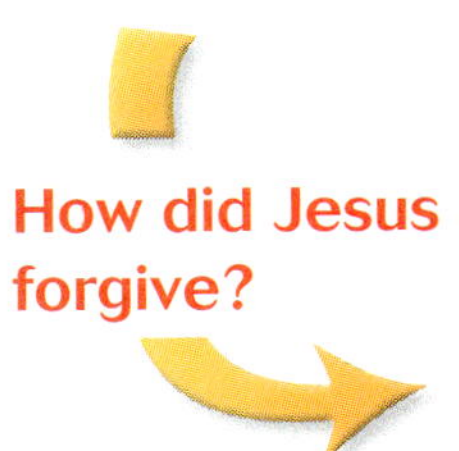
How did Jesus forgive?

Hear & Believe

Jesus Forgives

One day as Jesus ate dinner, a woman came to him. Everyone knew this woman was a sinner. Most people at the dinner ignored the woman. But Jesus welcomed her and let her speak to him.

The woman was so happy that she began to cry. Her tears washed over Jesus' feet. She dried them with her hair. Then she rubbed Jesus' feet with fine lotion.

"Your many sins are forgiven," Jesus told her. "Go in peace and sin no more. Remember that God is with you, helping you to be good."

Based on Luke 7:36–50

Our Church Teaches

The sacrament of Reconciliation helps us make peace with God and the Church. The gift of God's **grace** helps us stay away from sin. Grace is God's loving presence in our lives.

We Believe

In the sacrament of Reconciliation, we celebrate God's forgiveness.

Activity Use the correct word in each sentence.

Jesus welcomed the sinful woman. In the sacrament of Reconciliation the priest welcomes us.

Jesus let her speak to him. In the sacrament of Reconciliation we speak to a priest and confess our sins.

Jesus announced that her sins were forgiven. In the sacrament of Reconciliation the priest asks God to forgive our sins in the name of Jesus.

Jesus reminded the sinful woman that God will help her to do good. In the sacrament of Reconciliation, we receive the gift of God's grace.

welcomes

confess

forgive

grace

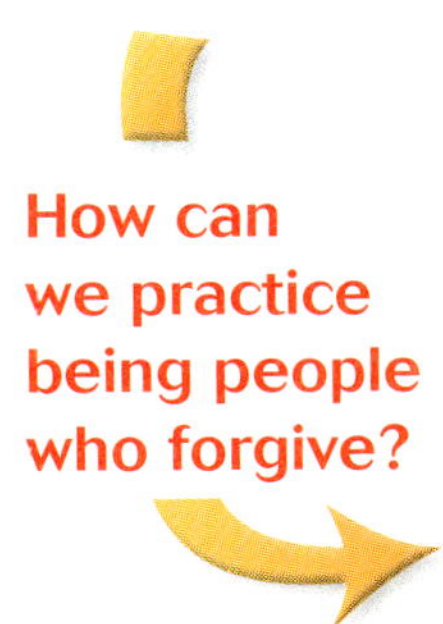

How can we practice being people who forgive?

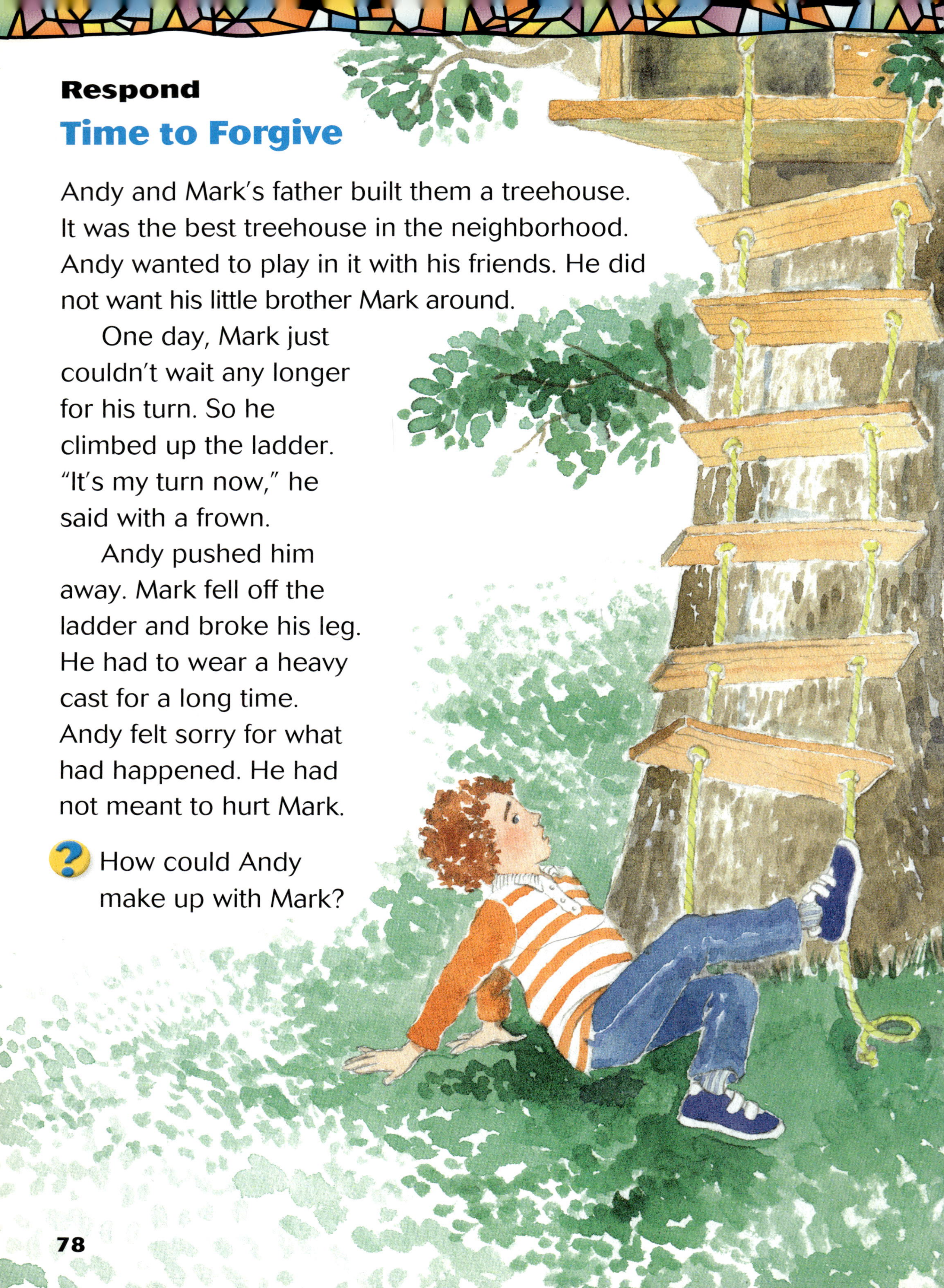

Respond

Time to Forgive

Andy and Mark's father built them a treehouse. It was the best treehouse in the neighborhood. Andy wanted to play in it with his friends. He did not want his little brother Mark around.

One day, Mark just couldn't wait any longer for his turn. So he climbed up the ladder. "It's my turn now," he said with a frown.

Andy pushed him away. Mark fell off the ladder and broke his leg. He had to wear a heavy cast for a long time. Andy felt sorry for what had happened. He had not meant to hurt Mark.

? How could Andy make up with Mark?

Activities

1. Complete the sentences with these forgiveness words.

sorry **forgive** **make up**

Andy and Mark should make up.

Andy should say to Mark, "I am sorry."

Mark should say to Andy, "I forgive you."

2. Write 1, 2, 3, and 4 to put the parts of the sacrament of Reconciliation in order.

3 pray a prayer of sorrow

2 be given a penance

4 receive absolution

1 confess sins

Prayer Celebration

Lord, Have Mercy

During Mass, we tell God we are sorry for our sins. We ask God to have mercy on us. Mercy is a generous type of love. It leads to forgiveness.

Pray this prayer of reconciliation.

Leader: Lord Jesus, you help us live in peace with one another and with God the Father.

All: **Lord, have mercy.**

Leader: Lord Jesus, you heal the hurt that is caused by sin.

All: **Christ, have mercy.**

Leader: Lord Jesus, you pray to your Father for us.

All: **Lord, have mercy.**

Leader: May almighty God have mercy on us, forgive us our sins, and bring us to everlasting life.

All: **Amen.**

The Order of Mass

Getting ready for Chapter 7

A choice of things to do at home

We Think About Our Choices

This chapter deals with making choices and presents the Ten Commandments. The Commandments serve as a guide against which we measure our choices. Children learn that they are responsible for their actions. They learn that when they choose to do wrong, they sin. They also consider the differences among mistakes, venial sins, and mortal sins.

Watching a movie

Rent the movie *Searching for Bobby Fischer* and watch it with your family. It shows a boy with an unusual ability, and the decisions his parents make about his education. The parents work to help Bobby as well as they can, not always agreeing on what is the best way to help.

Following the rules

Discuss with your child rules around the house and at school. Talk about the purpose of rules. Ask what happens when the rules are not followed, and what happens when they are followed.

Choose a game

Play a board game as a family. Board games that involve choices help to illustrate the point of this chapter. Playing one of these games will demonstrate how the choices we make lead to consequences.

A Prayer for the Week

Thank you, Lord,
for giving us
the Ten Commandments.
With your help, we believe that
we can do better every day.
Amen.

FAMILY TIME

Something to Do . . .

On Sunday

Talk with your family about ways to honor the Sabbath, such as going to Mass, avoiding conflict, and thinking about what God wants you to do.

Through the Week

Find examples of making everyday choices at home, work, and school. Which decisions are hardest to make?

Visit Our Web Site

www.blestarewe.com

Something to Think About . . .

Making Choices

I, the Lord, am your God, who brought you out of the land of Egypt, that place of slavery.
Exodus 20:2

With these words God gave Moses the Ten Commandments. God was reminding Moses and the Israelites that he was there for them when they were in trouble. God wasn't going to ask his People to honor him and keep his commandments without reminding them that he was a loving, caring God.

When we make choices in our lives, we try to make them according to the commandments. It is good to remember that God is there to help us. God's faithfulness is an example for parents. We need to be there for our children, even though their behavior is not always as good as we might wish.

Something to Know About . . .

Our Heritage in Film

The movie *E.T.: The Extraterrestrial*, made in 1982 and directed by Steven Spielberg, is a story in which characters take care of an extraterrestrial that is lost on Earth. These children are forced to make a number of decisions, many of which involve concealing E.T. from adults. Right or wrong, the children make their choices to protect E.T. out of love. The most difficult decision the children make is to help E.T. return home, even though they will miss the alien very much. E.T.'s relationship with Elliot, the main child character, is especially touching. The movie continues to be popular years after it was first shown.

7 We Think About Our Choices

Teach me, O LORD, your ways.
Guide me in goodness and truth.

Based on Psalm 25:4–5

Share

As we grow up, we learn to be responsible for our actions. We are responsible when we do our work. We are responsible when we take good care of things.

Check (✓) each sentence that tells about a responsibility you have.

- [ ] **1.** I feed the family pet.
- [ ] **2.** I help Mom and Dad.
- [ ] **3.** I do my homework.
- [ ] **4.** I listen to my teacher.
- [ ] **5.** I return my library books.
- [ ] **6.** I hang up my jacket.

Name some other responsibilities that you have.

How do church members show responsibility?

Hear & Believe

Moses on the Mountain

Moses was on a mountaintop when God spoke to him. God wanted to help everyone lead good lives. He gave Moses the laws called the **Ten Commandments**. God called the Hebrew people to love him and respect him. The Ten Commandments reminded people to rest and pray on the Lord's day, to obey their parents, and to avoid telling lies or stealing. The Commandments also said not to hurt other people nor be jealous of them.

When God had finished, Moses went down the mountain. He told the people about these laws of God, the Ten Commandments.

Based on Exodus 20:1–17

The Ten Commandments

The Ten Commandments are God's laws. God gave us the Ten Commandments as special responsibilities. They help us know right from wrong. They help us think about and make good choices. The Ten Commandments help us love God and love other people.

Activity What is one way you can show your love for God?

How can you show your love for other people?

What happens when we do not follow the Ten Commandments?

Hear & Believe

The Birthday Party

Sharon's birthday party was fun. Julie enjoyed the games, the cake, and the ice cream. But then Sharon opened her presents. One was a beautiful doll in a blue outfit.

Julie knew that Sharon already had a doll like that. But Sharon seemed happy anyway.

Julie was jealous. She wanted that doll for herself. When everyone else went outside to play a game, she picked up the doll.

Suddenly Sharon came back in. "Give me that," she shouted. "It's mine!"

"You have another one," Julie said. And she kept playing with the doll.

Sharon grabbed the doll, but Julie would not let go. They pulled and tugged. Before long, one of the doll's arms popped off.

"Now look what you've done!" Sharon cried loudly. She ran in tears to get her mother.

Julie started to cry, too. The beautiful doll was ruined.

Our Church Teaches

When we know that something is wrong, and we do it anyway, we sin. Sin turns us away from God and other people. **Mortal sins** are serious sins that separate us from our friendship with God. **Venial sins** are less serious sins. They weaken our friendship with God, but do not take it away.

We Believe

God gave us the Ten Commandments to help us know how to lead good lives.

Activity Answer these questions.

What wrong choice did Julie make in the story?

____

____

What wrong choice did Sharon make?

____

____

What did their wrong choices do to their friendship?

____

____

____

____

Talk about how Julie and Sharon could have made better choices.

Faith Words

mortal sin

A mortal sin is a serious sin that separates us from our friendship with God.

venial sin

A venial sin is a less serious sin. It weakens our friendship with God.

How can we think about the Ten Commandments?

Respond

An Examination of Conscience

Before we celebrate the sacrament of Reconciliation, we think about the Ten Commandments. We ask ourselves how well we have followed each one. This is called an examination of conscience.

God's Laws	My Actions
1. Believe that there is only one God.	Do I believe in God and love God with all my heart?
2. Respect the name of God.	Do I use the names of God, Jesus, Mary, and the saints with respect?
3. Go to Mass on Sunday.	Do I celebrate Mass every Sunday?
4. Respect your father and mother.	Do I respect and obey my parents?
5. Take care of all that God has made.	Do I treat all God's creatures, especially people, with respect?
6. Treat your body as a gift from God.	Do I take good care of my body and respect the bodies of others?
7. Respect the property of others.	Have I taken something that belongs to someone else?
8. Always tell the truth.	Do I sometimes lie?
9. Respect the families of others.	Do I treat other families with respect?
10. Be content with what you have.	Am I ever jealous or greedy?

Mistakes and sins are not the same. You might break a glass by mistake. You sin when you choose to do something you know is wrong.

Activity

Follow the stone path. If a **mistake** is described on a stone, color the stone blue. If a **sin** is described, color the stone red.

1. Oops! I spilled gravy on my new sweater.
2. I stole my brother's favorite cap.
3. I had a big fight with a friend.
4. I left the window open, and the rain came in.
5. I was jealous of my friend's new bike.
6. I lied about what happened to my homework.
7. I lost my lunch money.
8. I forgot to wish my cousin a happy birthday.

How can we celebrate thinking about our choices?

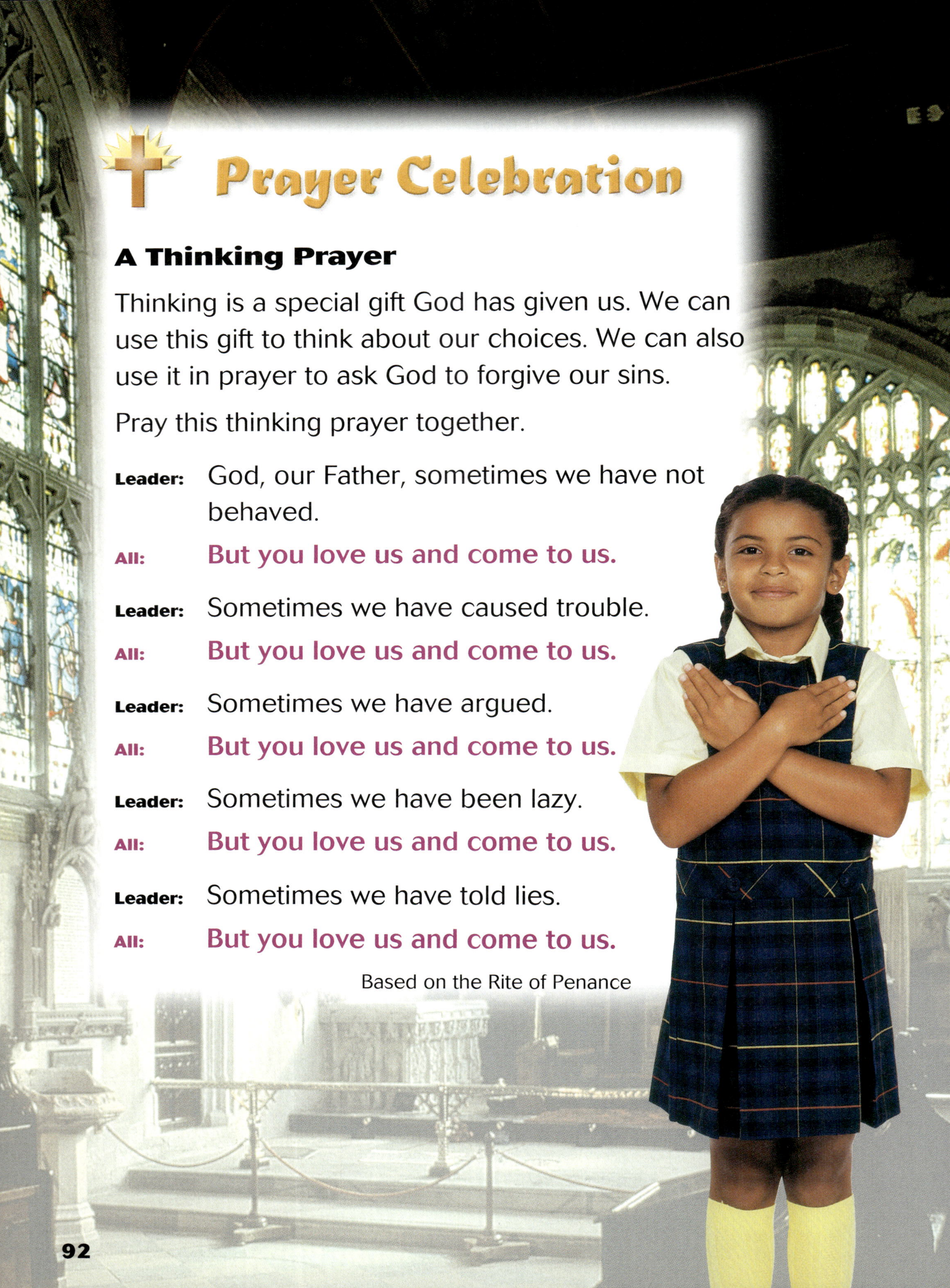

Prayer Celebration

A Thinking Prayer

Thinking is a special gift God has given us. We can use this gift to think about our choices. We can also use it in prayer to ask God to forgive our sins.

Pray this thinking prayer together.

Leader: God, our Father, sometimes we have not behaved.

All: **But you love us and come to us.**

Leader: Sometimes we have caused trouble.

All: **But you love us and come to us.**

Leader: Sometimes we have argued.

All: **But you love us and come to us.**

Leader: Sometimes we have been lazy.

All: **But you love us and come to us.**

Leader: Sometimes we have told lies.

All: **But you love us and come to us.**

Based on the Rite of Penance

7 Chapter Review

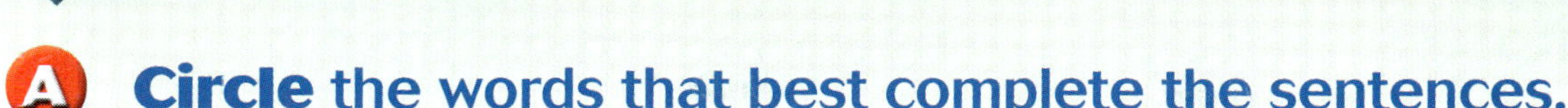

A Circle the words that best complete the sentences.

1. Returning library books on time is ____.
   responsible **not responsible** **not important**

2. Telling a lie is ____.
   responsible **not responsible** **okay**

3. God gave Moses the laws called the ____ Commandments.
   Two **Five** **Ten**

4. These commandments tell us to love God and ____.
   our friends **animals** **other people**

B Complete the definitions.

1. A mortal sin is a serious sin that

2. A venial sin is a less serious sin that

C **Complete** the commandments with words from the word list.

1. The first commandment tells us to believe that there is only ________ God.
2. The third commandment tells us to go to ________ on Sunday.
3. The fourth commandment tells us to respect our ________ and mother.
4. The seventh commandment tells us to respect the ________ of others.

father

Mass

one

property

D **Draw a line** between each term and its example.

Term	Example
1. Examination of conscience ●	● O God, I am sorry for causing trouble.
2. Mistake ●	● I stole my brother's favorite CD.
3. Prayer for forgiveness ●	● I spilled the ketchup.
4. Sin ●	● Am I ever jealous or greedy?

Getting ready for Chapter 8

A choice of things to do at home

We Say We Are Sorry

When we choose to do wrong, we need to say we are sorry, to God and to any person we have hurt. The focus of this chapter is to learn to use prayer to tell God that we are sorry. When we do this, we admit that we have done wrong and recognize that we need to acknowledge it. Children will learn that prayer brings us closer to God and that, with the Holy Spirit's help, we can change.

How many ways?

With your child, think of several ways to say or show that you are sorry. Some examples are "Please forgive me," "I didn't mean to hurt you," giving a hug, and shaking hands. You might want to make a list of all the expressions and actions you identified.

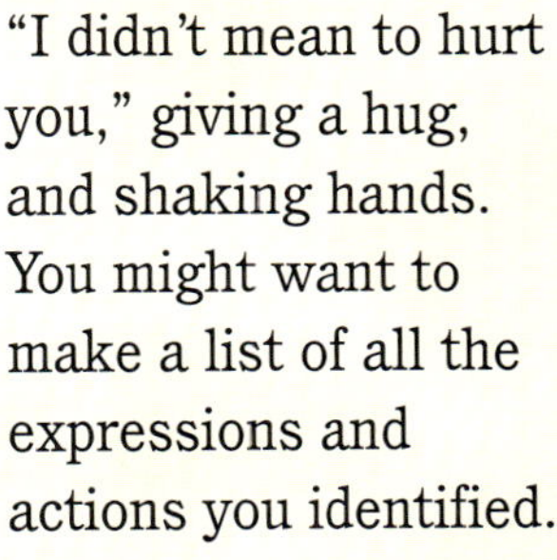

Sorry role-play

As a family, role-play situations from stories or TV episodes in which characters do something wrong and make an apology. For example, Cinderella's stepsisters have good reason to apologize!

Sorry state

"That's a sorry state you're in!" is an expression that means that something has gotten you into a mess. Talk about times when members of your family were in a "sorry state," needing to apologize to someone.

A Prayer for the Week

Lord, as we look back
on our day, we see
some things to be sorry for.
Please forgive us for our faults
and help us do better.
Amen.

FAMILY TIME

Something to Do . . .

On Sunday

During the Sunday liturgy, ask God's forgiveness for things that went wrong this week.

Through the Week

When stress occurs, call upon the Holy Spirit. Ask for God's grace to help you deal with your frustrations.

Visit Our Web Site

www.blestarewe.com

Something to Think About . . .

The Power of Baptism

At that time Jerusalem, all Judea, and the whole region around the Jordan were going out to him and were being baptized by him in the Jordan River as they acknowledged their sins.

Matthew 3:5–6

Baptism brings forgiveness of all sins. The Church teaches that water is the symbol for cleansing away the stain of sin. Daily we recognize that water refreshes, renews, and gives new life. Baptized persons have the sinful state of humanity blessed in baptism. Even though we often make wrong choices, the power of baptism, which has made us followers of Christ, offers us God's forgiveness. We know that God will have mercy on us.

Something to Know About . . .

Our Heritage in Music

Fiddler on the Roof was a long-running Broadway musical and a successful movie. It tells the story of a Russian Jewish family before the Russian Revolution. One of the most poignant songs, "Sunrise, Sunset," sung by the mother and father, is about how quickly time passes in a family and how quickly children grow up. This song echoes the sentiment of most parents. How do children grow up so fast? This timely song reminds us that we should nurture our relationship with our children, because they won't be with us forever.

8 We Say We Are Sorry

When a sinner is sorry, there is great joy in heaven.

Based on Luke 15:7

Share

There are many ways to say "I'm sorry."
You can say it with words like "Let's make up."
You can say it with an action like a hug.

Tell another good way to say "I'm sorry."

How can we tell God we are sorry?

Hear & Believe

Return to God!

John the Baptizer was a very holy man. He told other people how to find God's forgiveness.

John: Return to God! Repent, for God's kingdom is coming!

Woman: What does repent mean?

John: Repent means to be truly sorry for your sins.

Boy: What else does repent mean?

John: It means that you really want to change.

Girl: Is that all we need to do to return to God?

John: No. You must also do **penance**. Penance is a prayer or an act to make up for the harm caused by sin.

Many people heard John's words. They confessed their sins. They told God they were sorry. Then John baptized them in the river.

Based on Matthew 3:1–8

Returning to God

Sin separates us from God. John the Baptizer wanted people to go back to God. We can return to God by telling him we are sorry for our sins. When we are sorry for our sins, we feel **contrition**. Contrition means to be sorry and to want to do better. To show that we are sorry, we pray an **act of contrition**. This is a prayer of sorrow. In this prayer we promise to try not to sin again.

Faith Words

contrition

Contrition means to be sorry and to want to stay away from sin.

act of contrition

An act of contrition is a prayer that tells God we are sorry for our sins.

Activity Think about what you have said and done. For what are you sorry? Then go to page 370 and pray the prayer of sorrow.

How does God help us turn away from sin?

Julie and Sharon Make Up

Sharon's mother saw the broken doll. "What happened?" she asked the girls.

"She did it," Sharon said, pointing at Julie.

"No I didn't," Julie responded. "Sharon tried to take the doll away from me."

Sharon's mother shook her head. "Sharon, what do you have to say to Julie?"

Sharon wiped her eyes. "I'm sorry I didn't share my doll with you."

Sharon's mother then looked at Julie. "And Julie, what do you have to say to Sharon?"

Julie lowered her head. "I'm sorry. I should have asked if I could play with your doll."

Sharon's mother made both girls shake hands. Then she worked to put the doll's arm back on. "There," she said at last. "It's as good as new. Sharon, go get your other doll, so you and Julie can play together."

Soon the girls were playing happily with the two dolls. They were friends again.

Our Church Teaches

When we are truly sorry for our sins, the Holy Spirit helps us do better.

Activity The Holy Spirit helped Julie and Sharon to do better. Each girl showed contrition. Write a note to tell someone you are sorry for what you said or did.

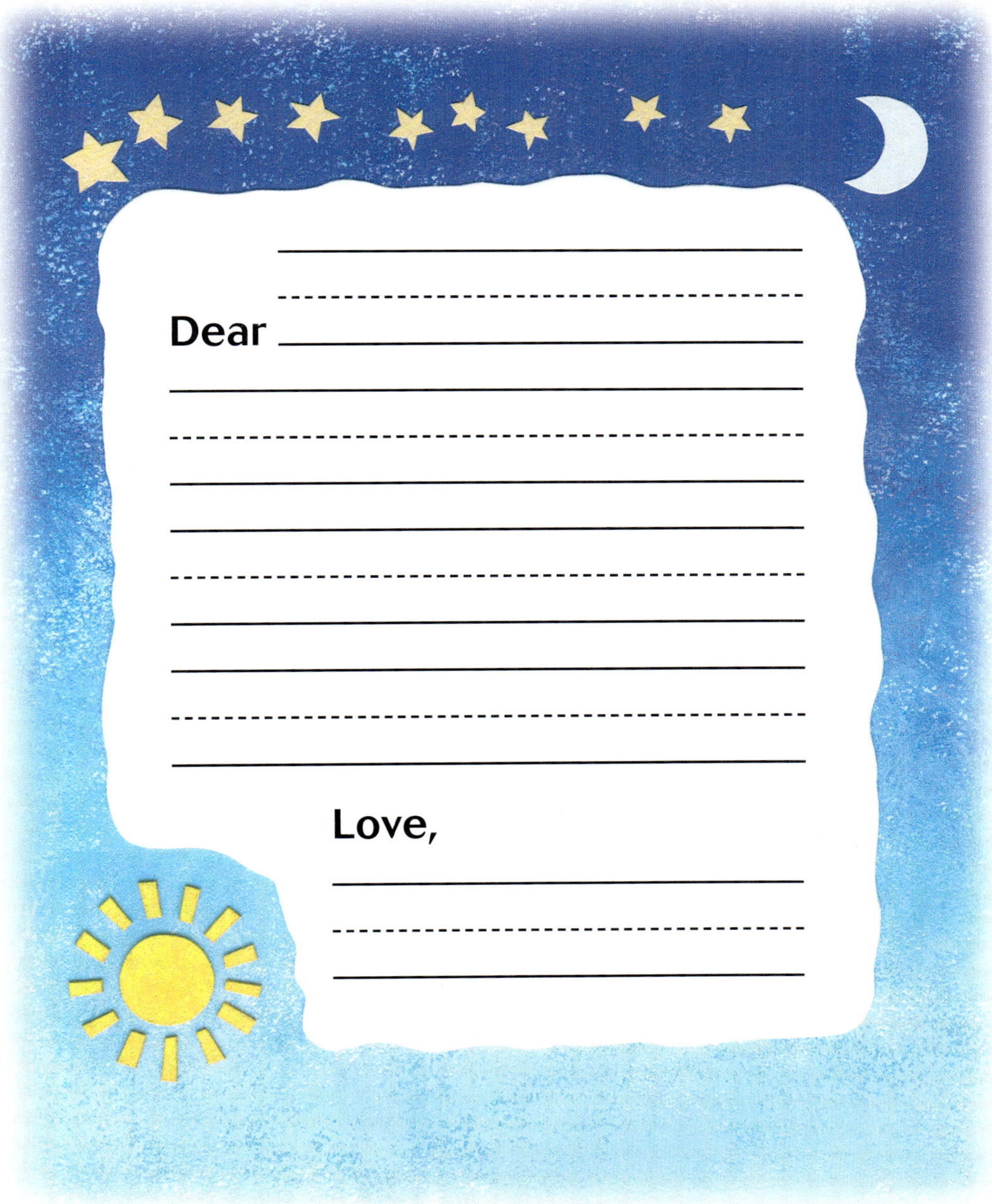

Dear ______________________

____

____

Love,

____

We Believe

When we sin, we can return to God with the help of the Holy Spirit. We ask the Holy Spirit to guide us. We make up our minds not to sin again.

Respond

A Penance Service

Matt and Susan went to a penance service. Many other people were there, too. Everyone had come to show that they wanted to return to God. They listened to a story that Jesus once told about a shepherd and a lost sheep.

God is like the shepherd who had one hundred sheep. One sheep was lost, and the shepherd went to look for it. When he found the sheep, the shepherd was very happy. In the same way, there is great joy in heaven when a sinner is sorry.

Based on Luke 15:4–7

Why is this a good story for a penance service?

Activity

Use the secret code to write the missing letters.

Then read the prayer of sorrow.

Secret Code

1	2	3	4	5	6	7	8	9	10	11	12	13
A	B	C	D	E	F	G	H	I	J	K	L	M
14	15	16	17	18	19	20	21	22	23	24	25	26
N	O	P	Q	R	S	T	U	V	W	X	y	Z

___ ___ ___ ___ ___ ___, ___
6 1 20 8 5 18 9

___ ___ ___ ___ ___ ___ ___
1 13 19 15 18 18 25

___ ___ ___ ___ ___ ___
6 15 18 1 12 12

___ ___ ___ ___ ___ ___.
13 25 19 9 14 19

How can we return to God?

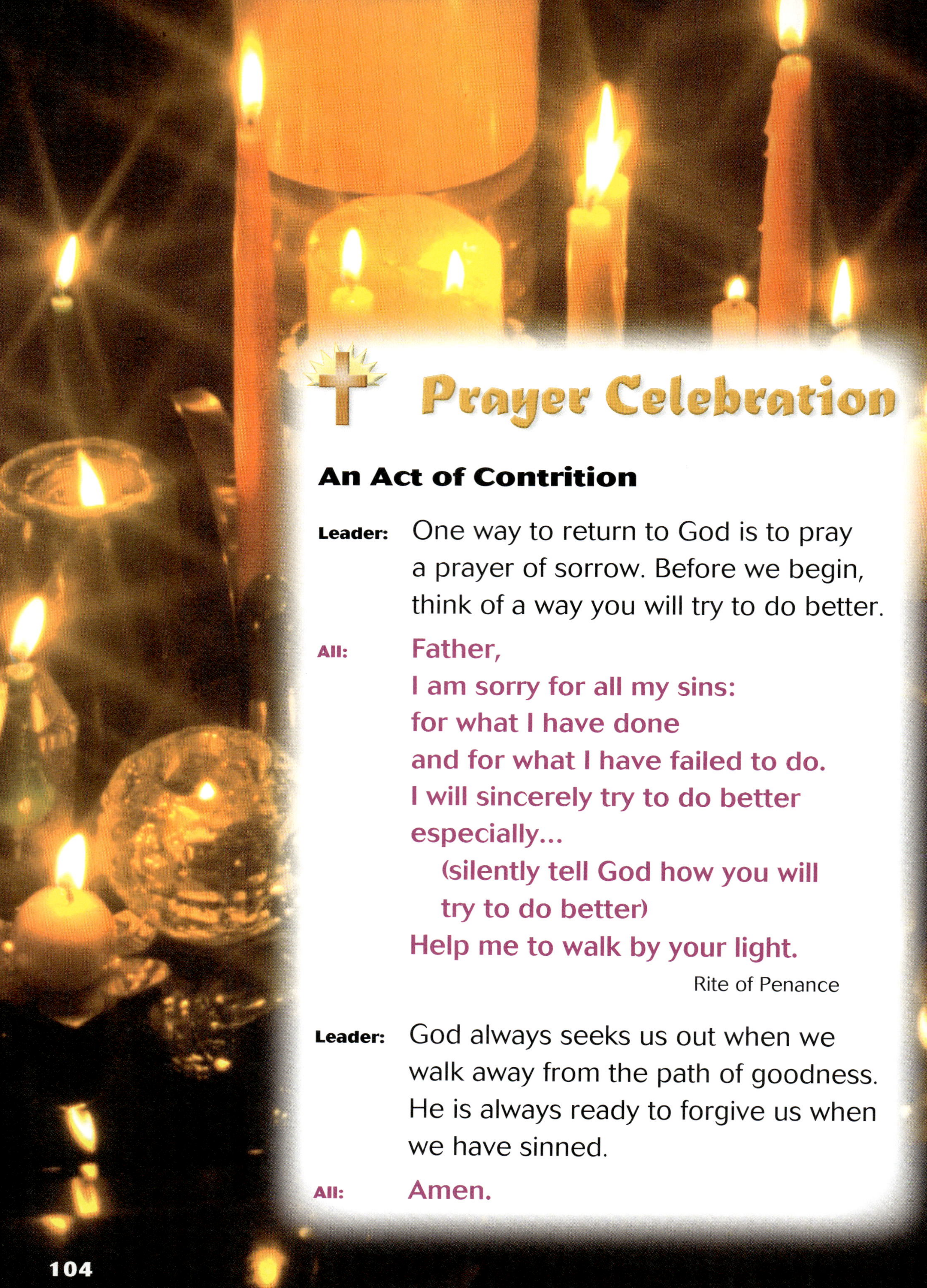

Prayer Celebration

An Act of Contrition

Leader: One way to return to God is to pray a prayer of sorrow. Before we begin, think of a way you will try to do better.

All: **Father,**
I am sorry for all my sins:
for what I have done
and for what I have failed to do.
I will sincerely try to do better
especially...
(silently tell God how you will
try to do better)
Help me to walk by your light.

Rite of Penance

Leader: God always seeks us out when we walk away from the path of goodness. He is always ready to forgive us when we have sinned.

All: **Amen.**

8 Chapter Review

A **Complete** each sentence by drawing a line to the correct word.

1. ____ means to be sorry and to want to do better. •	• act of contrition
2. A prayer or act to make up for the harm caused by sin is called a ____. •	• contrition
3. To show that we are sorry, we pray an ____ •	• penance
4. We can ____ to God by telling him we are sorry for our sins. •	• return

B **Complete** this part of the prayer of sorrow with words from the box.

avoid	love	penance	sins	wrong

I firmly intend, with your help, to do ____________,

to sin no more, and to ____________ whatever

leads me to sin. Amen.

C Circle the best answer.

1. When we are sorry for sins, who helps us to do better?
   a deacon **our religion teacher** **the Holy Spirit**

2. If we are truly sorry for our sins, we make up our minds not to do what?
   make mistakes **sin again** **obey the Commandments**

3. Jesus told a story about a shepherd who had 100 sheep. What did the shepherd do when he lost one sheep?
   He forgot about it. **He was happy.** **He looked for it.**

4. In Jesus' story, who is God like?
   shepherd **100 sheep** **lost sheep**

5. In Jesus' story, who are we like when we sin?
   shepherd **100 sheep** **lost sheep**

D Draw or write about what happens in heaven when a sinner is sorry and returns to God.

Pam Has a Problem

Pam Larsen is fourteen years old, Bobby is ten, and Sara is seven. Every Sunday, the Larsen family makes plans for the next week.

Last Sunday Bobby said, "Dad, I'll be coming home late on Tuesday. That's the day of our soccer game."

Sara said, "I need a ride after school on Friday, Mom. That's when I have my piano lesson."

Then Pam said, "I have a problem. For my school project, I will need to use our computer every day!"

Everybody in the family shares the computer. All of them talked about Pam's problem. Everybody agreed to let Pam use the computer whenever she needed it. Pam's problem was solved because everybody cooperated, or worked together.

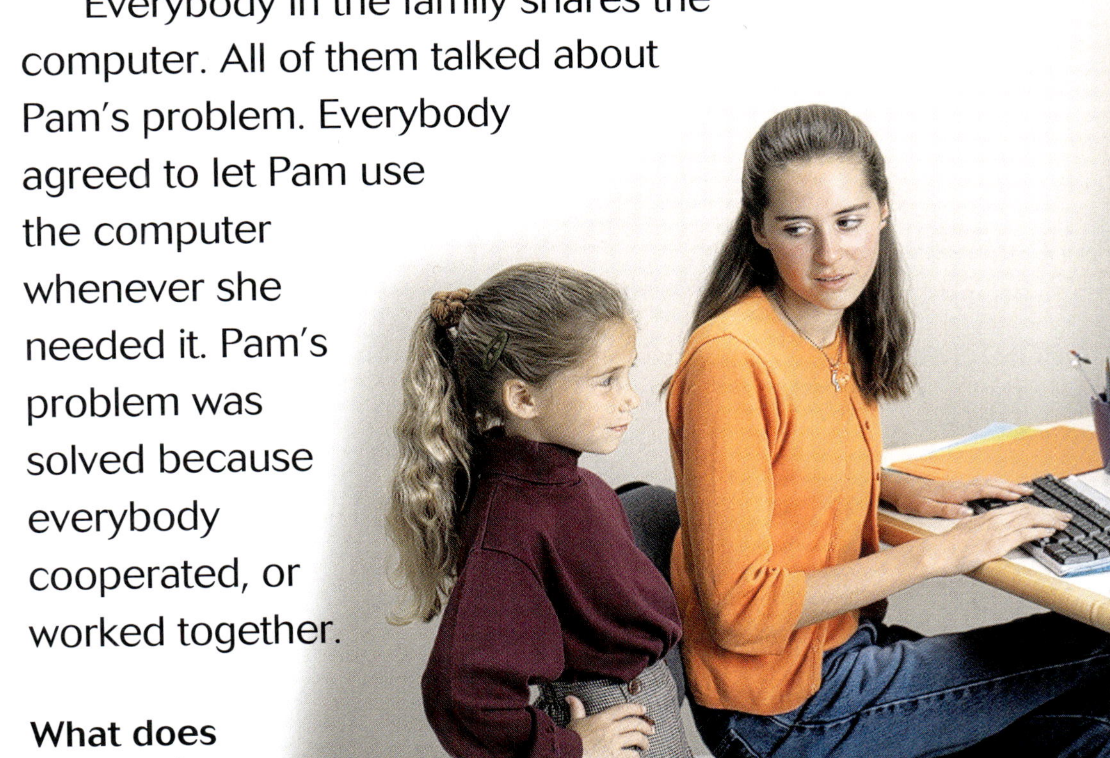

What does the word cooperate mean?

Think About It

What happens when people in the family cooperate? What happens when friends cooperate?

Circle the words that tell about how people feel when they cooperate.

laugh	angry
smile	cry
sad	happy

Learn About It

Jesus told us that he will come to judge all people. He will find the people who acted on God's word. Jesus will find the people who treated others fairly.

People in a family need to be fair with each other. Each person has rights. Each person has duties, too. To be fair, each person must respect the rights of all the others. Everybody needs to carry out their duties, too.

Do Something About It

What rights do you have in your family?
What duties do you have?

Draw a picture of a way you cooperate at home.

Organizer

Read the words on the signs. Then write the word that completes each sentence.

good

God's

sorry

1. We can choose ____________ what is ____________.

2. We celebrate ____________ ____________ forgiveness.

3. We think about ____________ our ____________.

4. We say we are ____________.

UNIT 2

Review

A **Remember the story "The Forgiving Father." Then put the story in order. Write the numbers 1, 2, 3, 4, and 5 in the boxes.**

☐ The young man moved far away from home.

☐ The father gave money to his son.

☐ They had a "welcome home" party.

☐ The father forgave the young man.

☐ The son was sorry for his wrong choices.

B **Circle the words that best complete the sentences.**

1. God wants us to be ________ for our sins.

   sorry **polite** **lonely**

2. God lets us choose between right and wrong. This is called ________.

   conscience **prayer** **free choice**

3. The gift of God's ________ helps us stay away from sin.

   grace **laws** **praise**

Review

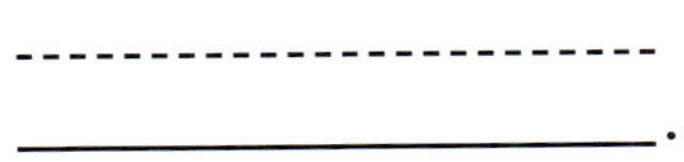

Complete the sentences with the words in the balloons.

1. The Ten Commandments are God's ________.

2. The Ten Commandments helps us make good ________.

3. Mistakes are never ________.

4. Sins turn us against God and other ________.

5. Sin weakens our friendship with ________.

UNIT 2

Review

D **Draw a line** to connect the parts of each sentence.

1. Our conscience •	• are venial sins.
2. We sin when we •	• turn away from God.
3. Serious sins that separate us from our friendship with God •	• helps us know right from wrong.
4. Less serious sins that weaken our friendship with God •	• are mortal sins.

E **Connect** the parts of each sentence by drawing lines.

1. Contrition means •	• a sacrament of healing that celebrates God's love and forgiveness.
2. Absolution is the forgiveness of God •	• to be sorry and to want to stay away from sin.
3. Reconciliation is •	• in the name of the Father, Son, and Holy Spirit.

F **Respond** to the following questions.

1. Who does the Fourth Commandment tell us we must ______________________

respect? ______________________

2. How do you keep the Fourth Commandment?

____

____

UNIT 3

We Celebrate the Word of God

The Word of God is Jesus Christ among us. When we listen to the Scripture readings, we are taught the way of the Gospel. We are inspired to live as true followers of Jesus.

But some seed fell on rich soil, and produced fruit, a hundred or sixty or thirtyfold. Whoever has ears ought to hear.

Matthew 13:8-9

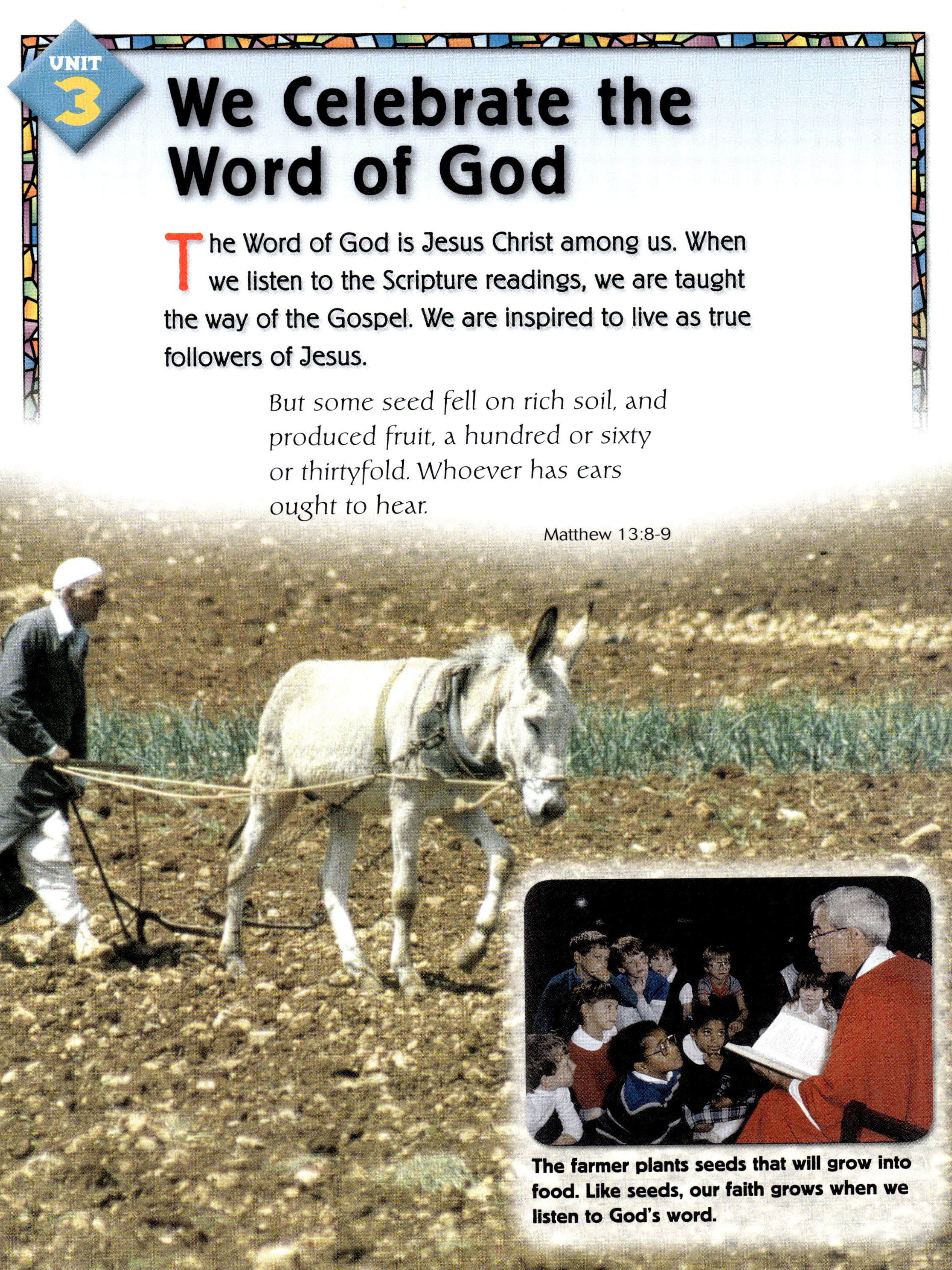

The farmer plants seeds that will grow into food. Like seeds, our faith grows when we listen to God's word.

Go and Listen

Words and Music by Robert J. Batastini

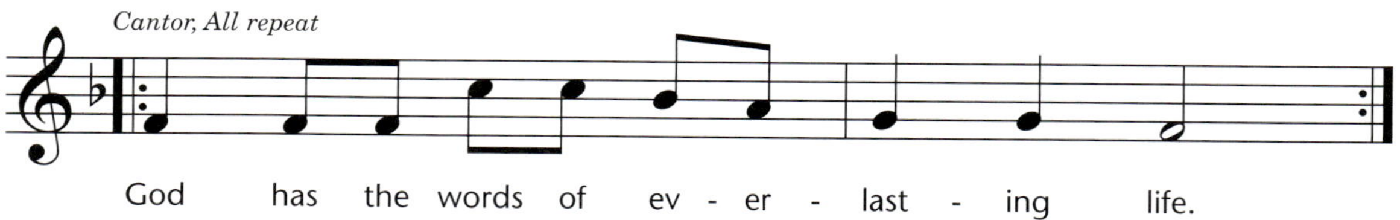

Getting ready for Chapter 9

FAMILY TIME

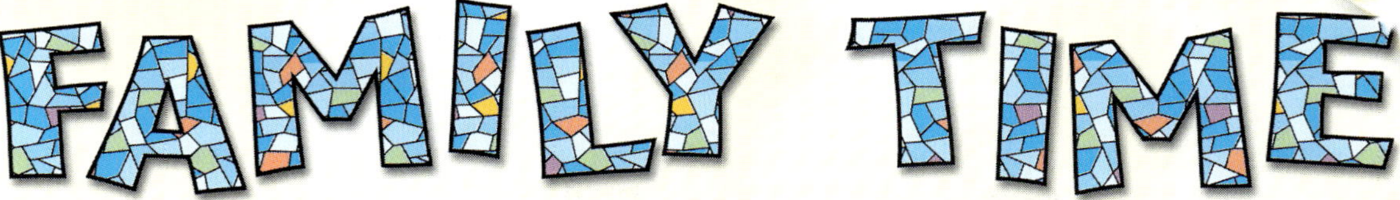

A choice of things to do at home

We Learn About God's Love

The Bible is a book filled with many kinds of literature, such as stories, letters, prayers, and songs. The Bible tells of God's love for us, from the moment of creation on. This chapter encourages children to be aware of the Bible as a tool for learning about God's gift of creation, his love for us, and his gift of his Son, Jesus.

Biblical current events

Think of an event that has happened in your family and write about it in Biblical style. There are many styles to use as models: the letters of St. Paul, the psalms of David, a prophecy, or an adventure story similar to the one about Jonah and the whale.

Creating with clay

God made us out of clay, according to one account in Genesis. Together, take some clay and make something that represents your thanks to God for creating each family member and continuing to love you throughout your lives.

Who came first?

With the members of your family, make a simple Bible timeline. We all know that Jesus came after Moses. But did Abraham come before or after Moses? How about Esther or David? Have fun discussing what everyone knows about who came after whom in the Bible.

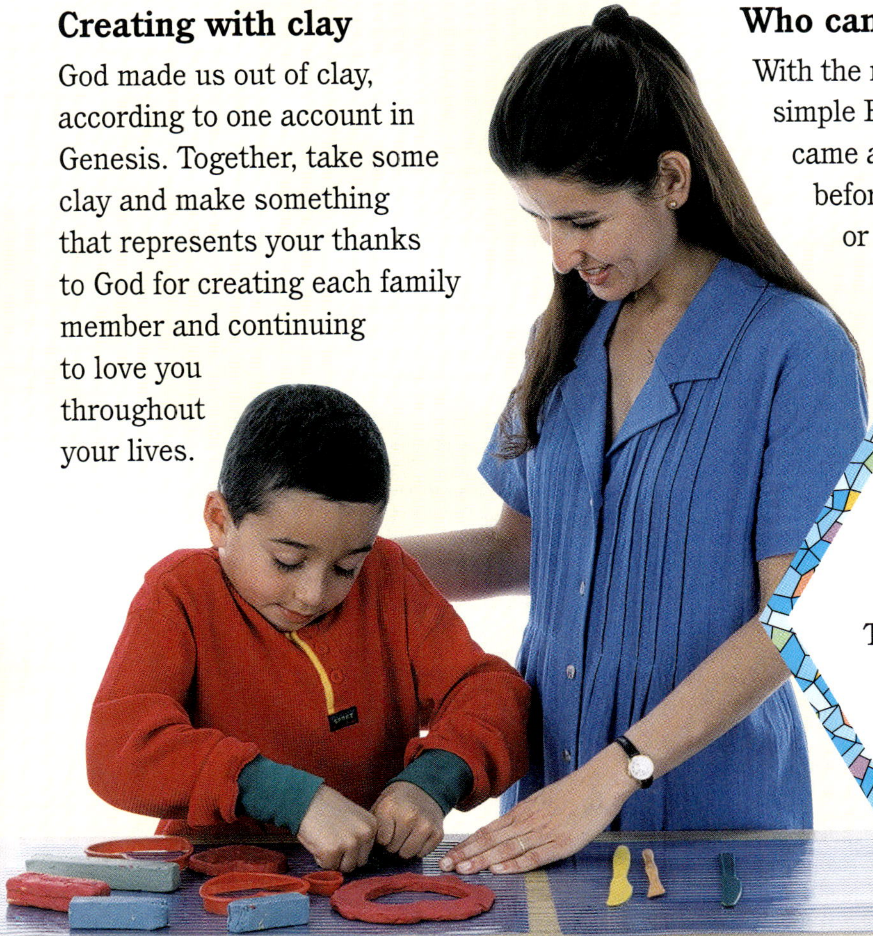

A Prayer for the Week

In the creation story, Lord, we learn of your goodness. Thank you for loving all your creatures. Your works are wonderful, Lord. Amen.

FAMILY TIME

Something to Do . . .

On Sunday

Listen to the readings at Mass. Then, later in the day, choose one of the readings to discuss with your family.

Through the Week

As a family, think about the good parts of being a son, a daughter, or a parent. Say a prayer of thanksgiving for the role God plays in all your lives.

Visit Our Web Site

www.blestarewe.com

Something to Think About . . .

In the Hands of God

Can any of you by worrying add a single moment to your life-span?
Matthew 6:27

This Gospel story from Matthew is about God's love. Jesus tells it to people who are worried about having enough food and clothing. Jesus tells the people not to worry about these things. He asks the people to trust that God will care for them, just as he cares for the birds in the sky and the flowers in the field.

From this story we can understand that God takes care of everything—including us—and that we shouldn't spend our time worrying. By not worrying, we put our trust in God and show that we appreciate his loving care.

Something to Know About . . . Our Heritage in Art

The painstaking work of monks and artists of the Middle Ages has left us with some priceless treasures of Scriptures copied and illuminated by hand. *Illumination* is a kind of decoration that was often used to illustrate and highlight the first letter of a passage. Artists used bright colors and gold to intertwine pictures of flowers and animals in the letter, making it so fancy that it was sometimes difficult to figure out what letter it was supposed to be. But the artworks are extraordinarily detailed and beautiful. They show the reverence in which the artists held the Holy Scriptures.

9 We Learn About God's Love

God looked at everything he had made.
He found it very good.

Based on Genesis 1:31

Share

The earth that God created has many kinds of land and water. It has mountains, forests, and deserts. It has rivers, lakes, and oceans.

The earth has many kinds of plants and animals, too. Name some plants and animals you know about.

Draw a picture that shows your favorite part of God's creation.

What does creation tell us about God?

God Loves All Creation

One day, Jesus told his followers this story about God's love.

"Some people worry about what they will eat and drink. Other people worry about what clothes to wear. But I say, do not worry. Instead, look at the birds in the sky. God takes good care of them. Look at the flowers in the field. God takes good care of them, too.

"So have faith. God loves you even more than the birds and flowers. God is a loving Father. You are his sons and daughters. God knows what you need. He will always take care of you."

Based on Matthew 6:25–34

Ways We Learn About God

The story Jesus told about God taking good care of all that he created is in the **Bible**. The Bible is also called the **Scriptures**. We learn about God's love for us from the Bible and from the teachings of Jesus.

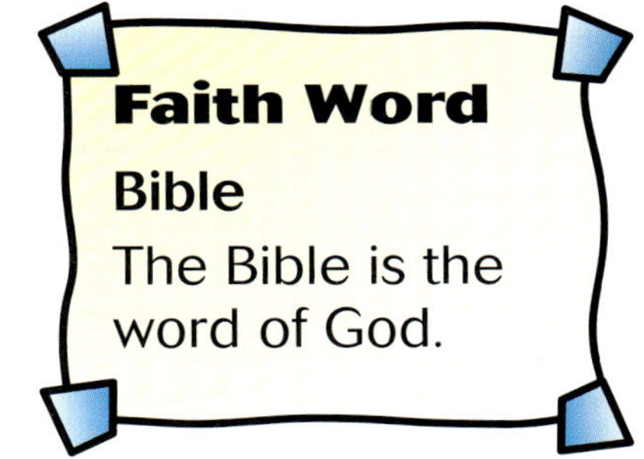

Faith Word

Bible

The Bible is the word of God.

Activity God loves each of us. What is one thing God has given you that shows his love?

____

____

What else do we learn from the Bible?

Who Jesus Is

When Jesus was twelve years old, he went to Jerusalem with Mary and Joseph. They joined many people to celebrate a holy time called Passover.

When Passover ended, Mary and Joseph started back for home. They thought Jesus was with relatives. But that night they could not find Jesus. He had not come back with the group.

Mary and Joseph looked everywhere for Jesus. Then they went back to Jerusalem. They looked for three days before they found him.

Jesus was in the Temple, talking with some teachers about the Scriptures. Mary hugged Jesus. "Why did you do this?" she asked him. Jesus smiled. "Did you not know that I must be in my Father's house?"

On the way home, Mary kept thinking about Jesus' words. Then she smiled. Her son was God's son, too. He was learning about God his Father.

Based on Luke 2:41–52

Our Church Teaches

God is the creator of all things. We read the **word of God** in the Bible.

Jesus is the **Son of God**. We read the teachings of Jesus in the Bible.

Activity Find the words from the chapter in the picture. Then color the picture.

Recall a story about God or Jesus in the Bible. What did you learn from the story?

We Believe

God made all creation good. Through creation, God shows himself to us in love. God wants us to know, love, and serve him.

Faith Word

Son of God

Son of God is a special title for Jesus. Jesus is God's only Son.

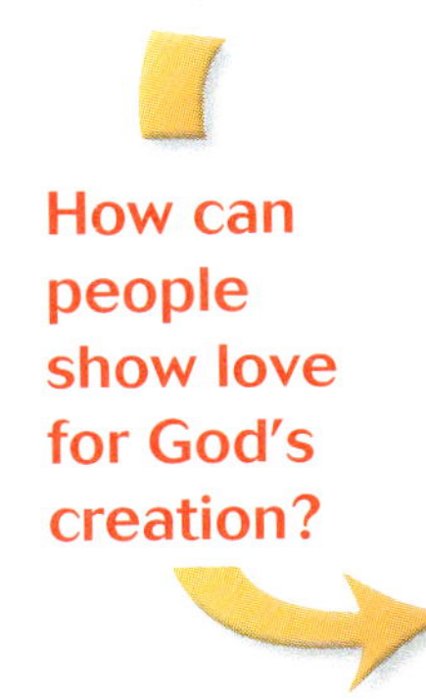

How can people show love for God's creation?

Respond

Caring for God's Creation

The Sisters of Earth are taking care of God's creation. Most of the Sisters of Earth are religious sisters. They want to heal the earth and protect it. Some Sisters of Earth live on farms, where they take care of the land. Others teach college students about farming, gardening, and caring for the earth. Others help people recycle things that can be used again.

? How can you care for God's creation?

Activities

1. Learn to sign the words "God cares for you."

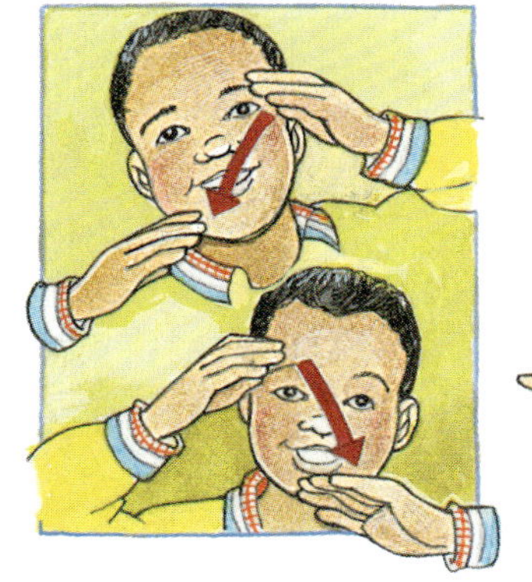

God cares for you.

2. Think of something God made that begins with each letter in the word creation. Write the words on the lines. The first one has been done for you.

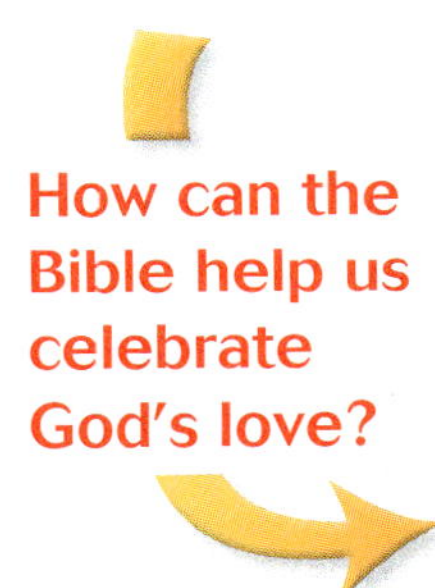

How can the Bible help us celebrate God's love?

Prayer Celebration

Bible Prayer

Celebrate the gifts of God's creation with this prayer of praise from the Bible. When you pray "O God, you are great indeed," lift your arms high, with the palms facing up.

Reader 1: You have made the clouds and wind.

All: **O God, you are great indeed!**

Reader 2: You have made the birds and trees.

All: **O God, you are great indeed!**

Reader 3: You have made the lakes and mountains.

All: **O God, you are great indeed!**

Reader 4: You have made the land and seas.

All: **O God, you are great indeed!**

Reader 5: How can we celebrate God's love?

All: **We will sing praise to God.**

Based on Psalm 104

9 Chapter Review

A **Make a list** of five things that the Bible tells us God created.

B **Complete** the sentences with words from the box.

all	always	love	more	Scriptures

1. The Bible is also called ______.
2. God takes care of ______ creation.
3. We learn about God's ______ for us from the Bible.
4. God loves us ______ than birds and flowers.
5. God will ______ take care of you.

C Circle the best answer.

1. Where was Jesus found when he was twelve years old?
   At the market **In the Temple** **At a relative's house**

2. What did Jesus talk about with the Jewish teachers?
   Mary **Roman law** **the Scriptures**

3. What do we read in the Bible?
   news **fables** **the word of God**

4. What is a special title for Jesus?
   Reformer **Son of God** **Baptizer**

D Draw a picture of one way you can care for God's creation.

Getting ready for Chapter 10

A choice of things to do at home

We Listen to God's Word

In this chapter, children will come to realize that when we hear the Scripture readings, we are listening to God's word. The children will learn the responses said during the Liturgy of the Word. They will also learn that the Nicene Creed is a prayer that states the beliefs that Catholics hold.

What is it for?

Assemble a group of varied reading materials, such as a newspaper, television guide, dictionary, math textbook, photo album, and Bible. Ask each family member to choose one item and describe its purpose. The Bible should be described as a holy book that contains stories about God's love for us.

Good listening

As a family, discuss ways to be a good listener. Create a chart to list the ideas. These may include being quiet, looking at the person who is speaking, and not talking until the person is finished. Decorate your chart and display it.

Good news

Put a "Remember the Good News!" sign on your refrigerator. Tell each other some good news this week. This will prepare your child to learn about the "Good News" of the Gospels.

A Prayer for the Week

Lord, we lift up our hearts,
our minds, and our ears to your
word. Help us understand your
Scriptures. Give us the gift
of understanding, Lord.
Amen.

FAMILY TIME

Something to Do . . .

On Sunday

Show your child the Old and New Testaments in the Bible. Point out that the New Testament contains the Gospel stories that tell about Jesus.

Through the Week

Read aloud some Bible passages. End your readings with the responses used at Mass.

Visit Our Web Site

www.blestarewe.com

Something to Think About . . .

The Sower and the Seed

Whoever has ears ought to hear.
Matthew 13:9

The Parable of the Sower that Jesus tells is about the importance of really hearing God's word and understanding it. Jesus equates the seeds the sower scatters with God's word. He categorizes people as those who hear God's word but don't understand it; those who hear God's word but believe it for only a short time; those who hear God's word but don't focus on it; or those who hear God's word and understand it. Jesus is saying that it is one thing to listen and hear, but we must also understand and act. This is what leads to Christian growth.

Something to Know About . . .

Our Heritage in Church Design

Catholic churches usually have a crucifix, statues, a baptismal font, an altar, and a lectern. The lectern reminds us that God speaks to us. A lectern may also be called an ambo. Starting around the ninth century, churches had two stands, called ambos. One was for Gospel readings and one was for readings from the letters. The one for the Gospel became more and more ornate until, by the thirteenth century, it became known as the pulpit. The word *pulpit* comes from the Latin *pulpitum*, meaning "stage." These ornate pulpits were at first built in Italian churches. Over time, they have been made in many styles and materials, such as stone and iron.

10 We Listen to God's Word

Listening to God's word is like building a house on rock.
A house like that will not fall down.

Based on Matthew 7:24–25

Share

Most people like hearing a good story. The story can be funny, sad, or even scary. To enjoy a story, we need to be good listeners.

1. Who is the best storyteller you know?

2. What story do you like to listen to again and again?

3. Why do you like this story?

When do church members listen to the stories of Jesus?

Hear & Believe

A Story About Listening

One day, Jesus told this story about listening to God's word.

"A farmer scattered seeds in his field. Some seeds fell on the path. Birds ate them up. Some seeds fell on rocks. The seeds dried up and died. Some seeds fell among weeds. The weeds grew up with the seeds and choked them. Other seeds fell on good soil. They took root, grew, and produced good fruit.

"People are like the different places where the farmer's seeds fell. Some people hear God's word but do not try to understand it. Some people hear God's word but only remember it for a short time. They are like the rocks. Some people hear God's word in church but then forget about it the rest of the week. They are like the ground that has many weeds. Other people hear God's word and really listen to it. They are like the good soil. Faith grows in them."

Based on Matthew 13:1–9, 18–23

Listening to God's Word

The Bible story tells us that when we really listen to God's word, our faith grows. At Mass we come together to listen to God's word from the Bible. This part of the Mass is the **Liturgy of the Word**.

Activity Review the Scripture story. Then, on the lines below, fill in where the seed fell.

_______________ They hear God's word, but forget about it during the week.

_______________ They hear God's word and listen to it. Faith grows in them.

_______________ They hear God's word, but only remember it for a short time.

What takes place during the Liturgy of the Word?

Hear & Believe

Father Andy's Visit

Father Andy smiled as he began to talk with the second graders. He had seen many of them in church on Sunday. Now he had the chance to talk with them in their classroom.

"Thank you for inviting me," he began. "Did Mrs. Evans tell you anything special about my visit today?"

Katie looked at her teacher and then raised her hand. "She told us to listen," said Katie.

Father Andy laughed as did a few of Katie's classmates. "What do you think it takes to really listen?" asked Father Andy.

"Our ears!" answered Katie, feeling more sure of herself.

"Oh yes—our ears, of course," said Father Andy. "But what else?"

No one answered. Everyone stared at Father Andy.

"We need to listen with our minds," he said. "We need to listen with our hearts."

What do you think it means to listen with your mind and with your heart?

Our Church Teaches

During the Liturgy of the Word on Sunday, we listen to three readings. The third reading is the **Gospel**. It tells the story of Jesus' life. Then the priest or deacon gives a talk called the homily. The **homily** helps us understand the Bible readings. After the Gospel and the homily, we state what Catholics believe in a prayer called the **Nicene Creed**.

We Believe

All the readings at Mass are from the Bible.

Activity What is happening in each picture?

The ______________ is giving the ______________.

Faith Words

Nicene Creed

Catholics tell what they believe when they pray the Nicene Creed at Mass. The creed tells about God's love for us and about how Jesus saved us.

The ______________ is reading the ______________.

How can we show we are listening during the Liturgy of the Word?

Respond

We Take Part at Mass

Jill loves Jesus. She wants to learn more about his life and teachings. That is why she tries her best to take part in Mass. She sings songs with other parish members. She answers "Amen" to the prayers. She stands, sits, and kneels with everyone else. And she listens to the Bible readings. She says the response at the end of each reading.

After the first Bible reading and after the second Bible reading, the reader says, "The Word of the Lord."

Jill answers, "Thanks be to God."

After the Gospel reading, the priest or deacon says, "The Gospel of the Lord."

Jill answers, "Praise to you, Lord Jesus Christ."

Then Jill sits down to listen to the homily.

Activity

What word is missing in each sentence?

1. The first part of Mass is the Liturgy of the ____.
2. After the first reading we say, "____ be to God."
3. The ____ tells the good news about Jesus' life and teachings.
4. After the Gospel we say, "____ to you, Lord Jesus Christ."
5. The talk given by the priest or deacon is called the ____.
6. The Nicene ____ is a prayer about what we believe as Catholics.

Now do the puzzle. Find and circle the missing words.

A	C	B	E	C	F	H	G
I	W	J	K	R	L	T	M
G	O	S	P	E	L	H	N
O	R	P	Q	E	R	A	S
U	D	T	V	D	X	N	Y
H	O	M	I	L	Y	K	Z
B	A	P	R	A	I	S	E

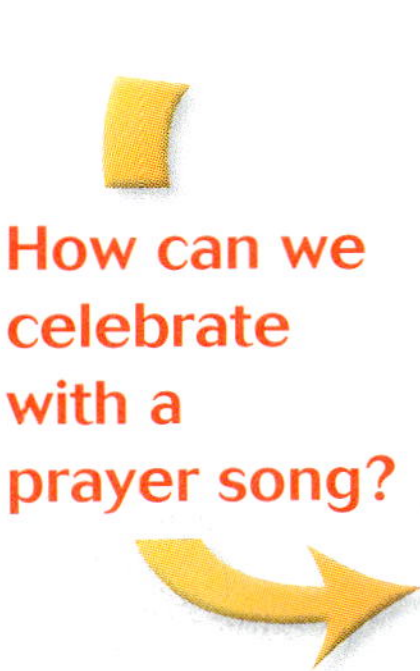

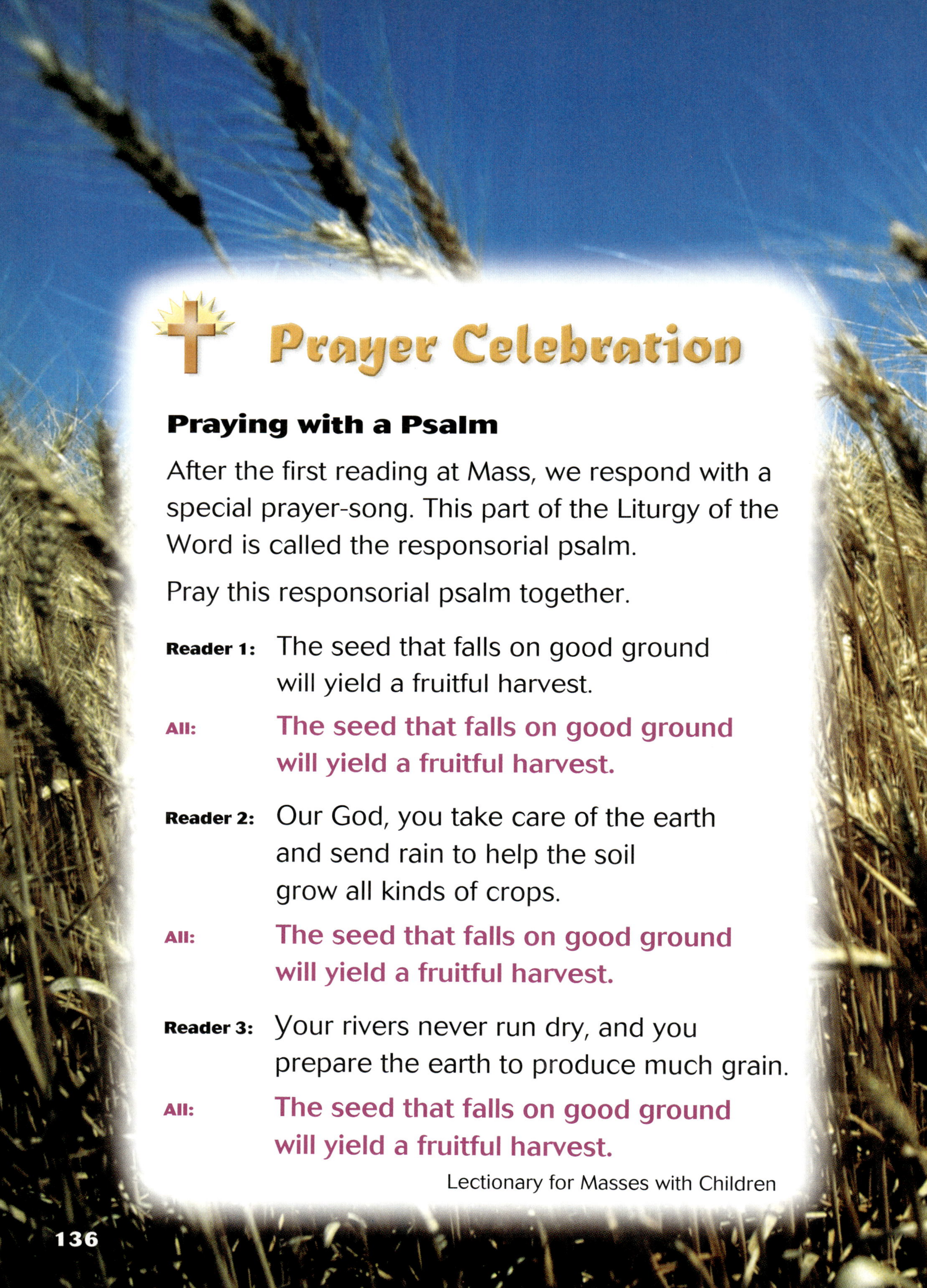

Prayer Celebration

Praying with a Psalm

After the first reading at Mass, we respond with a special prayer-song. This part of the Liturgy of the Word is called the responsorial psalm.

Pray this responsorial psalm together.

Reader 1: The seed that falls on good ground
will yield a fruitful harvest.

All: **The seed that falls on good ground**
will yield a fruitful harvest.

Reader 2: Our God, you take care of the earth
and send rain to help the soil
grow all kinds of crops.

All: **The seed that falls on good ground**
will yield a fruitful harvest.

Reader 3: Your rivers never run dry, and you
prepare the earth to produce much grain.

All: **The seed that falls on good ground**
will yield a fruitful harvest.

Lectionary for Masses with Children

10 Chapter Review

A **Draw a line** to connect the parts of each sentence.

1. People who listen to God's word are like seeds that fall on ____. •	• good soil
2. At Mass we come together to listen to God's word from the ____. •	• Word
3. We call this part of Mass the Liturgy of the ____. •	• Bible
4. ____ grows when we really listen to God's word. •	• faith

B **Unscramble** the words to complete the sentences.

1. During the Liturgy of the Word, we listen to readings from the **I B B E L**.

B______________________

2. The last reading is the **P L E S O G**.

G______________________

3. Catholics state what they believe in a prayer called the **C E E N I N E D R E C**.

N__________ C__________

C **Write** the answers to the questions.

1. After the first reading, the lector or reader says, "The Word of the Lord." What do we say?

2. After the Gospel reading, the priest or deacon says, "The Gospel of the Lord." What do we say?

3. After the readings at Mass, the priest or deacon gives a special talk. What do we call this talk? ____________

D **Number** the parts of the Liturgy of the Word in order.

____ The priest explains the Gospel reading.

____ We listen to the first Bible reading.

____ We state what we believe as Catholics.

____ We listen to the Gospel.

____ We sing a prayer-song.

Getting ready for Chapter 11

A choice of things to do at home

We Act on God's Word

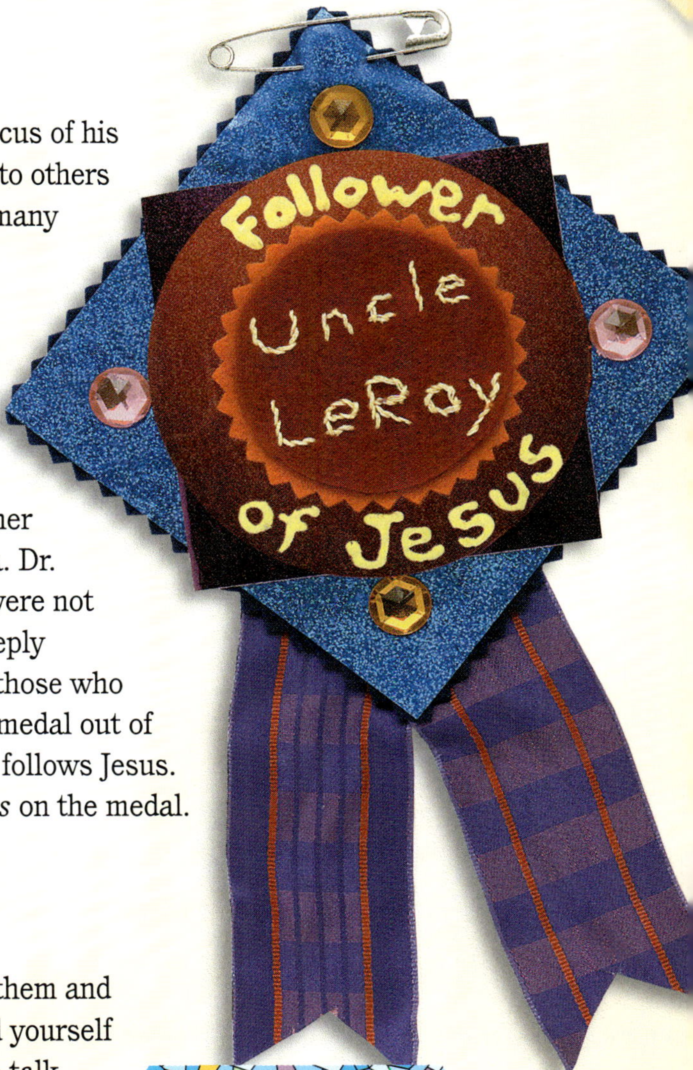

Jesus made the treatment of other human beings the focus of his time on earth. How we should think about and respond to others was the topic of many of Jesus' teachings. He gave us many examples of service. Children need to understand that Jesus cared for others to show his love for God. Jesus wants us to do the same by helping and serving others.

Followers of Jesus

Think of people who showed their love for others. Mother Teresa showed her love, especially for the poor of India. Dr. Martin Luther King Jr. showed his love for those who were not treated fairly by others. Mahatma Gandhi, who was deeply influenced by the New Testament, showed his love for those who treated each other peacefully. With your child, make a medal out of construction paper to honor any person you know who follows Jesus. Write the person's name and the words *Follower of Jesus* on the medal.

Hear no evil

Treating others well involves the way we speak about them and the things we listen to about them. Help your child and yourself avoid gossip. Don't talk negatively or listen to negative talk about others. Instead, help others and speak positively about them.

A quality person

Those who behave toward others as Jesus did have certain qualities in common. What are some of these qualities? Do you see these in your family? Discuss the qualities that make a good person.

A Prayer for the Week

Dear Jesus, give us the grace and strength to follow you. Help us trust as you did, love as you did, and care for others as you did. We trust you to help us. Amen.

FAMILY TIME

Something to Do . . .

On Sunday

What do today's readings tell you about being a good person? Pick one message from the homily to take home from this week's liturgy.

Through the Week

Using Jesus as your model, pick one thing that he did and try to make it part of your life.

Visit Our Web Site

www.blestarewe.com

Something to Think About . . .

In Loving Service

Amen, I say to you, whatever you did for one of these least brothers of mine, you did for me.

Matthew 25:40

The standard of behavior that Jesus sets for us is very high. He expects us to love and care for our family members, our friends, and even people we do not like. Jesus treated everyone with love and wants us to do the same.

In the Gospel story, Jesus told about the works of mercy. The works of mercy include feeding the hungry, giving drink to the thirsty, sheltering the homeless, clothing the naked, and visiting the sick and those in prison. Jesus is saying that when we help others in loving service, we show our love for God. We are challenged daily to treat all people with love.

Something to Know About . . .

Our Heritage in Literature

Thomas Merton was a Catholic monk who died in 1968. He was a convert to Catholicism as a young adult and wrote an autobiography in 1948 about how he moved from atheism to Catholicism. That book, *The Seven Storey Mountain*, became the most famous memoir ever written by an American Catholic. He was a social activist and spoke out on such topics as racial justice, violence, and world peace. His clear vision of how to live a Christian life, his wonderful writing, and his ever-questioning spirit are inspirations for those who have come after him.

11 We Act on God's Word

If you believe in me, you will act as I have acted.

Based on John 14:12

Share

So many actions
That we take.
We walk and ride.
We bake a cake.

So many actions
Every day.
We laugh and smile
We learn and pray.

Imagine yourself in each picture. What would you do? Write about an action you would take.

I would

____

____

____.

I would

____

____

____.

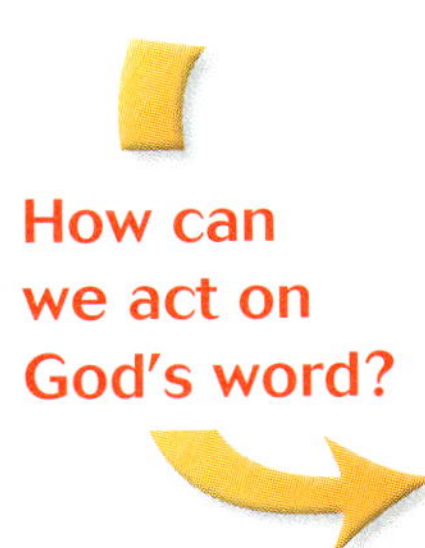

How can we act on God's word?

How Christians Act

Jesus told his followers, "I will return to earth at the end of time. Then I will judge all the people in the world. I will put the people in two groups. To the first group I will say, 'You have done well. I invite you to stay with me forever.' But I will tell the second group, 'Go far away. I don't want to see you again.'"

The people in the first group had treated everyone the same way as they would have treated Jesus. They gave food to the hungry. They gave drink to people who were thirsty. They made new people feel at home. They shared their own clothes with people who needed them. They cared for the sick. And they visited people in prison.

The first group of people had acted on God's word. That is why Jesus will welcome them to be with him forever.

Based on Matthew 25:31–46

Responding in Action

Jesus did good things because he loved God and wanted to please him. Jesus wants his followers to respond to God's word, too. Jesus wants us to treat others with love.

Activity How can we treat others with love? Write about or draw one thing you will do.

Jesus will welcome us to be with him

____

______________________________.

What else can you do to love others?

Kid's Kitchen

Sagen was only in second grade. But she knew there were many poor children in her school. These children ate free lunches during the school year.

"What do they eat during the summer?" Sagen wondered. She decided to try to help.

Sagen went to Sam, who ran the soup kitchen in her parish. He taught her how to organize her own kitchen.

Two summers later, Sagen opened the first Kid's Kitchen in her town. People from ten churches donated food. Sagen's friends prepared the food and served it.

That summer, Kid's Kitchen served 600 lunches to poor children every Wednesday. The children could take food home to share with their families.

Sagen spoke about Kid's Kitchen. "I feel the need to do something for others," she said. "That's what I hear on Sunday at church. I want to do something during the week that really helps other people."

Our Church Teaches

Jesus told his followers about some good actions. They are called the **works of mercy**. When we help others in loving **service**, we act as Jesus did.

The Works of Mercy
Feed the hungry.
Give drink to the thirsty.
Shelter the homeless.
Give clothing to the poor.
Visit the sick.
Visit those in prison.
Pray for those who have died.

Activity People in your parish practice the works of mercy. What is one thing they do?

____

____

? What will you do to serve others?

We Believe

Jesus shows us how to act on God's word. He teaches us that by loving our neighbor, we show our love for God.

Faith Words

works of mercy
The works of mercy tell how Jesus wants us to help others.

service
Service means doing work that helps others.

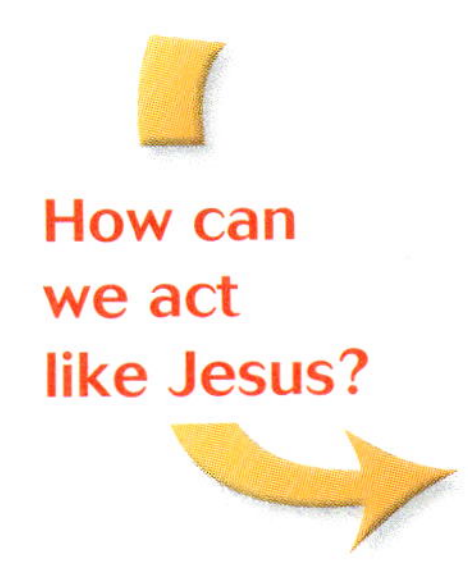

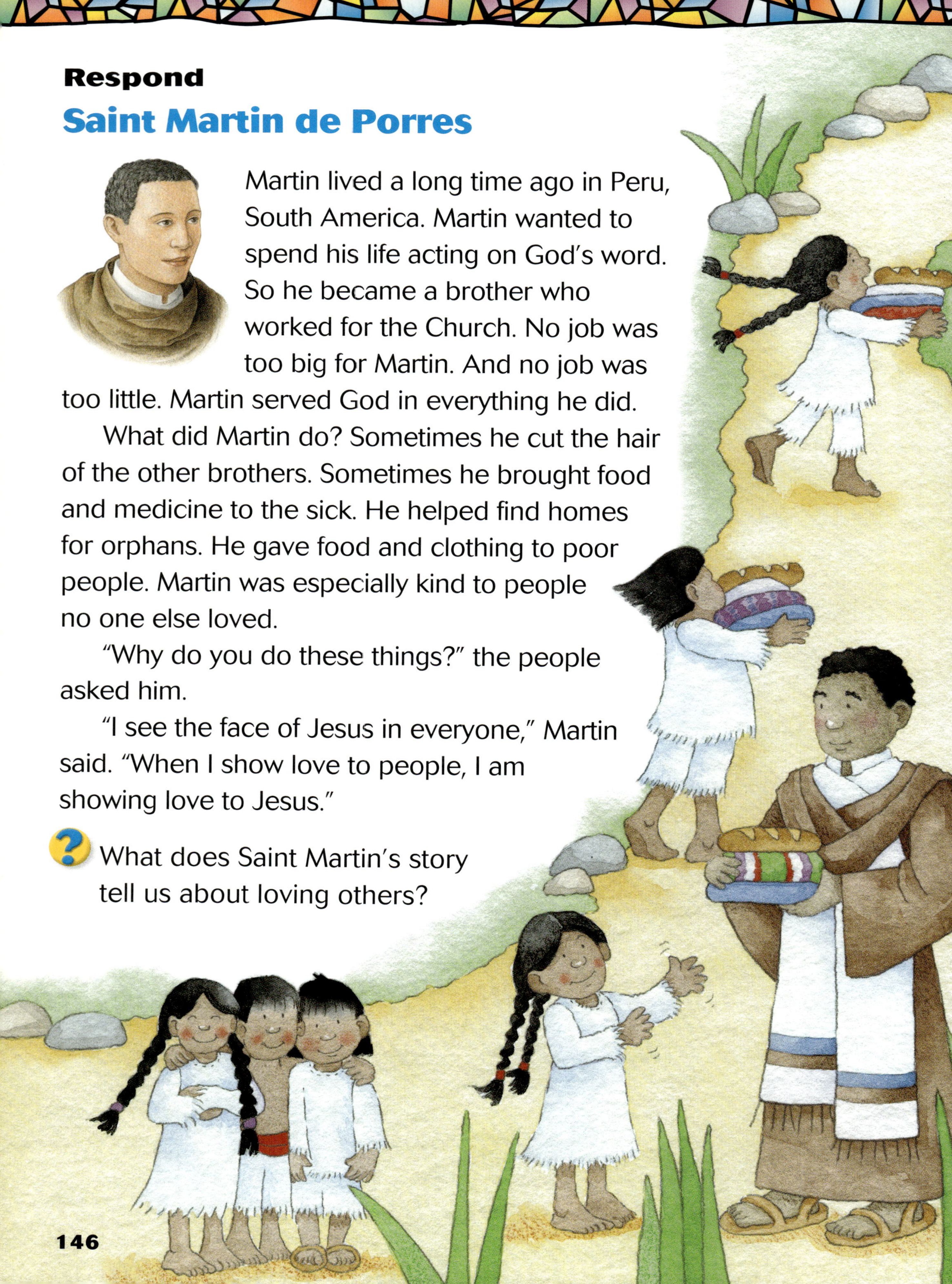

Respond

Saint Martin de Porres

Martin lived a long time ago in Peru, South America. Martin wanted to spend his life acting on God's word. So he became a brother who worked for the Church. No job was too big for Martin. And no job was too little. Martin served God in everything he did.

What did Martin do? Sometimes he cut the hair of the other brothers. Sometimes he brought food and medicine to the sick. He helped find homes for orphans. He gave food and clothing to poor people. Martin was especially kind to people no one else loved.

"Why do you do these things?" the people asked him.

"I see the face of Jesus in everyone," Martin said. "When I show love to people, I am showing love to Jesus."

What does Saint Martin's story tell us about loving others?

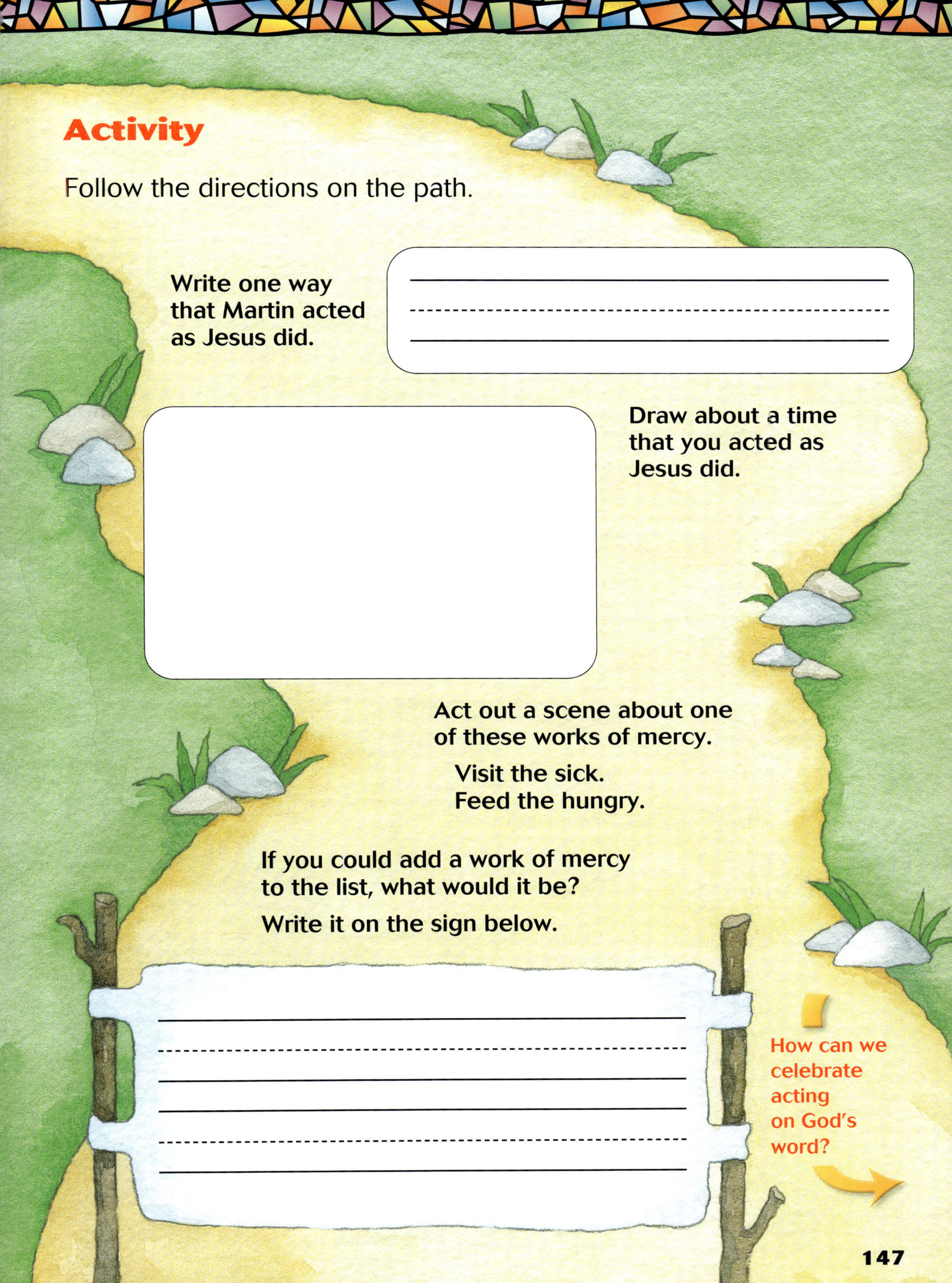

Activity

Follow the directions on the path.

Write one way that Martin acted as Jesus did.

Draw about a time that you acted as Jesus did.

Act out a scene about one of these works of mercy.

Visit the sick.
Feed the hungry.

If you could add a work of mercy to the list, what would it be?

Write it on the sign below.

How can we celebrate acting on God's word?

Prayer Celebration

A Saint's Prayer

Saint Frances Cabrini and some friends in Italy became famous for teaching children, caring for orphans, and helping the sick. Mother Cabrini was asked to come to the United States to help the many poor people who had come here from Italy. She directed the building of schools, orphanages, and hospitals. Mother Cabrini spent her life acting on God's word and helping others.

Listen to this prayer. It is based on a prayer that Mother Cabrini wrote.

Lord, you have made me see so many things.
I see that you are the one who acts.
You are the one who does everything.
I can do nothing without you.
You are the one who does all.
I stand in wonder
of your great and beautiful works.

Now read the prayer aloud together.

11 Chapter Review

A **Draw a line** to match each need with an action that responds to God's word.

1. People are hungry.	●	●	We give them something to drink.
2. People are thirsty.	●	●	We visit them.
3. People are cold.	●	●	We take care of them.
4. People are sick.	●	●	We give them clothes.
5. People are in prison.	●	●	We give them food.

B **Complete** each sentence with the correct word.

forever Jesus mercy respond

1. The works of ____________ tell how Jesus wants us to help others.
2. When we help others in loving ways, we act as ____________ did.
3. People who help others will be with Jesus ____________.
4. Acting with love is a way to ____________ to God's word.

C **Who am I?** Write the correct name on each line.

Martin de Porres   Mother Cabrini   Jesus Christ

1. I will return to earth at the end of time to judge all people.

2. I helped many poor people in Peru, South America.

3. I built schools, orphanages, and hospitals in the United States.

D **Draw or write** about one way you can give loving service as Jesus did.

Getting ready for Chapter 12

A choice of things to do at home

We Pray for Others

In this chapter, children will become more aware of the needs of others. Sometimes all we can do to help others is to pray for them. The children will come to realize that, when we pray, we trust God to care for people's needs. The children will also compose their own prayers for other people.

Trust walk

Blindfold one family member. Then have someone be the trust-walk leader. It is the leader's job to make sure that the blindfolded person doesn't bump into anything or get hurt. It is the blindfolded person's job to trust the leader. Take turns being the blindfolded person and the leader. Then talk about what it was like to play these roles.

Butterfly house

In order to survive, winter butterflies either migrate or hibernate. To help the ones that hibernate, you and your child can put a box with slits in it outdoors. Kits are available in hobby stores for building butterfly houses. It's a way to help some of God's fragile creatures.

What's wrong?

With your child, practice solving a pretend or real problem, such as making up with a friend or finding time to do homework. First, state the problem. Next, propose and discuss possible solutions. Finally, decide on the best solution.

A Prayer for the Week

Lord, sometimes we are caught up with our own needs and we ignore the needs of those around us. Open our hearts to see the needs of others. Amen.

FAMILY TIME

Something to Do . . .

On Sunday

Listen for the priest to say the words "Let us pray." When he pauses, use the opportunity to be quiet and prayerful. When he continues, listen with attentive ears and an open heart.

Through the Week

Take time each day to quiet yourself and pray for the needs of others.

Visit Our Web Site

www.blestarewe.com

Something to Know About . . .

Our Heritage in Prayer

Do not despise my poor prayer. Do not let my trust be confounded!

The prayer above is part of a novena to Saint Jude, the patron saint of impossible causes. A novena is a repeated prayer asking for a specific intention. N*ovena* comes from the Latin word *novem*, or *nine*. Most novenas are said nine times in a row for nine days in a row. Often said as a last resort by the desperate or the hopeless, novenas may be made to saints, to angels, and to God himself. Mary, the mother of Jesus, is perhaps the person most often addressed in this form of devotion.

Something to Think About . . .

Praying for Ourselves and Others

Ask and it will be given to you; seek and you will find; knock and the door will be opened to you.
Matthew 7:7

Just as Jesus told his friends and followers to trust God, so he tells us to do the same. Jesus taught that God gives us what we need when we pray. He also said to pray for the needs of others. As Christians we pray for our needs in prayers called *petitions*. God gives us the support and strength to deal with whatever comes our way. When we pray for the needs of others, the prayers are called *intercessions*. We often pray for those we love, since we know their needs. We trust God to care for others when we pray for them.

Saint Jude, also called Saint Jude Thaddeus

12 We Pray for Others

O God, hear me and answer my prayer.

Based on Psalm 17:6

Share

Have you ever made a list of things you wish you could do? Perhaps you want to learn to ice skate. Maybe you would like to see the ocean.

Write three of your wishes here.

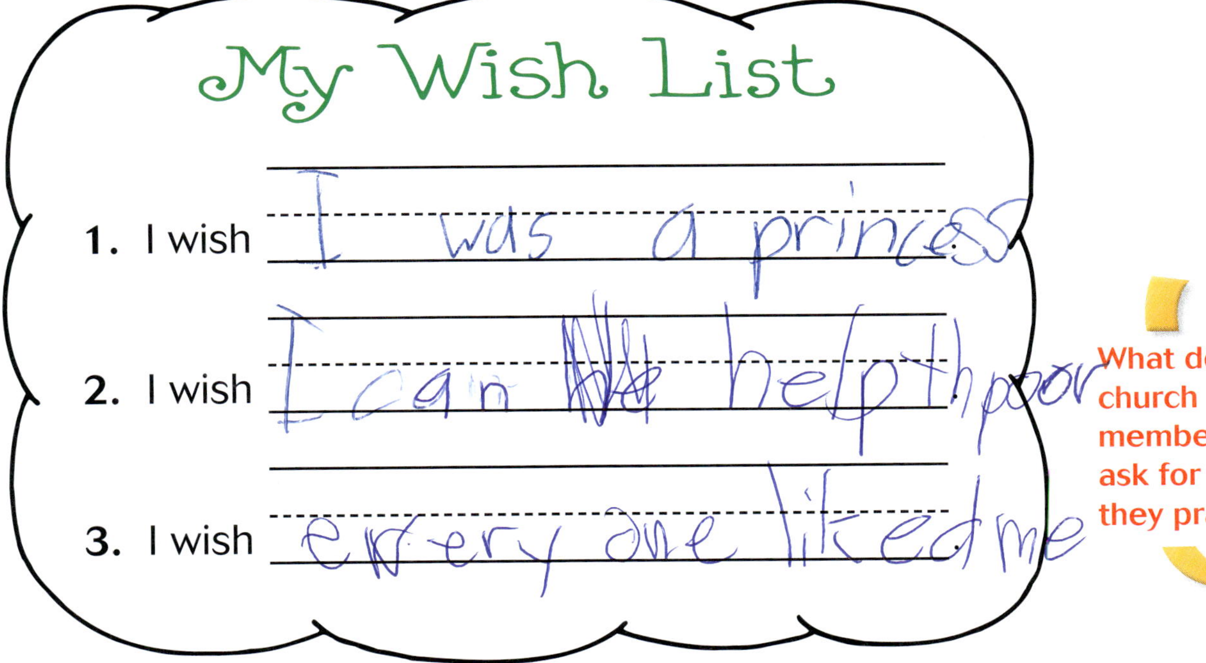

What do church members ask for when they pray?

Jesus and Prayer

On the night before he died, Jesus ate dinner with his friends. After dinner, Jesus prayed for his friends. “Father, please help my friends in their work. Help them tell others about your love.”

Jesus taught about different kinds of prayer. One time, Jesus said we should ask God for what we need for ourselves. “Ask, and you shall receive,” Jesus said. “Pray for what you need, and God will give it to you.”

Another time, Jesus said we should pray for the needs of other people. “When you come together to pray for others, I will be with you,” Jesus promised. “God will give you whatever you ask for in my name.”

Based on John 17:9–21; Matthew 7:7–8; 18:19–20; John 16:23

Christian Prayer

Jesus told his friends to place their trust in God. When we pray for ourselves, we know that God will answer us. When we pray for other people, we trust that God will care for them.

Activity Make a prayer list. Write the names of people for whom you will pray.

1. ______________________________
2. ______________________________
3. ______________________________
4. ______________________________
5. ______________________________
6. ______________________________

What are petitions and intercessions?

Hear & Believe

A Full Time Job

Most people go to Las Vegas to have fun. There are many hotels, restaurants, swimming pools, and places to play games. But Agnes went to Las Vegas to pray.

Agnes joined a group of religious sisters there called the Carmelites. These sisters almost never leave their house. They spend most of the day in prayer.

One day, Agnes had a visitor. It was Carla, her youngest sister.

"Who do you pray for?" Carla asked.

Agnes smiled. "I pray for you and our family. I pray for members of the Church. I pray for the people who work here. I pray for the people who visit here. I pray for the people I read about in the newspaper. I pray for the people I hear about on the TV news."

"That's a lot of people to pray for," Carla said.

Agnes laughed. "Maybe that is why Jesus told us to pray always. It's a full-time job!"

Our Church Teaches

As Christians we pray for our own needs. We call these prayers petitions. We ask God to give us what we need to be good followers of Jesus.

Activity Use your own words to make up a prayer of petition. Think about what you need in order to be a good follower of Jesus. Ask God to answer your prayer.

We also pray for the needs of others. We call these prayers intercessions. At Mass the Liturgy of the Word ends with the **Prayer of the Faithful**. In this prayer of intercession, we pray for people everywhere.

We Believe

We trust our heavenly Father to answer our prayers. We know that God loves us and gives us what is truly good for us.

Faith Words

Prayer of the Faithful

The Prayer of the Faithful is the last part of the Liturgy of the Word at Mass. During this prayer we pray for ourselves and for people everywhere.

How can we pray a prayer of intercession?

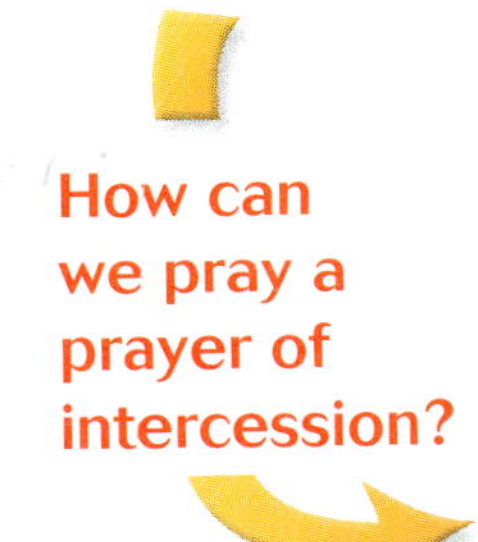

Respond

The Needs of Others

Before we can pray for others, we need to know what they need. The photos on this page tell stories. Talk about what the people need.

How would you ask God to care for these people?

Activities

The prayer below is a prayer for people in need.

For those who are sick,
we pray to the Lord.

1. Use your own words to complete these prayers for other people.

For those who ______________________________,
we pray to the Lord.

For those who ______________________________,
we pray to the Lord.

2. Color each space that has an **X**. What is the hidden message?

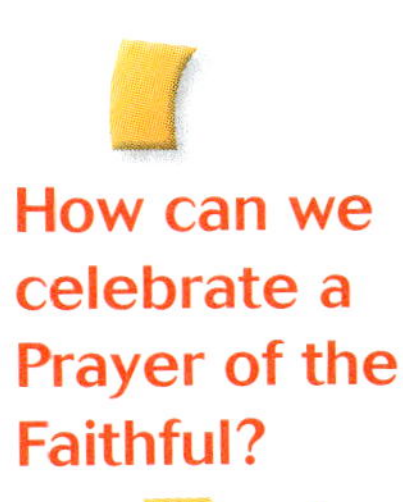

How can we celebrate a Prayer of the Faithful?

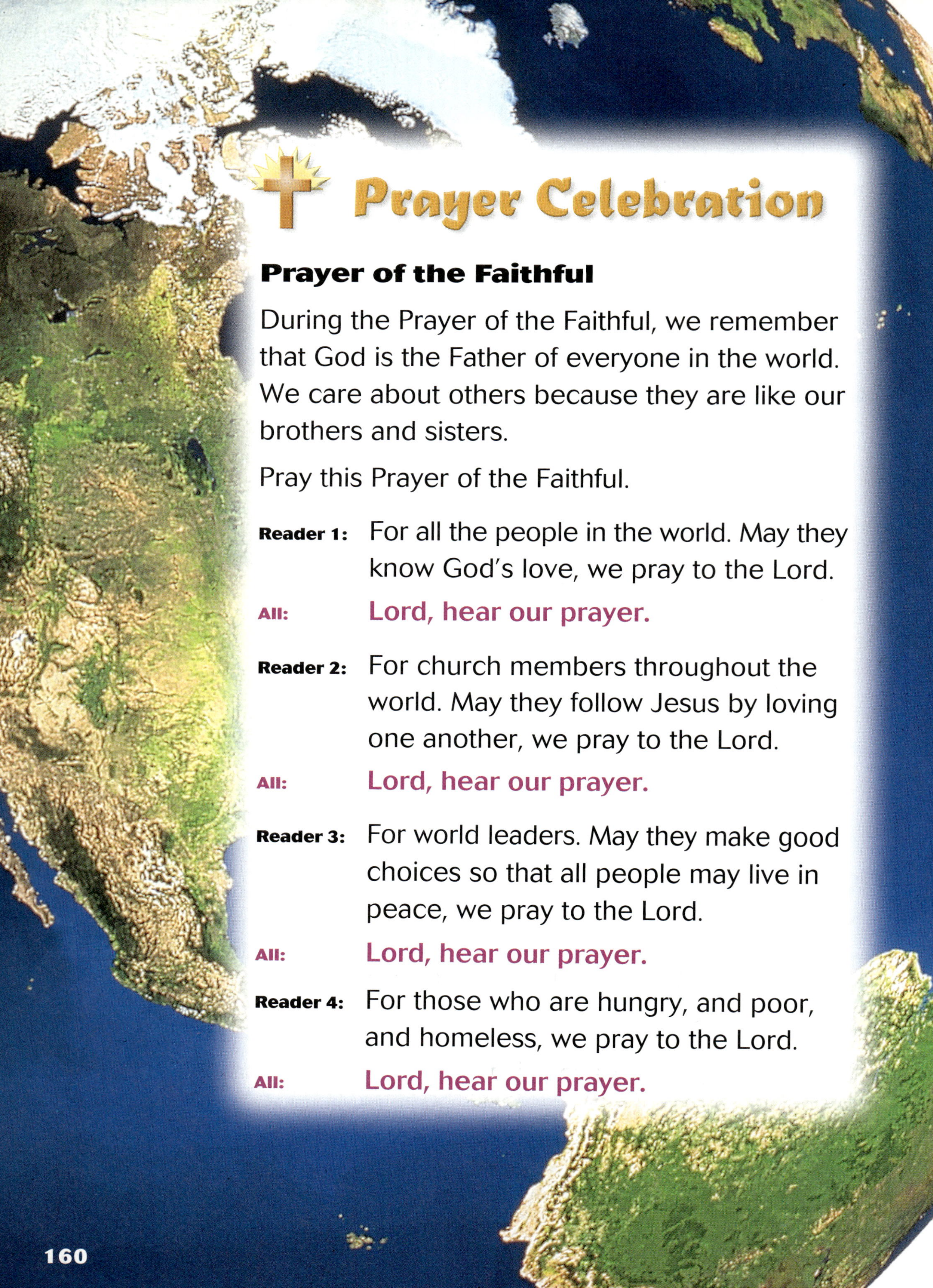

Prayer Celebration

Prayer of the Faithful

During the Prayer of the Faithful, we remember that God is the Father of everyone in the world. We care about others because they are like our brothers and sisters.

Pray this Prayer of the Faithful.

Reader 1: For all the people in the world. May they know God's love, we pray to the Lord.

All: **Lord, hear our prayer.**

Reader 2: For church members throughout the world. May they follow Jesus by loving one another, we pray to the Lord.

All: **Lord, hear our prayer.**

Reader 3: For world leaders. May they make good choices so that all people may live in peace, we pray to the Lord.

All: **Lord, hear our prayer.**

Reader 4: For those who are hungry, and poor, and homeless, we pray to the Lord.

All: **Lord, hear our prayer.**

12 Chapter Review

A **Draw a line** to complete the parts of each sentence.

1. After dinner on the night before he died, Jesus ____ •	• receive."
2. "Ask and you shall ____ •	• in my name."
3. "God will give you whatever you ask for ____ •	• prayed for his friends.

B **Circle** the best answer.

1. Jesus told us to pray ____.
   sometimes **always** **only in church**
2. Carmelite Sisters spend most of the day ____.
   teaching school **praying** **at Mass**
3. Prayers for our own needs are called ____.
   intercessions **petitions** **litanies**
4. Prayers for the needs of others are called ____.
   intercessions **petitions** **praise prayers**
5. The ____ is a prayer of intercession at the end of the Liturgy of the Word.
   Prayer of the Faithful **Nicene Creed**

C **Circle** the four words hidden in the puzzle. Then use these words to answer the questions.

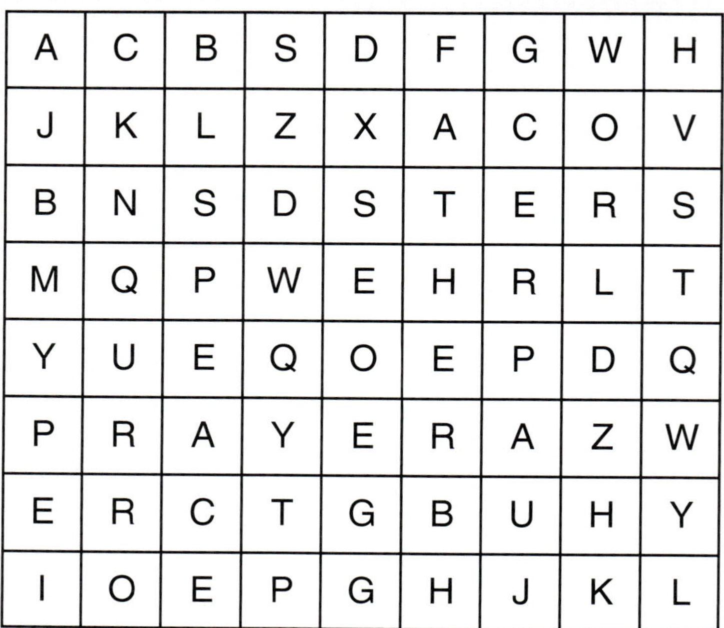

A	C	B	S	D	F	G	W	H
J	K	L	Z	X	A	C	O	V
B	N	S	D	S	T	E	R	S
M	Q	P	W	E	H	R	L	T
Y	U	E	Q	O	E	P	D	Q
P	R	A	Y	E	R	A	Z	W
E	R	C	T	G	B	U	H	Y
I	O	E	P	G	H	J	K	L

1. During the Prayer of the Faithful, we remember that God is the ______________________ of everyone.

2. In the Prayer of the Faithful, we pray for church members throughout the ______________________.

3. In the Prayer of the Faithful, we pray that all people may live in ______________________.

4. One way to respond to each petition during the Prayer of the Faithful is, "Lord, hear our ______________________."

Partners in Planting

Father Garcia found something out about the senior citizens in the parish. It seems that many of them wanted to have a garden! A friend of Father Garcia's let these older people use some empty land. Now they had a place to plant their gardens.

But gardening is very hard work. So Father Garcia asked some religious education students to help. Each student became a partner with an older gardener. They became friends. The children learned so many things! First, they learned to respect their partners. But most of all, they learned to respect God's wonderful creation!

What have you learned from a senior citizen?

Think About It

Do you know anyone who has a vegetable garden or a flower garden? Do they like taking care of it?

What is your favorite vegetable or flower? Draw a picture of it.

Learn About It

The Earth that God has given us is a wonderful place. But God tells us we must respect the Earth. We must take care of it. We must use it well.

Today many children live in cities. It is not easy to learn to respect the Earth in a city. Mostly you see roads, parking lots, and buildings. The children in Father Garcia's parish are lucky. They have the vegetable gardens. And they have older people to teach them how to respect our Earth.

Do Something About It

You may not have a garden. But you can still learn to respect the Earth.

Use a ✔ to show things you could do to respect our Earth:

- ☐ pick up litter
- ☐ grow plants outdoors
- ☐ recycle plastic
- ☐ throw cans on the grass

Organizer

Use these words to complete the sentences.

pray love act listen

1. In the Bible we learn about God's
______________.

2. In the Bible we learn to
______________ to God's word.

3. In the Bible we learn how to
______________ on God's word.

4. We learn we must
______________ for others.

Unit 3 Review

A **Circle** the best answer.

1. God made all creation (**good** **fair** **bad**).
2. God is a loving (**angel** **father** **shepherd**).
3. God will always (**take care of** **ignore** **refuse**) you.
4. Mary and Joseph took Jesus to the feast of the (**Temple** **Passover** **Trinity**).
5. Mary knew that her son was God's (**cousin** **son** **father**).

B **Recall** an event from the life of Jesus in the Gospel. Draw or write about this event in the space below.

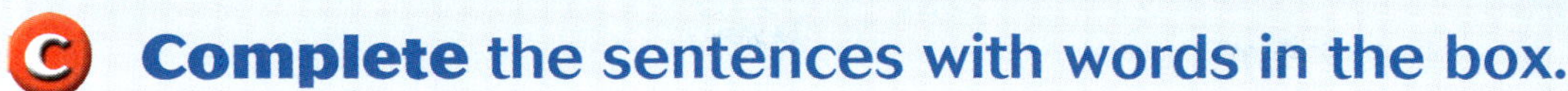

UNIT 3 Review

C Complete the sentences with words in the box.

word love news

1. Jesus told his followers about some good

______________________.

2. Jesus shows us how to act on God's

______________________.

3. Jesus tells us when we love our neighbor, we

show our ______________________ for God.

D Draw a line to connect the parts of each sentence.

1. The prayers we pray for ourselves •	• give us what is truly good for us.
2. The prayers we pray for others •	• are called intercessions.
3. We know that God will •	• spend most of their day in prayer.
4. The Carmelite Sisters •	• are called petitions.

UNIT 3
Review

E Circle the best answer.

1. During this prayer we pray for ourselves and for people everywhere. It is called the ____.

   Hail Mary **Nicene Creed** **Prayer of the Faithful**

2. A special title for Jesus is ____.

   Son of the Earth **Son of God** **Son of Bethlehem**

3. Good actions that help others are called ____.

   works of grace **works of the Bible** **works of mercy**

4. Doing work that helps others is called ____.

   service **visiting** **projects**

5. Catholics recall God's love for us and Jesus' saving actions in the ____.

   Novena **Nicene Creed** **Our Father**

F Respond to the following questions.

1. How does Jesus want us to treat others?

   ____

2. What is one way that you treat others as Jesus wants?

   ____

3. Who told us that God the Father will always take care of us?

   ____

UNIT 4

We Celebrate the Gift of Eucharist

God's greatest gift to us is his only Son, Jesus Christ. We celebrate the Eucharist to praise and thank God for this gift. We celebrate to share more fully in the life of Christ.

I am the bread of life.
Those who eat this bread
will never be hungry.

Based on John 6:35

Jesus was buried in a tomb very much like the one shown here. We remember Jesus' death and Resurrection each time we receive Holy Communion.

Eat This Bread

John 6, Adapted by Robert J. Batastini and the Taizé Community *Music by Jacques Berthier*

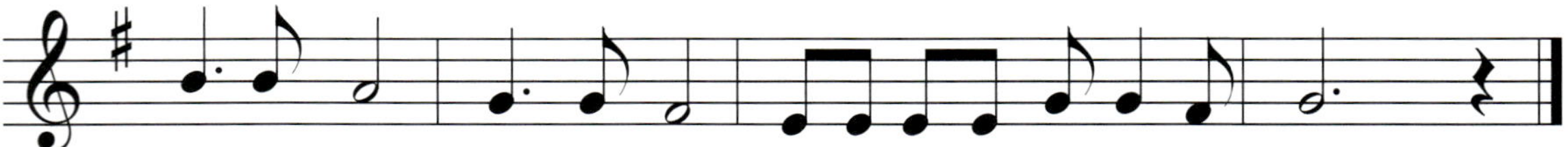

Getting ready for Chapter 13

A choice of things to do at home

Jesus Saves Us from Sin

We know that Jesus gave up his life to save all of us from sin. We all share the benefit of his great sacrifice. This chapter presents the story of Jesus' death and Resurrection. Children will consider the concept of sacrifice as it applies to everyday life, and they will learn about the ultimate sacrifice made by Jesus when he gave up his life so that we could be saved from sin.

Gift giving

Help your child write a brief description of something (such as a handcrafted item or a picture) that could be made as a gift for a friend. The description should tell why the friend would like the gift. Then help your child make the item.

It's a sacrifice

Discuss the meaning of sacrifice by using an example, such as a sacrifice fly in baseball. Explain that sacrifice is the act of giving up one thing for the sake of something else. Help your child think of some advantages in making sacrifices.

The rugged cross

Together, make a cross of twigs held together with a piece of twine or a pipe cleaner. Display your work in a prominent place. Let it serve as a reminder that Jesus sacrificed his life to save us from sin.

A Prayer for the Week

Your cross is a sign
of your gift to us, O God.
You gave the life of your Son,
Jesus, so that we would
be saved from sin.
Amen.

FAMILY TIME

Something to Do . . .

On Sunday

After the consecration, say (or sing) the words "Christ has died, Christ is risen, Christ will come again" with a new sense of appreciation.

Through the Week

In gratitude for the gift of salvation that Jesus gave us, praise and thank God in prayers throughout each day.

Visit Our Web Site

www.blestarewe.com

Something to Think About . . .

The Greatest Gift

Having bought a linen cloth, he took him down, wrapped him in the linen cloth and laid him in a tomb that had been hewn out of the rock.

Mark 15:46

Jesus loved us so much that he accepted a punishment for a crime he had not committed. Jesus sacrificed his life when he died on the cross. He gave us the gift of his life, and it all stemmed from his love. Jesus is God's greatest gift to us. His Resurrection from the dead to new life is central to our faith. He is our Savior, having saved us from sin and given us everlasting life. How blessed we are to have received such a love!

Something to Know About . . . Our Heritage

Many have been inspired by God's raising Jesus to glory. One person was a French priest named Basil Anthony Moreau. He was born in 1799, at the end of the French Revolution. The country was devastated, and many people were needed to minister. Father Moreau gathered a group of priests and brothers and established the Congregation of Holy Cross in 1837. Today there are four Holy Cross congregations who follow the spirit and ministry of Father Moreau: the Congregation of Holy Cross (priests and brothers), the Marianites of Holy Cross, the Sisters of the Holy Cross, and the Sisters of Holy Cross. All of these groups conduct ministries around the world.

13 Jesus Saves Us from Sin

The greatest love you can show is to give up your life for your friends.

Based on John 15:13

Share

Acting on God's word is not always easy. Sometimes we have to give up what we want. Sometimes we have to put the needs of others first.

What is the boy giving up?
Why is he doing this?

What is the girl giving up?
Why is she doing this?

Draw a picture that shows a time when you gave up something.

What did Jesus give up for us?

Jesus Gives Up His Life

Jesus gave up his life to save us from sin. On the night before he died, Jesus was arrested by his enemies. The next day, soldiers led Jesus to a place where they nailed him to a large wooden cross. Then they waited for Jesus to die.

After Jesus died, some of his friends took him away and buried him.

Three days later Jesus' friends went to visit his grave, or tomb. When they got there, Jesus was gone. An angel told the friends that Jesus had been raised from the dead.

Based on Mark 15:1–47; 16:1–6

God's Gift of Jesus

Jesus is God's greatest gift to us. Jesus gave up his life as a **sacrifice** for our sins. A sacrifice is a special gift that is given out of love.

We call Jesus our **Savior**. A savior is someone who rescues others from danger. Jesus saves us from sin and death.

Faith Words

sacrifice

A sacrifice is a special gift that is given out of love.

Activity What can we say to Jesus who sacrificed his life for us? Fill in the letters.

T__ __ __K Y__ __, JE__ U__, __O__ S__V__ __ __ U__!

Say these words each day as a prayer.

What do we call Jesus' rising from the dead?

Hear & Believe

Jesus Rises from the Dead

Three days after Jesus died, Mary and another woman went to Jesus' tomb. When they got there, a great earthquake shook the ground. An angel rolled aside the huge stone that covered the entrance to the tomb. The soldiers guarding the tomb fainted from fear.

Mary and her friend were afraid, too. But then the angel said, "Do not be afraid! I know you are looking for Jesus. He is not here because he has been raised from the dead. Come and see the place where he lay. Go and tell his disciples the good news."

Mary and her friend saw the empty tomb. Then they hurried away to tell everyone the good news. On their way, they met Jesus! The women were so happy. They bowed down and kissed his feet as a sign of love and respect.

Then Jesus said, "Do not be afraid. Go tell my brothers to go to Galilee. There they will see me."

Based on Matthew 28:1–10

Our Church Teaches

Jesus died on the cross to save us from our sins. Three days later, God raised Jesus to new life. By his life, death, and **Resurrection**, Jesus showed us God's love.

Activity Complete each sentence.

1. Jesus died on a large wooden C______.
2. Jesus gave up his life as a S______ for our sins.
3. By his life, death, and Resurrection, Jesus showed us God's l______.
4. We call Jesus being raised from the dead the R______.
5. Jesus is our S______ because he saves us from sin and death.
6. Jesus, our Savior gives us everlasting l______.

We Believe

Jesus' Resurrection is an important belief of our faith. Because of our Savior's Resurrection, we are saved from sin and given everlasting life.

Faith Words

Resurrection

Resurrection is Jesus' being raised from the dead to new life.

Respond

Saint Elizabeth of Hungary

Elizabeth was born a long, long time ago. She was the daughter of the King and Queen of Hungary. Elizabeth was rich, and she spent her money wisely.

Elizabeth loved Jesus very much. To show her love, she fed people who were poor and hungry. She took care of people who were sick and alone. Because of Elizabeth, hospitals were built in two towns. Elizabeth sold her fancy clothes and jewelry to help the poor. She gave everything she had to people in need.

? Why did Saint Elizabeth of Hungary make sacrifices?

Activities

1. Think of one sacrifice you could make this week. Write about how this sacrifice will show your love for someone.

2. At Mass we listen as the priest prays, "Let us proclaim the mystery of faith."

Trace over the dotted words below. You will find "the mystery of faith."

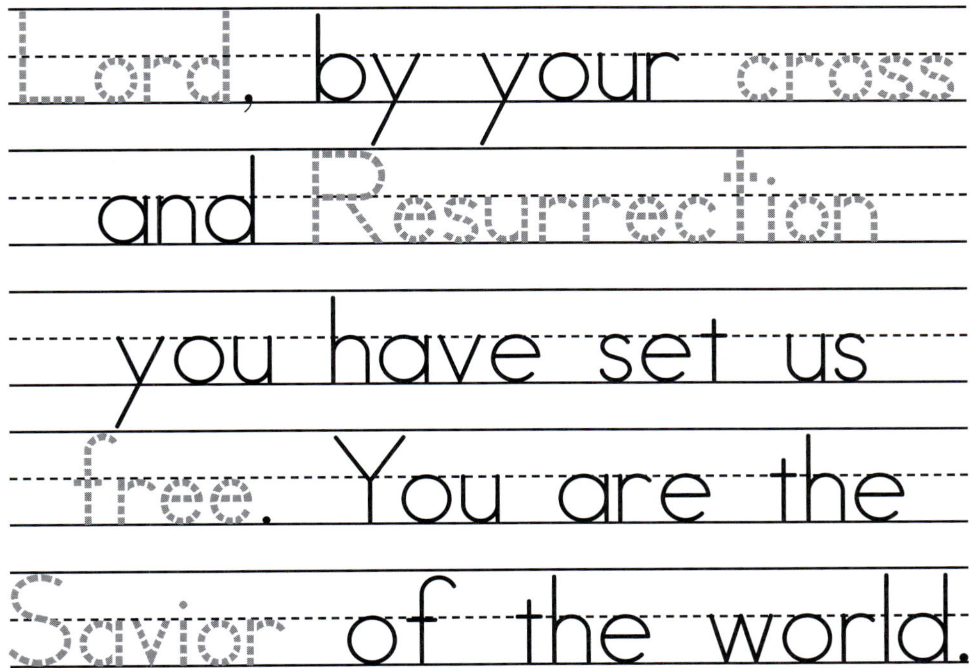

How can we celebrate the sacrifice of Jesus?

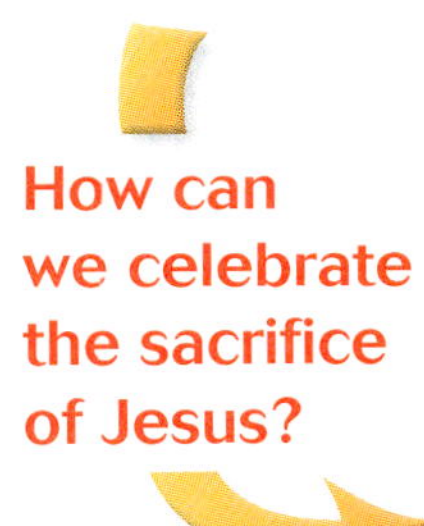

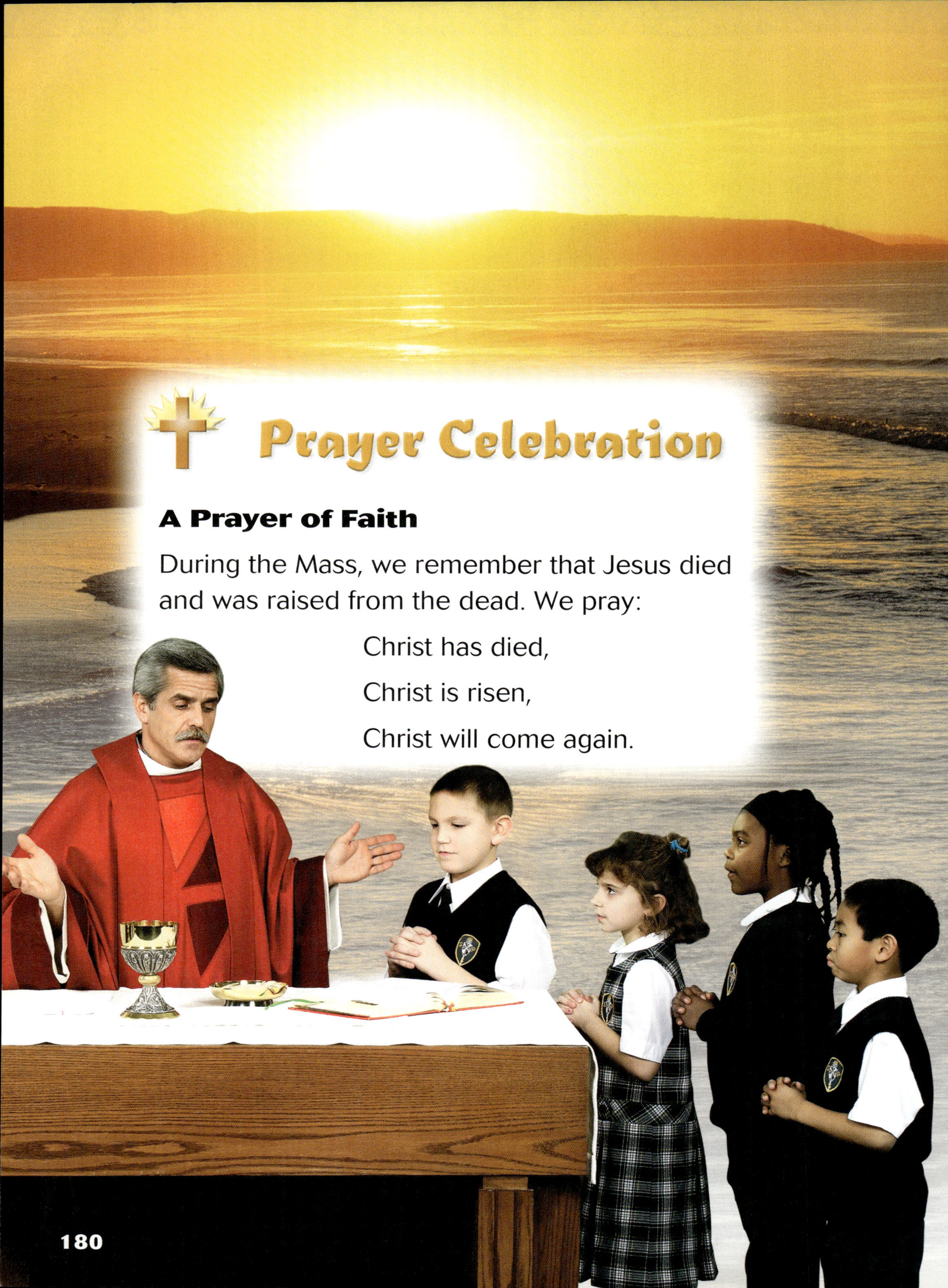

Prayer Celebration

A Prayer of Faith

During the Mass, we remember that Jesus died and was raised from the dead. We pray:

Christ has died,
Christ is risen,
Christ will come again.

13 Chapter Review

A **Draw a line** to connect the parts of each sentence.

1. Acting on God's word sometimes means that ____ •	• someone who rescues others from danger.
2. Giving up something we want out of love is ____ •	• we have to give up what we want.
3. Jesus is ____ •	• he saves us from sin and death.
4. A savior is ____ •	• called a sacrifice.
5. Jesus is our Savior because ____ •	• God's greatest gift to us.

B **Circle** the best answer.

1. How did Jesus die?
   He got sick. **He died on a cross.**

2. What happened three days after Jesus died?
   He was buried. **He rose from the dead.**

3. What do we call Jesus' rising from the dead?
   Resurrection **Ascension** **the empty tomb**

C Respond to the following questions.

1. What is one sacrifice that Saint Elizabeth made?

____

2. Why did Saint Elizabeth make this sacrifice?

____

____

D Complete the sentences with words from the box.

come	died	Jesus	risen

1. During Mass, we remember that ______________ died and was raised from the dead.

2. Complete this prayer from the Mass.

"Christ has ______________,

Christ is ______________,

Christ will ______________ again."

Getting ready for Chapter 14

A choice of things to do at home

We Receive the Gift of Jesus

Some gifts are so great that we remember them for a lifetime. Other gifts, such as fresh air and clean water, we hardly give any thought to at all. This chapter presents the concept of Jesus in the Eucharist as gift.

Children will learn that we remember the Last Supper at Mass. They will discover that Jesus is present in the bread and wine. Lastly, they will learn how to receive Jesus in the Eucharist.

It's all set

Teach your child how to set the table. Show where to put the plates, glasses, napkins, and silverware. If possible, put candles and flowers on the table. Explain that, just as the altar is set in a particular way for Mass, so the family table should be set for a meal.

A dinner to remember

Talk about some memorable meals that you and your child have eaten together. Who ate with you? Was it the food, the company, or the conversation that made these meals so special?

Eucharist word web

Make a word web for Eucharist. In the middle of a piece of paper, draw a circle big enough to write the word Eucharist inside. Then draw lines out from the circle and write and circle words that your child associates with Eucharist, such as *Jesus*, *bread*, *wine*, and *church*.

A Prayer for the Week

Thank you for the
gift of Eucharist, Lord.
We believe that you are truly
present and that you give us
forgiveness, life, and peace.
Amen.

FAMILY TIME

Something to Do . . .

On Sunday

Listen carefully to the words of consecration. As you receive communion, think about what you have heard.

Through the Week

Find times to say, "My Lord and my God." This prayer will remind you of receiving Jesus in the Eucharist.

Visit Our Web Site

www.blestarewe.com

Something to Think About . . .

The Body and Blood of Christ

While they were eating, Jesus took bread, said the blessing, broke it, and giving it to his disciples said, "Take and eat; this is my body."
Matthew 26:26

The Liturgy of the Eucharist is a memorial that makes present the sacrifice of Christ. Jesus is here with us as he was with his disciples at the Last Supper.

If we want to be close to Jesus, there is no better way than to receive communion. In the Eucharist the Holy Spirit changes the bread and wine into the Body and Blood of Christ. After receiving communion, we offer a prayer of thanks to show that we do not take Jesus' gift for granted.

Something to Know About . . .

Our Heritage in Music

Jesus Christ Superstar is a rock opera about the life of Christ with music by Andrew Lloyd Webber and lyrics by Tim Rice. The story is about the last week of Jesus' life, and it tells about the guilt Judas experiences when he betrays Jesus. The scene that depicts the Last Supper recreates the relationship of Jesus with the Twelve Apostles.

Originally performed on Broadway in 1971, the show ran from 1972 to 1980 in London. It opened on Broadway again in April, 2000. *Jesus Christ Superstar*, the first musical to incorporate rock music, gives us an opportunity to take a new look at a very familiar story and think about it in a fresh way.

14 We Receive the Gift of Jesus

I am the bread of life. Those who eat this bread will never be hungry.

Based on John 6:35

Share

We all need food and water to stay healthy. But we have other needs, or hungers, too. Look at these pictures. How is each person hungry?

Rosemary is very, very tired. She is hungry for

______________________________________.

Matt has not eaten since lunch. He is hungry for

______________________________________.

Luis can't rake all these leaves. He is hungry for

______________________________________.

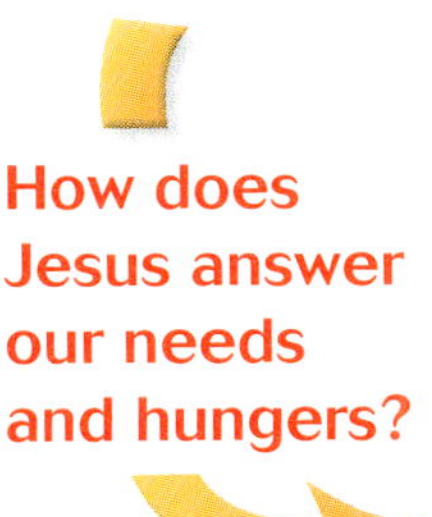

How does Jesus answer our needs and hungers?

The Gift of Eucharist

At Mass, the priest prays as he prepares the bread and wine for the sacrament of Eucharist.

On the night before he died for us, he had supper for the last time with his friends.
He took bread
and gave thanks to God his Father.
He broke the bread
and gave it to his friends, saying:
Take this, all of you, and eat it:
this is my body which will be
given up for you.
In the same way he took a cup of wine.
He gave thanks to God
and handed the cup
to his friends, saying:
Take this, all of you,
and drink from it:
this is the cup of my blood,
the blood of the new and
unending promise.
It will be shed for you
and for all
so that sins may be forgiven.
Then he said to them:
do this in memory of me.

Based on Eucharistic Prayer for Masses with Children III

The Meal of God's People

The Mass is both a sacrifice and a celebration. During the **Liturgy of the Eucharist**, we remember the Last Supper. We also remember the death and Resurrection of Jesus Christ.

The Mass is also a holy meal for God's People today. In the **Eucharist**, the Holy Spirit changes the bread and wine into the Body and Blood of Jesus Christ.

Faith Words

Eucharist

The Eucharist is a sacrifice and a special meal of thanks. In the Eucharist, God gives us the Body and Blood of Christ.

GO TO pages 364–367 to learn more about the Liturgy of the Eucharist.

Activity Complete the sentence.

The bread and wine change ______________________

to the ______________________

____

and ______________________

of Jesus Christ.

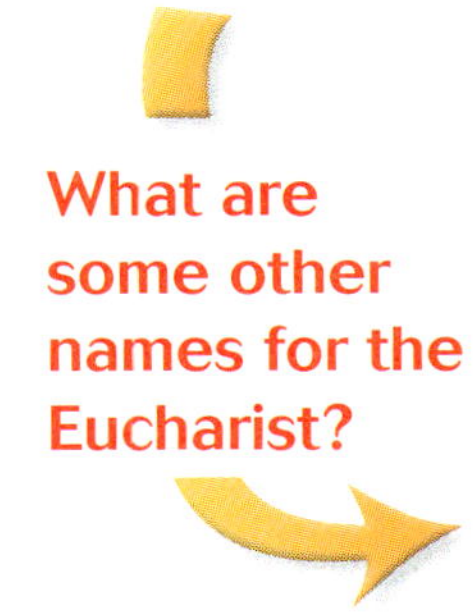

What are some other names for the Eucharist?

Walking with Jesus

Cleopas and his friend were very sad. Jesus had died on a cross three days earlier. Some women had gone to the tomb and now were telling everyone that Jesus was alive. But the two disciples had not seen Jesus with their own eyes. So they decided to leave Jerusalem and walk home.

As Cleopas and his friend walked down the road, a stranger joined them. They told him why they were sad. Then the stranger said, "How foolish you are! The Scriptures tell us that the Savior must suffer, die, and then enter into glory." The stranger helped them to see that Jesus was the Savior sent by God.

That night, the two men asked the stranger to stay and eat with them. When they sat down to eat supper, he took bread and gave thanks to God. He gave the bread to them to eat. Then he disappeared from their eyes.

All of a sudden, their eyes were opened. Cleopas and his friend knew that the stranger was Jesus! They recognized him in the breaking of the bread. He truly was alive!

Based on Luke 24:13–35

Our Church Teaches

Only a priest can preside over, or lead, the celebration of the Eucharist. We receive the Body and Blood of Christ in **Holy Communion**. The Eucharist unites us with Jesus, our Savior, who gives us the gift of everlasting life.

We Believe

Christ is truly present in the bread and wine at Mass. In them, Christ gives us himself, the Bread of Life.

Activity Place the events in the correct order. Use 1 for the event that happened first.

_____ Cleopas and his friend recognized Jesus.

_____ A stranger joins Cleopas and his friend on the road.

_____ Cleopas and his friend ask the stranger to stay and eat with them.

_____ The stranger explains the Scriptures.

_____ The stranger gives thanks to God and shares bread with them.

Cleopas and his friend recognized Jesus in the

breaking of the ______________________.

Respond

Going to Communion

Sister Christine was meeting with a group of girls and boys. She said, "Tell me what you know about receiving communion."

Up shot every hand in the group!

Paolo answered first. "I must have already received Reconciliation before my First Communion," he said.

Mike added, "I must be free of serious sin."

Lucy said, "I shouldn't eat or drink anything but water for one hour before receiving communion."

April added, "I can receive communion either in the hand or on the tongue."

"And when the priest or the eucharistic minister says **the Body of Christ**, I should answer **Amen**," said Paolo

Mike said, "I also say Amen when I hear **the Blood of Christ** if I receive from the cup, or chalice."

Then Lucy said softly, "After communion, I return to my seat. I give thanks, because I have received the gift of Eucharist."

"Wow!" said Sister. "You didn't forget a thing!"

? What do you do after receiving communion?

Activity

Where you see a **Q**, an **X**, or a **Z** in the puzzle, cross it out.

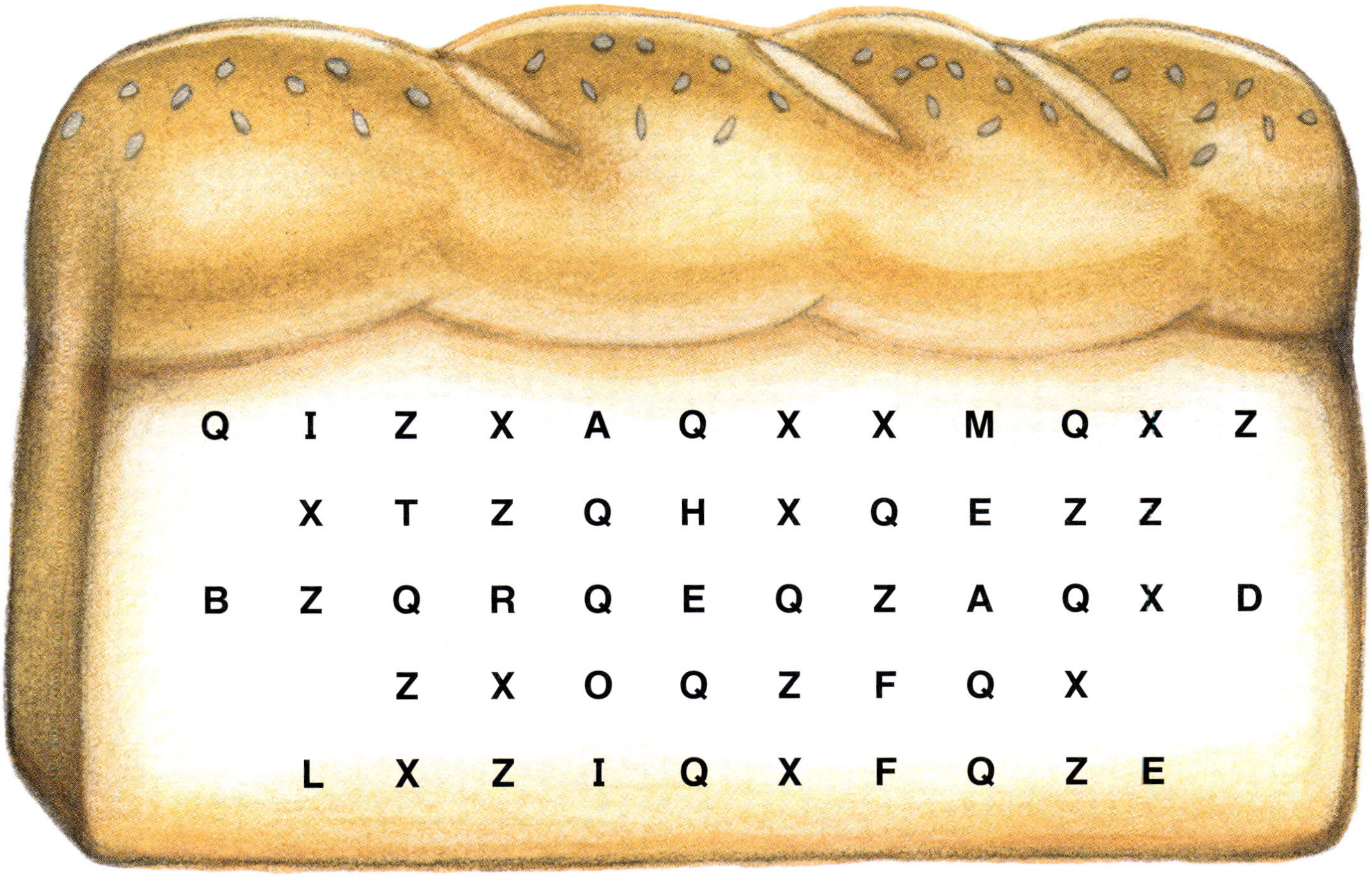

Q I Z X A Q X X M Q X Z
X T Z Q H X Q E Z Z
B Z Q R Q E Q Z A Q X D
Z X O Q Z F Q X
L X Z I Q X F Q Z E

Write the sentence you found in the puzzle.

How can we celebrate being one with Jesus?

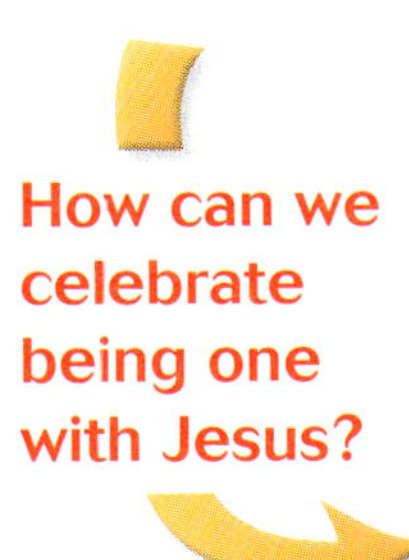

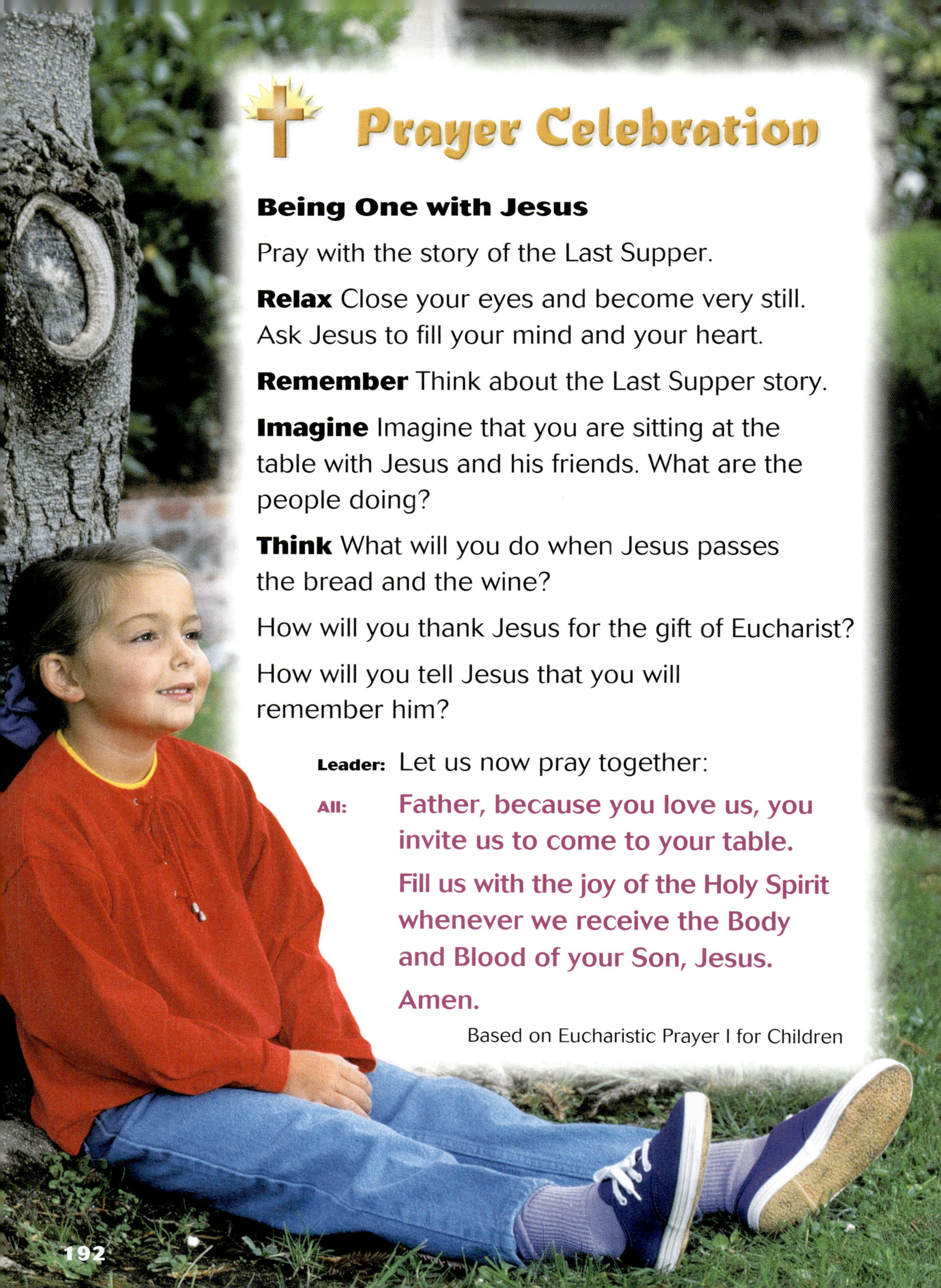

Prayer Celebration

Being One with Jesus

Pray with the story of the Last Supper.

Relax Close your eyes and become very still. Ask Jesus to fill your mind and your heart.

Remember Think about the Last Supper story.

Imagine Imagine that you are sitting at the table with Jesus and his friends. What are the people doing?

Think What will you do when Jesus passes the bread and the wine?

How will you thank Jesus for the gift of Eucharist?

How will you tell Jesus that you will remember him?

Leader: Let us now pray together:

All: **Father, because you love us, you invite us to come to your table.**

Fill us with the joy of the Holy Spirit whenever we receive the Body and Blood of your Son, Jesus.

Amen.

Based on Eucharistic Prayer I for Children

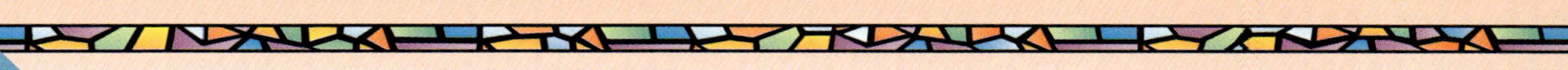

14 Chapter Review

A **Write** the answers to the questions.

1. Jesus said, "I am the bread of ______."

2. Jesus said, "Those who eat this bread will never be ______."

3. What do you think Jesus meant by these words?

______

______

______

B **Complete** the sentences with words from the box.

Liturgy	Eucharist	Body	Blood

1. The ______ is a sacrifice and a special meal of thanks.

2. During the ______ of the Eucharist, we remember the Last Supper.

3. In the Eucharist, the Holy Spirit changes the bread into the ______ of Jesus Christ.

C **Draw or write** about how Cleopas and his friend recognized the Risen Jesus.

D **Draw a line** to match the descriptions with the correct words.

1. Another name for receiving the Body and Blood of Christ •	• in the hand
2. Our answer when the eucharistic minister says, "The Body of Christ" •	• everlasting life
3. One way to receive Holy Communion •	• Amen
4. Who presides over, or leads, the Eucharist •	• Holy Communion
5. What Jesus gives us through Holy Communion •	• priest

Getting ready for Chapter 15

A choice of things to do at home

We Carry On the Work of Jesus

Chapter 15 presents the New Commandment that Jesus gave us about loving one another. Children will discover how Jesus showed his love for people. They will also identify ways that they can show their love for others.

What matters most?

We carry on the work of Jesus by knowing what our priorities are. With your family, talk about priorities. To explain the meaning of *priority*, use phrases such as *most important* and *do first things first*. Then have a quiz game. Ask each other "Which is most important. . ." questions, such as ". . .watching a video, writing a thank-you note, or filling the ice-cube trays?"

Choose one

With your child's help, think of different tasks any family member could do, such as putting away toys or folding towels. Together, write the tasks on slips of paper, fold them, and place them in a bowl. Then have each person take one slip from the bowl each day and complete the task.

Have a heart

With your child, make a large red paper heart and put it on display. Keep a box of adhesive bandage strips nearby. Have your child put one on the heart whenever any family member does an act of healing to make someone feel better.

A Prayer for the Week

Through your works,
Lord, you showed your love.
Help us carry on your work
with acts of kindness,
healing, and love.
Amen.

FAMILY TIME

Something to Do . . .

On Sunday

As you pray silently during the prayer after communion, reflect on how you will love others as Jesus loves you.

Through the Week

To show love for their family, members can make an effort to lend a hand with indoor and outdoor tasks.

Visit Our Web Site

www.blestarewe.com

Something to Think About . . .

The Example of Jesus

My daughter is at the point of death. Please, come lay your hands on her that she may get well and live.
Mark 5:23

In the Gospel story about Jairus and his daughter, Jesus heals a girl who relatives and friends think is dead. When he takes the girl's hand and tells her to get up, she rises immediately. Through the healing power of Jesus, she is completely well, to the utter astonishment of her family.

This is a striking account of the way Jesus showed his love for everyone, setting an example for us to love others.

Something to Know About . . .

Our Heritage in Holy People

Damien de Veuster is a holy person who risked his life as he cared for others. Born in Belgium in 1840, as a young man he entered the Congregation of the Sacred Hearts. He volunteered to serve in the Hawaiian missions. Father Damien spent eight years in the missions, carrying on the work of Jesus.

In 1866 a sickness called Hansen's disease, better known as leprosy, spread across the Hawaiian Islands. The lepers were exiled to the island of Molokai. Father Damien volunteered to care for them. He kept their bodies and their bandages clean; he built houses and coffins; he practiced untold works of charity. Father Damien contracted the disease himself in 1876, dying of leprosy in 1889.

This holy man represents Hawaii in Statuary Hall in Washington, D.C. On June 4, 1995, Damien de Veuster was beatified by Pope John Paul II.

15 We Carry On the Work of Jesus

Love one another as I have loved you.

Based on John 13:34

Share

What kind of workers do you see?

What kind of work would you like to do when you grow up? Show it in a drawing.

What work did Jesus do?

Jesus and the Little Girl

Storyteller: Jesus was speaking to a crowd of people. A man named Jairus was there.

Jairus: (kneels in front of Jesus) Lord, please come to my home and see my sick daughter.

Jesus: Show me the way. I will help her.

Jairus: (gets up) Thank you, Jesus. Let's go!

Storyteller: They started walking. Then a servant girl ran up to them.

Servant: Sir, your daughter just died.

Storyteller: Jairus was very sad.

Jesus: Do not be afraid, Jairus. I can still help.

Storyteller: When they got to the house, Jesus went in. The dead girl was lying on the bed.

Jesus: (holding her hand) Little girl, get up!

Storyteller: The little girl got up at once. She ran to hug her father.

Jairus: Jesus, how can I ever thank you?

Jesus: Try to love everyone as I have loved you.

Based on Mark 5:21–24, 35–42

The Work of Jesus

Jesus showed his love for Jairus and his daughter. Jesus always loved everyone. Jesus also taught people about God's love for them. He did this in many ways. He told stories. He shared food. He forgave sinners. He comforted people who were sad. Jesus healed the sick. He even brought dead people back to life.

Activity How do you love as Jesus did? Write one way here.

____

____

What is the New Commandment?

Father Damien and the Lepers

Long ago most people in Hawaii were afraid of lepers. The lepers were sick people with a terrible skin disease. People thought that if they got near the lepers, they would get sick, too. So they sent the lepers far away. The lepers had to live all alone on an island, Molokai, with no one to help them.

When Father Damien learned about the lepers, he remembered the work of Jesus. Jesus was not afraid of sick people, not even lepers. Jesus spent time with them. Often, he healed them.

Father Damien wanted to act like Jesus. He decided to go to the island and live with the lepers. He would help them build houses and grow food. He would teach them about Jesus. He would keep their bandages clean. He would try to nurse them back to health.

Father Damien lived and worked on the island for twelve years. Then he became sick and soon died. To this day, the people on the island give God thanks for Father Damien's help. He had been like Jesus for them.

Our Church Teaches

In the **New Commandment** Jesus said, "Love one another as I have loved you." This is the law of love. We are called to love others the way God loves us. We live by Jesus' law of love when we show our love for others.

Activity Place the words of Jesus in the correct order.

have	you.	another	Love
one	I	as	loved

____

____

____

We Believe

When we love others, we are following Jesus. We are also showing our love for God.

Faith Words

New Commandment
Jesus gave us the New Commandment. He said "Love one another as I have loved you."

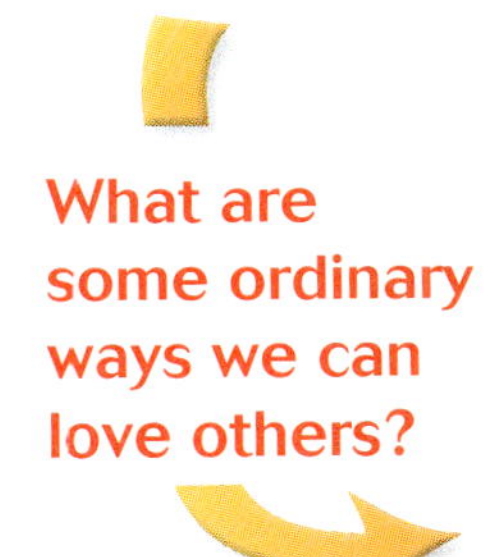

What are some ordinary ways we can love others?

Respond

Taking Care of Others

"Mrs. Nye wasn't at Mass today," said Mattie. "She was at home, sick and alone. She couldn't even cook!

"Everybody wanted to help. Dr. Ray stopped in to see Mrs. Nye. Joey Garcia brought her a nice lunch. He stayed and visited for a while. The Grant family prepared her dinner."

"So that took care of Sunday. What about the rest of the week?" asked Kim.

"We'll deliver Mrs. Nye's meals every day. Many people will visit her. And I will ask everybody in the parish to pray for Mrs. Nye.

"You know, Jesus taught us to love one another as he loved us. When we take care of Mrs. Nye, we show our love for God!"

Activities

Show how you can carry on the work of Jesus.

1. Write four words you can say to someone who is sad.

2. Draw a picture that shows how you can help a sick person.

How can we pray a simple prayer for others?

Prayer Celebration

The Thumb Prayer

You can pray for others by using just your thumb. Trace a small Sign of the Cross with your thumb. On the downward stroke of the cross, whisper "Jesus." On the sideways stroke, whisper the name of someone you are praying for. You might whisper "Jesus," then "Uncle Tim." You can trace the thumb cross anywhere—in the palm of your hand, on a book, on your pillow at night, or on the seat of a car.

Choose one of the thumb prayers below. Decide where you will make your crosses. Then say your prayer over and over again.

Jesus, the Pope.
Jesus, all parents.
Jesus, those in need.
Jesus, Father Doyle.
Jesus, all children.
Jesus, (your own prayer).

15 Chapter Review

A **Draw a line** to match what Jesus did to show love to these people.

1. Sad people •	• Jesus shared food.
2. Sinful people •	• Jesus brought them back to life.
3. Hungry people •	• Jesus forgave them.
4. Sick people •	• Jesus comforted them.
5. Dead people •	• Jesus healed them.

B **Circle** the best answer.

1. How did Jesus help the daughter of Jairus?
   He fed her. **He forgave her.**
   He brought her back to life.

2. Who did Father Damien help?
   children **lepers** **adults**

3. How did Father Damien help?
   He sent them money. **He wrote them letters.**
   He kept their bandages clean.

4. How can we follow Jesus?
   We can fight. **We can show love.**

5. "Love one another as I have loved you." What do we call this law?
   Ten Commandments **New Commandment**

C **Draw** a picture or write about ways to love others as Jesus did.

D **Respond** to the following questions.

1. In the Thumb Prayer, what sign do you make with your thumb?
   Sign of Peace **Sign of the Cross** **Stop Sign**

2. In the Thumb Prayer, what do you whisper during the first part of the motion?
   Jesus **Lord's Prayer** **the name of someone who is sick**

3. In the Thumb Prayer, what do you whisper during the last part of the motion?
   Jesus **Hail Mary** **the name of someone in need**

4. Where can we pray the Thumb Prayer?
   in church **in school** **anywhere**

Getting ready for Chapter 16

A choice of things to do at home

We Pray Like Jesus

We call God "our Father" because Jesus asked us to, and we pray the Lord's Prayer because Jesus taught it to us. In Chapter 16, children learn to pray the Lord's Prayer with an understanding of its meaning. The children will also identify the parts of the day in which they might pray.

Daily bread

The bread that we eat every day may be very different from the bread Jesus ate, or from the breads eaten in other parts of the world. Serve a variety of breads this week (raisin, pita, sourdough, French, Italian, cornbread). Talk about how daily bread is needed by everyone.

Making conversation

Some conversations focus on asking for things, while others focus on solving problems. Still others focus on praising or apologizing. With your child, list several purposes of conversation. Remind your child that when we pray, we talk to and listen to God.

Pray all ways

Discuss with your child different ways you can pray, such as by singing, by using gestures, by meditating, by praying words you have learned by heart, or by using your own words. Practice using some of these prayer forms together.

A Prayer for the Week

Jesus, thank you for teaching us the Lord's Prayer. It reminds us that we can ask God our Father for what we need. Help us always pray it with an open heart. Amen.

FAMILY TIME

Something to Do . . .

On Sunday

Say a prayer of gratitude for the life-affirming bread of the Eucharist.

Through the Week

Each day this week, say a family prayer at a different time. Some suggested times are bedtime, mealtime, before leaving home in the morning, or before doing homework.

Visit Our Web Site

www.blestarewe.com

Something to Think About . . .

The Essence of Prayer

This is how you are to pray:
Our Father in heaven,
hallowed be your name.
Matthew 6:9

Jesus taught the Lord's Prayer to his followers when they asked him how they should pray. The Lord's Prayer is so important that we pray it at every Mass; it summarizes the whole Gospel of God's love. In a concise series of statements, Jesus taught us how to pray. He praised God and asked for food, forgiveness, and to be kept from temptation. Through the years we have repeated this prayer, regarding it as the very essence of prayer. As we teach the Lord's Prayer to our children, we share our recognition of its value, its beauty, and its centrality to Christian life.

Something to Know About . . .

Our Heritage in Symbols

In Jesus' time, people sometimes used objects as they prayed. Palm branches were used during prayers of praise. The waving branches symbolized victory. Jesus' followers held palm branches during his triumphant entry into Jerusalem before his passion and death.

Traditionally, palms are blessed at the beginning of the liturgy on Palm Sunday. The ashes that are crossed on our foreheads on Ash Wednesday come from burned palms. Some families place palms behind a hanging crucifix or holy picture. Other traditions include braiding palms into crosses or burning them slightly when there is a bad storm or some other such crisis.

16 We Pray Like Jesus

Let us call to the Lord at all times.
Let us praise God both day and night.

Based on Psalm 34:2

Share

Many people do things at the same time each day.

At 7:00 A.M., Betsy wakes up.
What time do you usually wake up?

At 8:00 A.M., Willie gets on the bus.
What time do you go to school?

At 6:00 P.M., the Diaz family eats dinner.
What time does your family eat dinner?

Talk about what time things happen on Saturday.

Tell what is different about Sunday.

How did Jesus pray?

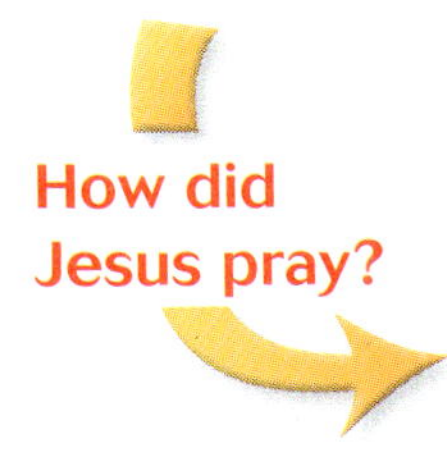

The Prayer of Jesus

One day, Jesus' friends asked him to teach them to pray. So Jesus taught them this prayer:

Our Father,
who art in heaven,
hallowed be thy name.
Thy kingdom come,
thy will be done on earth
as it is in heaven.
Give us this day
our daily bread;
and forgive us
our **trespasses**
as we forgive those
who trespass against us;
and lead us not
into **temptation**,
but deliver us from evil.
Amen.

Based on Luke 11:1; Matthew 6:9–13

The Lord's Prayer

We call the prayer Jesus taught the Lord's Prayer. We pray the Lord's Prayer at every Mass. In this special prayer, we remember that God is the Father of all people. Everyone is like our brother or sister. That is why we sometimes join hands with others when we pray the Lord's Prayer.

Activity Ask God to bless the person who taught you the Lord's Prayer.

Lord, bless ______________________________
for teaching me to pray.

Faith Words

hallowed
Hallowed is another word for "holy."

trespasses
Trespasses are sins or wrongs.

temptation
A temptation is wanting to do something that is wrong.

What do the words of the Lord's Prayer mean?

Hear & Believe

The First Christians

The first Christians prayed the Lord's Prayer three times a day. They said the same words we say today as members of the Church. Read the chart to find out what the words mean.

The Lord's Prayer	What It Means
Our Father, who art in heaven, hallowed be thy name.	We praise God the Father for being good and holy.
Thy kingdom come, thy will be done on earth as it is in heaven.	We pray God will bring about a time of perfect happiness and peace. We pray that everyone will obey God's laws.
Give us this day our daily bread;	We pray for our needs and the needs of others.
and forgive us our trespasses as we forgive those who trespass against us;	We ask God to forgive our sins. We forgive people who have hurt us.
and lead us not into temptation,	We ask God to help us choose right instead of wrong.
but deliver us from evil.	We ask God to protect us from things that may harm us.
Amen.	We say "Yes, I believe. It is true."

Our Church Teaches

The Lord's Prayer is a perfect prayer. That is why the Lord's Prayer is an important part of Baptism, Confirmation, and Eucharist—the three sacraments of belonging to the Church.

Activity We can pray the Lord's Prayer at any time during the day. Look at each picture. Decide what time of day it is. Then place the time on the clocks.

We Believe

Jesus taught us how to pray the Lord's Prayer. It is the prayer of Christians all over the world.

How do church members pray?

Respond

Time for Prayer

One day in religion class, Mrs. Santos asked, "What is your favorite time to pray?" Almost all the students raised their hands.

Mrs. Santos called on Maria first. "I like to pray on Sunday in church," she said.

Steven was next. "My favorite time to pray is at night, before I fall asleep."

"I like to pray best in the morning," Trish said, "when I first wake up."

"My favorite time is meal time," Alex explained. "My family prays together then."

Fiona said shyly. "I like to pray when I'm walking to and from school." "Sometimes I pray in the car or in the grocery store," Trent added.

Mrs. Santos smiled and praised the students for their responses. "I can see that there are many different times that we can pray. Every time is a good time to talk to God!"

? When do you pray during the day?

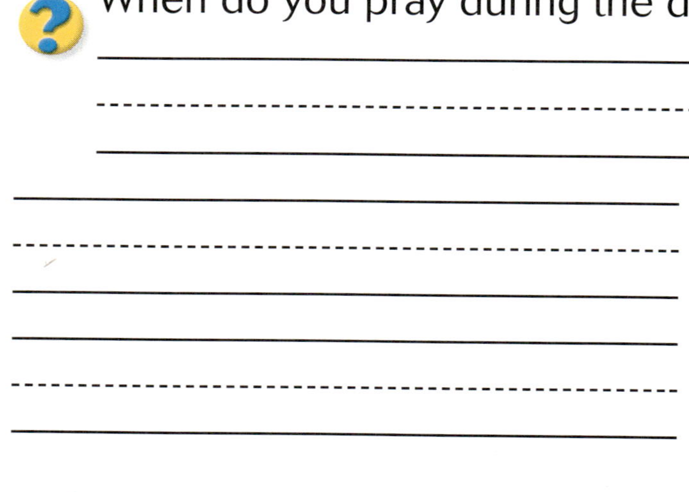

Activities

Before eating, Catholics pray the Grace Before Meals. After eating, we pray the Grace After Meals.

1. Choose words from the box to complete these mealtime prayers. The pictures will help you.

 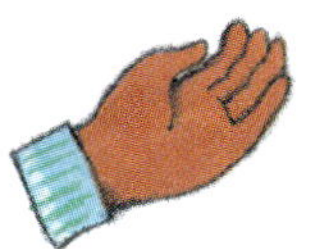   

gifts **receive** **Christ** **thanks** **forever**

Bless us, O Lord, and these your  ____________________, which

we are about to 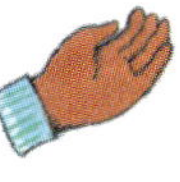 ____________________ from your goodness,

through  ____________________ our Lord. Amen.

We give you  ____________________ for all your

 ____________________, almighty God, living and

reigning now and  ____________________. Amen.

2. Learn the mealtime prayers by heart.

When can we pray the Lord's Prayer?

Prayer Celebration

Prayer Time

Every time of day is a good time for prayer. Be very quiet now, and remember that God is always near. Then pray together the prayer that Jesus taught us.

The Lord's Prayer

Our Father,
who art in heaven,
hallowed be thy name.
Thy kingdom come,
thy will be done on earth
as it is in heaven.
Give us this day
our daily bread;
and forgive us
our trespasses
as we forgive those
who trespass against us;
and lead us not
into temptation,
but deliver us from evil.
Amen.

Chapter Review

A **Circle** the words to complete the sentences.

1. Jesus taught the ____ to his followers.
   Hail Mary **Lord's Prayer** **Sign of the Cross**

2. We pray this prayer at every ____.
   meal **party** **Mass**

3. Another word for "holy" is ____.
   hallowed **hollow** **holly**

4. ____ are sins or wrongs.
   Temptations **Trespasses** **God's laws**

B **Complete** the Lord's Prayer.

1. Our ______________________, who art in heaven, hallowed be thy name.

2. Thy ______________________ come, thy will be done on earth as it is in heaven.

3. Give us this day our daily ______________________;

4. And ______________________ us our trespasses as we forgive those who trespass against us;

5. And lead us not into temptation, but deliver us from ______________________. Amen.

C Respond to the following questions.

1. What do we mean when we call God "Our Father"?

2. When we ask God for daily bread, what are we really asking for?

D Complete the prayer and respond to the question.

1. Bless us, O Lord, and these your ____________, which we are about to ____________ from your goodness, through ____________ our Lord. Amen.

2. What do we call this prayer? ____________

Caring and Sharing

The children in the parish that Taylor belongs to did something really neat. They brought some of their used books to the Parish Hall. Their religion teacher had told them about some poor children in town. These boys and girls had no money to buy picture books, or storybooks, or comic books. The parish gave the used books to the poor children.

Many boys and girls gave away their old books. Some books were about sports. Others were about famous people. Others told exciting stories. The boys and girls thought about how much they had enjoyed reading them! They hoped that the poor children would like them that much, too!

Do you have anything you could share with poor children?

Think About It

Suppose that you have never had a book to read and enjoy. Imagine what that would be like! It's hard to believe, but some poor children have no books at all!

Write the name of your favorite book.

Learn About It

Jesus said, "Love one another as I have loved you." He teaches us to treat everyone fairly and to help poor people. That is what the children did in the story on page 219.

Do Something About It

Do you have books or other things that you could give away? Think of things like clothes and sneakers that don't fit you anymore. Do you have toys, a bike, or video games that you don't use?

Write words that name extra things you could share with poor children.

Organizer

Use the chapter titles to complete the sentences.

Jesus saves us from

________________________.

We carry on the

____

of Jesus.

We receive the gift

____

of ________________________.

We ________________________

like Jesus.

Review

A Circle the best answer.

1. Jesus gave up his life to save us from (**death** **sin** **life**).
2. The soldiers nailed Jesus to a wooden (**door** **cross** **pole**).
3. After Jesus died some of his (**friends** **enemies** **family**) buried him.
4. The entrance to the tomb was covered with a huge (**stone** **gate** **tree**).
5. The tomb was empty because Jesus had been raised from the (**dead** **sleep** **dream**).

B Draw a line to connect parts of each sentence.

1. The Mass is both a •	• preside over or lead the celebration of the Eucharist.
2. Cleopas and his friend recognized Jesus •	• sacrifice and a celebration.
3. Only a priest can •	• present in the bread and wine at Mass.
4. Christ is truly •	• in the breaking of the bread.

C Connect the parts of each sentence by drawing lines.

1. The Mass is a •	• because Jesus had died on the cross.
2. At Mass we remember •	• the death and Resurrection of Jesus.
3. Cleopas and his friend were sad •	• holy meal.

Review

D **Draw** a picture that shows you understand the story of Jesus, Jarius, and his daughter.

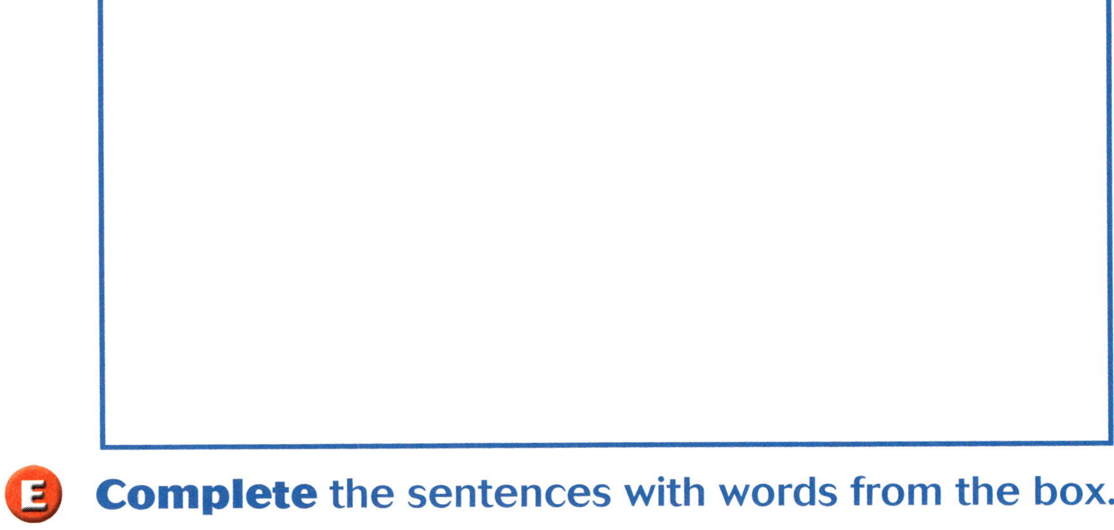

E **Complete** the sentences with words from the box.

Mass three sacrament time perfect

1. We pray the Lord's Prayer at every ________________.

2. The first Christians prayed the Lord's Prayer ________________ times a day.

3. Every ________________ of day is a good time to pray.

UNIT 4

Review

F **Circle** the words that best complete the sentences.

1. Hallowed is another word for ____.

   true **holy** **prayer**

2. A sacrifice is a special ____ that is given out of love.

   gift **deed** **belief**

3. Resurrection is Jesus' being raised from the dead to new ____.

   love **times** **life**

4. The ____ is a sacrifice and a special meal of thanks.

   Resurrection **Eucharist** **Lord's Prayer**

5. Jesus gave us the New Commandment. He said, "____ one another as I have loved you."

   Respect **Love** **Like**

G **Respond** to the following questions.

1. What does "Give us this day our daily bread" mean?

____

____

2. When do you pray the Lord's Prayer?

____

UNIT 5

We Go in Peace

Made stronger by the Eucharist, we work to be more like Christ in all we do. We can help others know about Jesus by the way we treat them.

Blessed are the peacemakers,
for they will be called
children of God.

Matthew 5:9

Christ's first disciples may have walked this street in Jerusalem spreading a message of peace. At the end of Mass we also go in peace to serve all people.

Alleluia

Music by Fintan O'Carroll

Getting ready for Chapter 17

A choice of things to do at home

God Gives Us the Holy Spirit

God gives us the Holy Spirit to guide us in our daily lives. The children will come to understand that the Holy Spirit is our helper, guide, and teacher. They will think about and appreciate the spiritual gifts that Paul writes about in the Scripture passage.

Matching gifts

Have a gift night! Each person can give a small present to one other family member. Choose names beforehand so that everyone gets a present. The present should represent a gift the person has. For example, if someone draws well, the gift might be a sketch pad.

Wisdom

A wise person considers things from different points of view and thinks about the outcome of the things he or she says. With your child, make a list of people you consider wise—in your family, in school, in your community, or in the news.

We are gifted

Talk with your child about some qualities you and other adults in your family may have, such as kindness and helpfulness. Explain that these are gifts that God has given and that people have developed. Then discuss with your child which of God's gifts he or she can develop.

A Prayer for the Week

Holy Spirit,
thank you for the gifts of
wisdom and knowledge. Your
gifts help us be faithful
followers of Jesus.
Amen.

FAMILY TIME

Something to Do . . .

On Sunday

Pray for the people who, in the name of the congregation, bring the gifts in the offertory procession.

Through the Week

In many cultures, the elders of the community are considered especially wise. Talk to or visit an elderly relative or neighbor this week.

Visit Our Web Site

www.blestarewe.com

Something to Think About . . .

Different Gifts

There are different kinds of spiritual gifts but the same Spirit; there are different forms of service but the same Lord; there are different workings but the same God who produces all of them in everyone.

1 Corinthians 12:4–6

Saint Paul explains what spiritual gifts are and how they are distributed. Some of the gifts that he discusses include the gifts of wisdom, knowledge, faith, and healing. He says that one Spirit produces all of these gifts, which are distributed individually to each person. We all have different functions in the community and therefore receive different gifts. In our family, the same is true. People have different functions in the family and therefore need different gifts. It's not up to us to decide which gifts we think people should have. We should be thankful for the gifts we have, and we should use them to help others.

Something to Know About . . . Our Heritage in Architecture

The Hagia Sofia, Greek for "holy wisdom," was built in the sixth century by the emperor Justinian I in Constantinople, now Istanbul, Turkey. The cathedral was named for the gift of the Holy Spirit and remains one of the finest examples of Byzantine architecture. After the Turks conquered Constantinople in the fifteenth century, the Hagia Sophia became a mosque, or Islamic house of worship. Its mosaics and Christian symbols were covered with plaster. The Hagia Sofia stayed that way until the twentieth century, when it became a museum and some of its original mosaics were uncovered.

17 God Gives Us the Holy Spirit

God has sent the Holy Spirit into our hearts.

Based on Galatians 4:6

Share

All people have special gifts. These gifts are part of who we are. We can use these gifts to help others.

Some people are smart. They can help others learn.

Some people are funny. They can cheer up people who are sad.

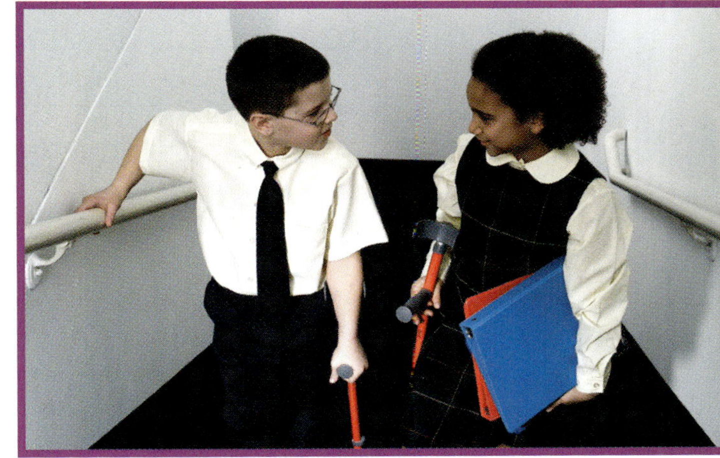

Some people are kind and helpful. They can make life easier for others.

What is one special gift you have?

I can ______________________________.

How can you use this gift to help others?

The Special Gifts

Paul had friends who lived in the city of Corinth. These friends asked Paul about the best way to serve God and their community. Paul wrote them this letter.

Dear Friends,

God loves you very much. He sent the Holy Spirit to help you live as good followers of Jesus.

One way the Holy Spirit helps is by giving special gifts to each person. These special gifts are called **spiritual gifts**. Some of these gifts are wisdom, healing, knowledge, and faith. The Holy Spirit may give one person the gift of wisdom. He may give another person the gift of healing. To someone else, he may give knowledge or faith.

God wants you to show your love for him by sharing your gifts with each other and with the Church. Remember, the Church needs each person's gifts!

Peace and love,
Paul

Based on 1 Corinthians 12:4–11

Gifts to Share

Paul wrote in his letter that the Holy Spirit gives each of us special, spiritual gifts. Some examples are knowledge, wisdom, healing, and faith. We show our love for God by using our gifts to help others.

Activity Share the gift of understanding to help someone to learn.

I will help ______________________________

____

learn about ______________________________.

Faith Words

spiritual gifts
Spiritual gifts help us follow Jesus. Some of these gifts are knowledge, wisdom, healing, and faith.

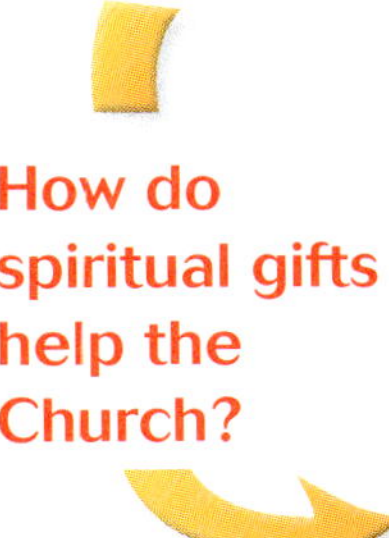

How do spiritual gifts help the Church?

Hear & Believe

One Church, Many Gifts

The Holy Spirit gives us spiritual gifts to share with other people. Here are two saints who used their spiritual gifts wisely. They used their gifts to help the Church.

God gave Saint Thomas Aquinas the gift of knowledge. He wrote many books about the Catholic faith. These books helped people to learn about their faith. Saint Thomas is the patron saint of students and Catholic schools. We celebrate his feast day on January 28.

God gave Saint Catherine of Siena the gift of wisdom. She used this gift to give advice and guidance on living a good Christian life. When there was fighting, she helped people make peace. She even helped the Pope to make important decisions. Her feast day is on April 29.

Our Church Teaches

The Holy Spirit is our helper, guide, and teacher. He leads us in our daily lives. The Holy Spirit helps us share our spiritual gifts with other people and with the Church.

Activity Each sentence below describes a spiritual gift. Write the correct name of the gift below each sentence.

knowledge	wisdom	healing	faith

Gift that helps people learn many things.

____

Gift that helps people grow in friendship with God.

____

Gift that helps people return to health after sin or sickness.

____

Gift that helps people have good sense and understanding.

____

We Believe

The Holy Spirit gives each of us spiritual gifts. God wants us to use these gifts to help other people and the Church. The Holy Spirit helps us share our gifts.

What can we do with the gifts we have been given?

Respond

Using Our Gifts

Religion class had just started. Mrs. Foy asked, "How do you use your spiritual gifts to help others?"

Gino said, "I help my little sister learn to count. That's how I use my gift of knowledge."

"Sometimes Dad gets hot and tired from working outdoors. I bring him a nice cold drink. That's how I use my gift of healing," added Tara.

Kathy said "I use the gift of wisdom when I make good choices."

"All of us use the gift of faith when we trust in God," said Jake.

? How do you use your spiritual gifts to help others?

Activities

1. Sometimes we use symbols to stand for the Holy Spirit. Some symbols are a white dove, wind, flames, and rays of light. Color the symbols and the words in the banner.

2. God wants us to open our hearts to the Holy Spirit. God wants us to use the gifts we have been given.

Put a ✓ under **Yes** if the person is using his or her gifts. Put a ✓ under **No** if the person is not using his or her gifts.

	Yes	No
a. Janet receives a letter from Grandma. She does not answer it.	☐	☐
b. Carlos shares his popcorn with Miguel and Ricardo.	☐	☐
c. Mike can read. He does not want to help his little sister learn to read.	☐	☐
d. Debra can draw beautiful pictures. She draws one for Aunt Sue.	☐	☐
e. Susan likes to sing. She sings in the children's choir at Mass.	☐	☐
f. Robert plays the piano very well, but he will not play for others.	☐	☐
g. Tanya tells bedtime stories to her little sister.	☐	☐

How can we celebrate our spiritual gifts?

Prayer Celebration

We Pray to the Holy Spirit

The Holy Spirit helps us pray. Here is a prayer you can pray to the Holy Spirit.

Leader: We have been given gifts by the Holy Spirit. Close your eyes now, and think about a special gift that you have. (pause)

Leader: Let us pray that we may always use our gifts to help others.

Side 1: Breathe in me, O Holy Spirit,

Side 2: That my thoughts may be holy;

Side 1: Act in me, O Holy Spirit,

Side 2: That my work may be holy;

Side 1: Fill my heart, O Holy Spirit,

Side 2: That I love only what is holy;

Side 1: Strengthen me, O Holy Spirit,

Side 2: To defend all that is holy;

Side 1: Guard me, O Holy Spirit,

Side 2: That I always may be holy.

Based on the Holy Spirit Prayer of St. Augustine

17 Chapter Review

A **Complete** the sentences with words from the box. Use these words to fill in the puzzle.

faith	healing	knowledge	spiritual	wisdom

Down

2. The gift of ____ helps people have good sense and understanding.

3. The gift of ____ helps people return to health after sin or sickness.

Across

1. The gift of ____ helps people learn many things.

4. The Holy Spirit gives each of us ____ gifts.

5. The gift of ____ helps people grow in friendship with God.

1. 2. 3. 4. 5.

B **Write** something you know about Saint Thomas Aquinas or Saint Catherine of Siena.

C **Respond** to the following questions.

1. What is one spiritual gift that the Holy Spirit has given you?

2. What does the Holy Spirit want us to do with our spiritual gifts?

D **Circle** the words that best complete the sentences.

1. The Holy Spirit helps us to ____.
   play **pray** **tell lies**

2. God wants us to open our ____ to the Holy Spirit.
   wallets **books** **hearts**

3. The Holy Spirit gives us gifts to help us be ____.
   happy **holy** **rich**

Getting ready for Chapter 18

A choice of things to do at home

We Celebrate Peace and Service

The children will learn that we greet each other at Mass by offering those around us a Sign of Peace. This sign reminds us that Jesus wants us to get along with everyone and to serve one another.

Greetings

Play a game with your child in which you take turns making different gestures to say Hello, such as waving. Be creative and see how many turns you can take without repeating the same gesture.

Switch with me

To better understand how each person serves the family, switch chores and responsibilities in the family. At the end of the week, change again, so that everyone has a chance to serve in different ways.

Called to service

Talk with your child about different people who work in your church. Ask your child to think of as many people as possible. Explain how these people are actively serving in the life of your parish.

A Prayer for the Week

Welcome us to your table,
Lord. Help us see your presence
in everyone we know.
Help us be people
who share and serve.
Amen.

FAMILY TIME

Something to Do . . .

On Sunday

Remind each other to think about making peace in the family as you share the Sign of Peace at Mass.

Through the Week

Talk with your family about the importance of getting along with everyone and serving one another in your family and parish.

Visit Our Web Site

www.blestarewe.com

Something to Think About . . .

Cooperating in Service

The peace of the Lord be with you always.
The Order of Mass

The Sign of Peace is a sign of the Holy Spirit, a greeting, and a reminder that we should get along with everyone. The Sign of Peace is also a reminder that we are to serve others. Belonging to the Catholic Church is not like membership in a club. It is more like being part of a cooperative endeavor, where everyone has a job to do. Because everyone cooperates, the Church is able to accomplish things it otherwise would have neither the money nor the personnel to do. Because some church members conduct worship, others raise families, and still others take on church-related jobs of education and service, the community runs smoothly. On Sunday we come together to celebrate our unity.

Something to Know About . . .

Our Heritage in Religious Life

Blessed Jeanne Jugan, Marie of the Cross (1792–1879), grew up as a poor French girl. From her youth she felt that she was called to do something special. In 1837, with another woman and a teenage orphan girl, she formed a community of prayer and good works. From that small beginning, she established an order called the Little Sisters of the Poor, whose mission is to care for the needy elderly. In addition to the vows of poverty, chastity, and obedience, this group takes a vow of hospitality. On October 3, 1982, Jeanne Jugan was beatified by Pope John Paul II. Today, there are Little Sisters of the Poor in thirty countries, on five continents.

18 We Celebrate Peace and Service

Greet one another with a sign of peace.

Based on 2 Corinthians 13:11

Share

We greet other people with words or with actions.
How can you greet someone without using words?

The people in the pictures want to say "Hello."
But each of them wants to say it in a different way.
Write a different greeting in each person's balloon.

How do we greet each other at Mass?

 The Sign of Peace

At each Eucharist, we offer those around us a Sign of Peace. Peace is a sign that the Holy Spirit is with us. The Sign of Peace reminds us that Jesus wants us to get along with everyone. It also reminds us that we are to serve one another each day.

Here is the Sign of Peace you take part in during Mass.

Priest: Lord Jesus Christ, you said to your apostles:
I leave you peace, my peace I give you.
Look not on our sins, but on the faith of your Church,
and grant us the peace and unity of your kingdom
where you live for ever and ever.

All: Amen.

Priest: The peace of the Lord be with you always.

All: And also with you.

Priest: Let us offer each other
the sign of peace.

The Order of Mass

We Take Part and Serve

The Sign of Peace reminds us that Jesus wants us to love one another and to have peace. It calls all members of the Church to serve one another. The Sign of Peace reminds us to take part in parish activities.

Activity Complete the sign-up sheet.

Name ______________________

Look at the list of parish activities. What would you like to do?

___ sing in the children's choir

___ bring the gifts to the altar

___ read the Scriptures at Mass

___ act to help the poor and hungry

___ help out at a parish festival

___ read to preschoolers in a nursery

What other parish activities can you be a part of?

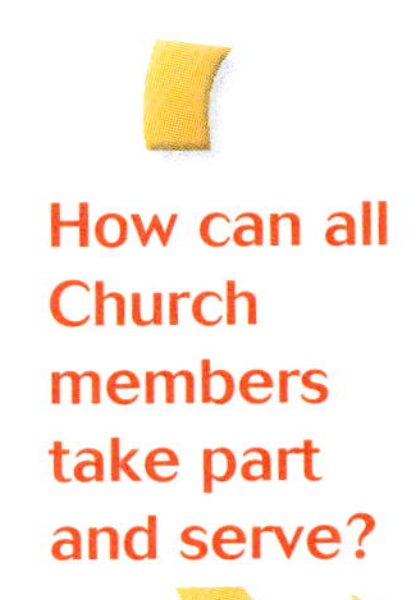

How can all Church members take part and serve?

Hear & Believe

The Way of Peace

One day, Saint Paul wrote a letter to the Christian community in the city of Philippi. In the letter, he spoke of ways to live in peace.

- Try to understand one another.
- Be kind to everyone.
- Pray for your own needs as well as the needs of others.
- Tell the truth and be fair.
- Make giving to others more important than getting things for yourself.

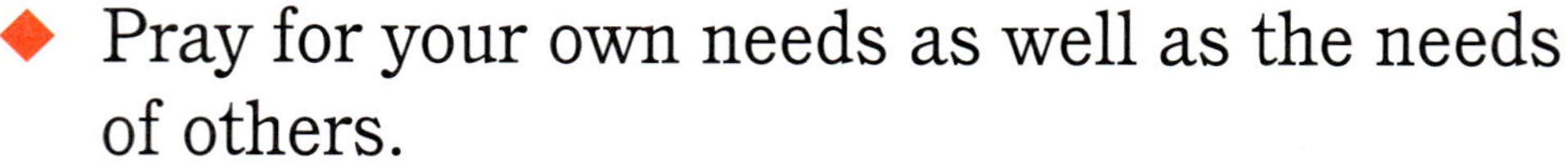

Then the God of peace will be with you.

Based on Philippians 4:1–9

Our Church Teaches

Men who become deacons, priests, and bishops receive the sacrament of **Holy Orders**. They lead the Church community in celebrating the sacraments and teaching the Gospel.

Baptized men and women receive the sacrament of **Matrimony** from each other. They promise to be faithful to each other for their whole lives. They serve the Church by caring for their families and sharing in the work of their parish.

We Believe

Holy Orders and Matrimony are sacraments of service. All members of the Church are called to live in peace and serve others.

Activity Find the seven hidden words from this lesson.

A	C	H	O	L	Y	H	J	K	L
J	K	L	Z	X	A	C	O	V	Q
S	B	N	O	R	D	E	R	S	O
A	S	D	S	T	H	Z	R	T	M
C	Y	U	E	I	O	E	P	D	A
R	N	P	T	O	U	K	G	H	T
A	S	E	R	V	I	C	E	J	R
M	E	A	R	A	Y	H	A	V	I
E	E	C	T	G	B	U	U	W	M
N	M	E	Q	P	W	R	H	L	O
T	I	K	A	F	B	C	M	N	N
S	W	F	Q	R	R	H	L	C	Y

Faith Words

Holy Orders

Holy Orders is a sacrament of service.

Matrimony

Matrimony is a sacrament of service.

How can we celebrate our call to service?

Respond

Choosing to Serve

Joseph Ratzinger was born in a tiny village in Germany in 1927. When he was five years old he met a cardinal for the first time. Joseph was part of a group of children who presented the visiting cardinal with flowers. After that visit he decided to become a cardinal himself. Before then he had wanted to be a bricklayer.

Joseph did not like sports but enjoyed walks in the mountains. He still enjoys music and plays the piano.

Joseph and his older brother, George, studied for the priesthood together. In 1951 both brothers celebrated the sacrament of Holy Orders. In 1977 Pope Paul VI named Joseph archbishop and then cardinal. He was living his childhood dream!

Cardinal Ratzinger later became an advisor to Pope John Paul II. He served as advisor until the pope's death. He did not expect to be named the new pope. But on April 19, 2005 other cardinals chose him to serve as pope. He took the name Benedict XVI. He said, "I am a humble servant in God's vineyard."

Activities

1. Find the hidden message. Write it on the line below the picture. Then color the picture.

____.

2. Complete these sentences.

A bride and groom celebrate the sacrament of

____.

When a man becomes a priest, he receives

____.

How can we celebrate people who serve others?

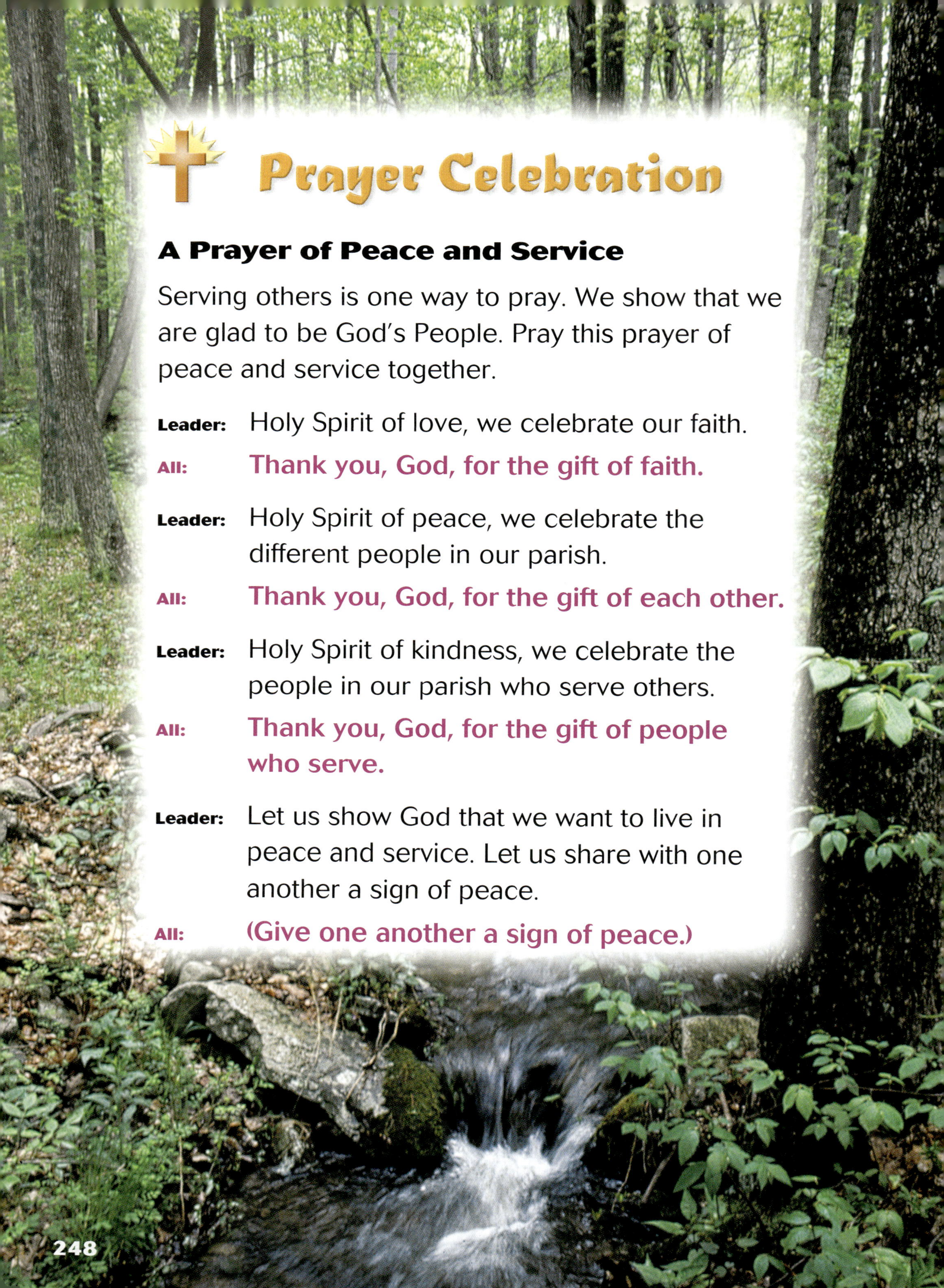

Prayer Celebration

A Prayer of Peace and Service

Serving others is one way to pray. We show that we are glad to be God's People. Pray this prayer of peace and service together.

Leader: Holy Spirit of love, we celebrate our faith.

All: **Thank you, God, for the gift of faith.**

Leader: Holy Spirit of peace, we celebrate the different people in our parish.

All: **Thank you, God, for the gift of each other.**

Leader: Holy Spirit of kindness, we celebrate the people in our parish who serve others.

All: **Thank you, God, for the gift of people who serve.**

Leader: Let us show God that we want to live in peace and service. Let us share with one another a sign of peace.

All: **(Give one another a sign of peace.)**

18 Chapter Review

A **Circle** the words that best complete the sentences.

1. One way to greet people at Mass is to ____.
   ask them a question **share the Sign of Peace** **talk all through Mass.**

2. Peace is a sign that the ____ is with us.
   Holy Spirit **pope** **priest**

3. The Sign of Peace reminds us that Jesus wants us to ____ with everyone.
   live **get along** **fight**

4. When the priest says, "The peace of the Lord be with you always," we answer:
   Amen. **And also with you.** **Alleluia**

5. The Sign of Peace reminds us to take part in ____ activities.
   family **school** **parish**

B **Write** about one way you can serve others in your parish.

C Complete each sentence by drawing a line to the correct word.

1. Karol Wojtyla was born and raised in •		• priest.
2. Karol celebrated the sacrament of •		• Poland
3. Karol first served the Church as a •		• pope
4. Karol took the name John Paul II when he became •		• Holy Orders

D Complete the sentences.

1. Deacons, priests, and bishops receive the sacrament of ______________________________.

2. A baptized bride and groom receive the sacrament of ______________________________.

3. Deacons, priests, and bishops serve the Church by ______________________________ teaching the ______________________________.

4. Married people serve the Church by sharing in the ______________________________ of their parish.

Getting ready for Chapter 19

A choice of things to do at home

We Work for Peace and Justice

The saying "If you want peace, work for justice" sums up the Christian belief in the interconnectedness of the two. We are called to treat others fairly and with respect. In Chapter 19 children will consider the concepts of peace and justice and identify actions they can take to promote these concepts. The children will realize that Jesus taught us to treat others fairly and respectfully.

Certificate of fairness

With your child, make a simple certificate with construction paper and bright-colored decorations. Help your child write the words *Fairness Counts* at the top. List words associated with fairness, such as *sharing*, *helping*, and *giving*. Each time your child acts fairly this week, give her or him a sticker to add to the certificate.

Peace party

With your child, plan a family peace party. Instead of the Nobel peace prize, give a prize named after your family. Tell what the winner did to earn the prize. Pencils with peace signs on them or chocolate coins make good prizes.

Just desserts

The phrase "get one's just deserts" means "get a fair reward or punishment." But the sound-alike word *desserts* also presents a good way to learn about fairness. Try using a system in which one person cuts a piece of dessert in two, and another person chooses which piece to take.

A Prayer for the Week

In your eyes we are
all equal, Lord. You have made
all of us in your image. Help us
learn, in your name, to love
everyone equally.
Amen.

FAMILY TIME

Something to Do . . .

On Sunday

Other than in the Sign of Peace, when is peace mentioned in the liturgy? Listen for other mentions of peace.

Through the Week

Find peaceful, fair ways to resolve differences that arise in your family. Encourage family members to respect one another.

Visit Our Web Site

www.blestarewe.com

Something to Think About . . .

Sharing Earthly Goods

The community of believers was of one heart and mind, and no one claimed that any of his possessions was his own, but they had everything in common.

Acts 4:32

The early Christians followed Jesus' teachings of peace and justice by making things fair for everyone and by treating others as they wanted to be treated themselves. The sharing of earthly goods was characteristic of the early Christians. They were able to claim that there was no one in their community who went without what they needed to live.

We are challenged to share our goods cheerfully, out of love for the Lord. As we work toward the goal of meeting everyone's needs, we are spreading the Gospel because we are sharing with people who have less than they need. When we do what is right, God's Spirit is with us.

Something to Know About . . . Our Heritage in Art

Edward Hicks was a Pennsylvania Quaker minister, a carriage maker, a sign and furniture painter, and an artist. He lived in the late eighteenth– and early–nineteenth centuries. Hicks became one of the best–known American folk artists. He painted more than one hundred versions of *The Peaceable Kingdom*, based on the prophecy of Isaiah 11:6-9. Isaiah prophesied that in God's peaceable kingdom, the wolf would lie down with the lamb and a little child would lead all creatures. Hicks painted wild animals and children existing in peace together. Because Jesus was born as a human baby, some people thought that Jesus fulfilled Isaiah's prophecy.

19 We Work for Peace and Justice

Happy are those who are fair with others.
Happy are those who make peace.

Based on Matthew 5:6, 9

Share

Life is not always fair. Some people are rich, while others are poor. Some people are healthy, while others are sick.

Look at the pictures. Use a ✔ to mark each one **fair** or **unfair**.

She shares.

☐ fair ☐ unfair

He steals.

☐ fair ☐ unfair

She helps.

☐ fair ☐ unfair

He gives.

☐ fair ☐ unfair

She peeks.

☐ fair ☐ unfair

How does Jesus want us to act?

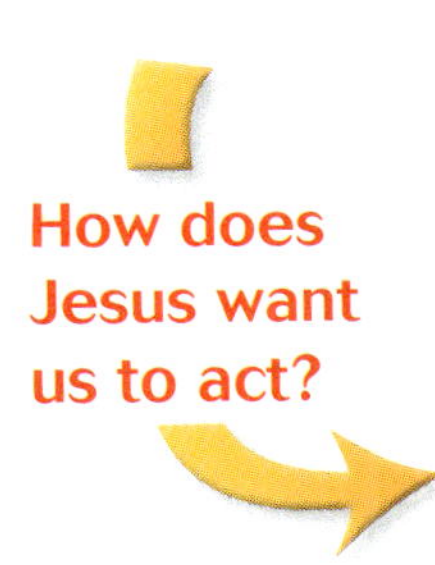

The First Followers of Jesus

The first followers of Jesus tried to be fair to everyone. If life was not fair, they tried to help make it more fair. Here is how the early Christians treated one another.

The Christians were all of one heart and
 one mind.
They tried to make peace and they tried to
 be kind.
They shared what they had, both the rich and
 the poor,
So no one went hungry or wanted for more.
Those who had extra would sell what they had
To take care of those who were sick or were sad.
If someone was needy, the church members came
With food and with money in Christ Jesus' name.

Based on Acts 4:32–35

What Jesus Taught

Jesus taught us to live in **peace**. When there is fighting, Christians try to make peace. Jesus also taught us to treat everyone with **justice**. We help people who need extra help. We share with people who have less.

Activity Look at the artwork. What do you see?

What can you hand to someone in need?

____

____

Faith Words

peace
Peace means getting along with others.

justice
Justice means treating people as they deserve to be treated.

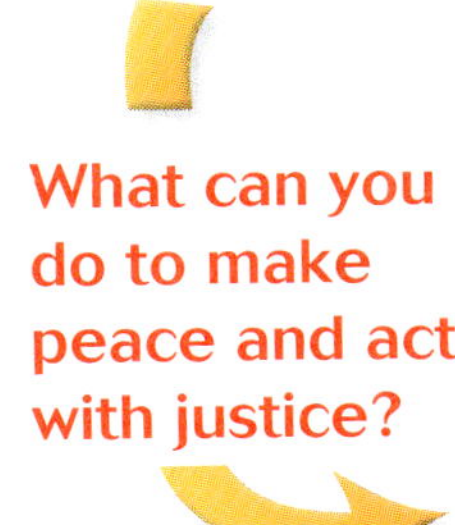

What can you do to make peace and act with justice?

Hear & Believe

A Parish Responds

When Carlos and Maria came to St. Joan's Parish from a city in South America, they were refugees. Refugees are people who are seeking a better way of life in a new country. When Carlos and Maria came, they brought their baby and only a few clothes.

The people of St. Joan's Parish decided to help.

The Kent family found Carlos and Maria a place to live. They also paid for the first month's rent.

Mr. Gonzales and men from the parish collected furniture. Soon they had a crib, a bed, a table, chairs, a TV, and a sofa.

Mrs. Smith got her friends to bring food for Carlos and Maria. Before long, their cupboards were full of good food.

Other people helped the new family find work and make friends. Different church members gave them rides to work and to church.

Today, Carlos and Maria are happy members of St. Joan's Parish. Carlos helps with Bible study. Maria sings in the choir. They help others whenever they can.

Our Church Teaches

We should treat people the way we want others to treat us. We grow in holiness when we make peace and treat others fairly. We follow Jesus and grow closer to God.

Activity Draw a picture of or write about one way you would welcome new people to your parish.

We Believe

God's Spirit is with people who do what is right. Christians believe that all people deserve to be treated with justice.

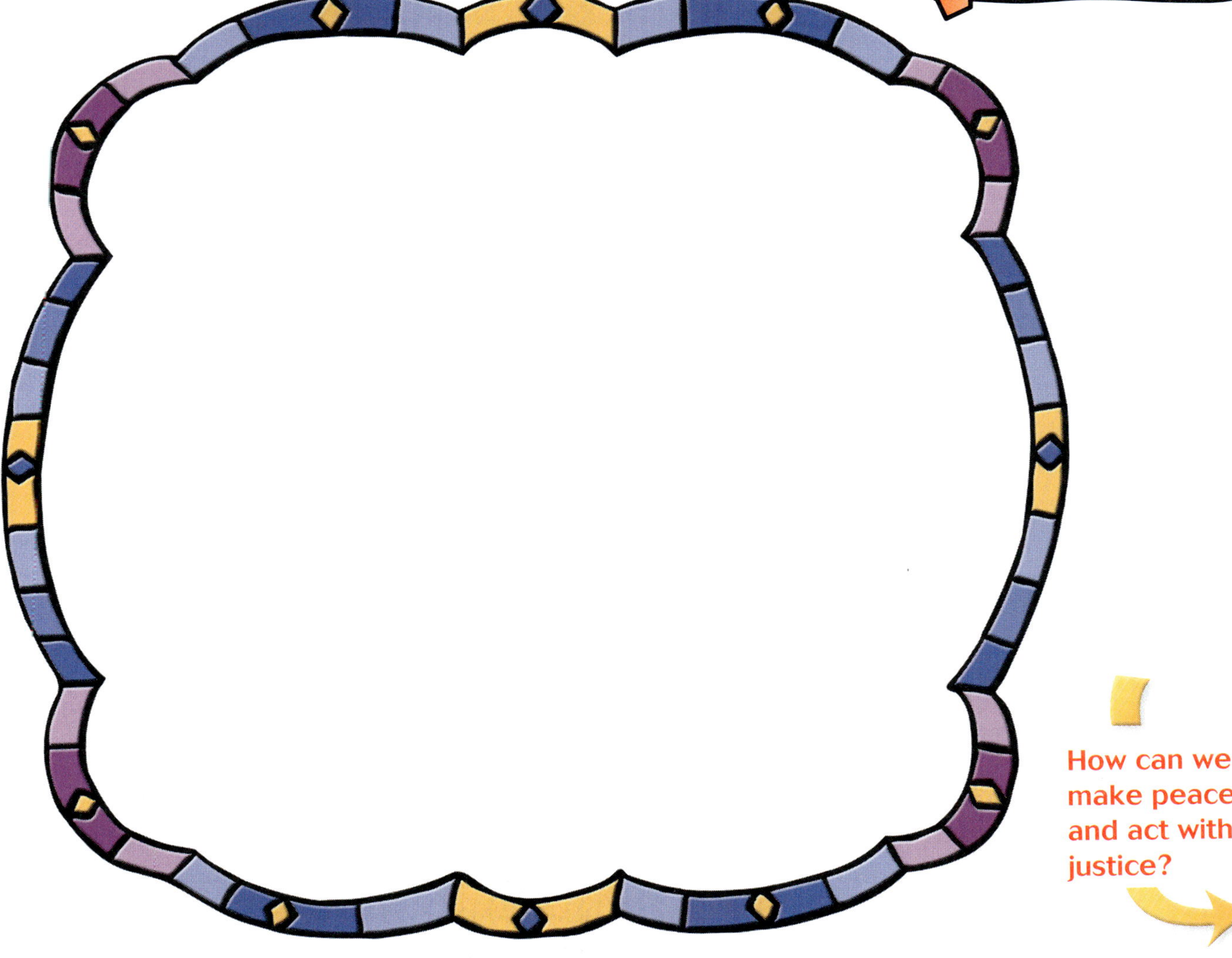

How can we make peace and act with justice?

Respond

Christian Peacemakers

Peacemakers try to make peace when there is fighting and trouble. They try to bring justice to people who need it. Here are some Christians who are peacemakers.

Doctor Johnson works with Operation Smile. He helps poor children by fixing their mouths so they can smile again.

Sammy helps keep peace in another country. He makes sure that fighting does not start again.

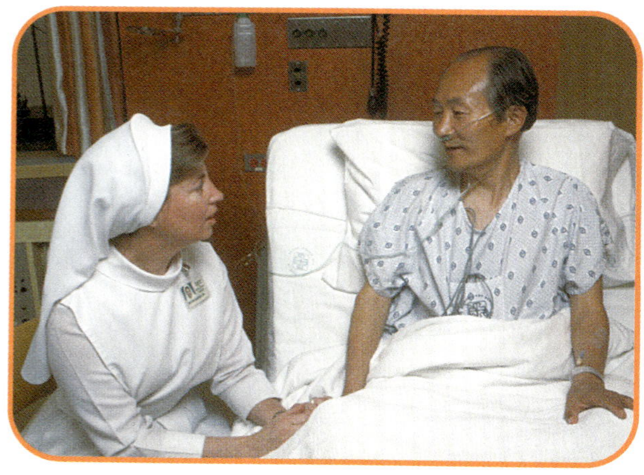

Sister Carole Martin helps people who are sick and dying. She shows them that God has not forgotten them.

Angela works in a shelter for women and children. She protects them from people who want to hurt them.

Activity

Get ready for the Prayer Celebration on page 260. Learn to sign the words "Blessed are the peacemakers, for they will be called children of God" (Matthew 5:9).

Blessed **peacemakers,**

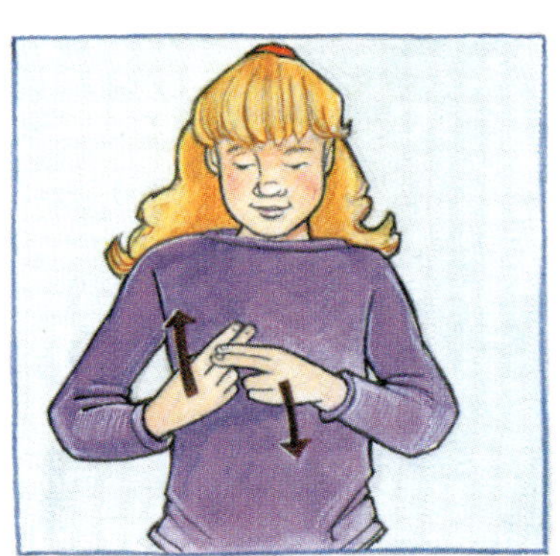

they **will be** **called**

children **God**

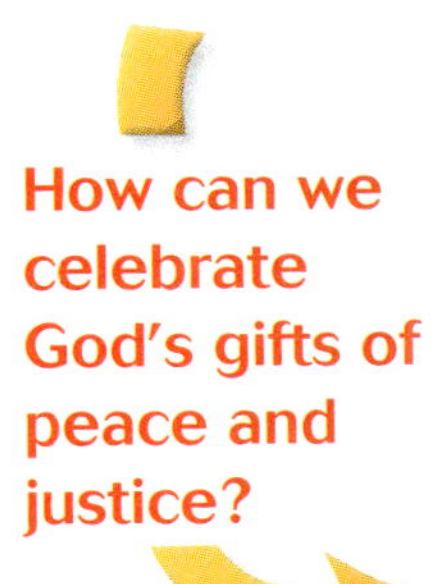

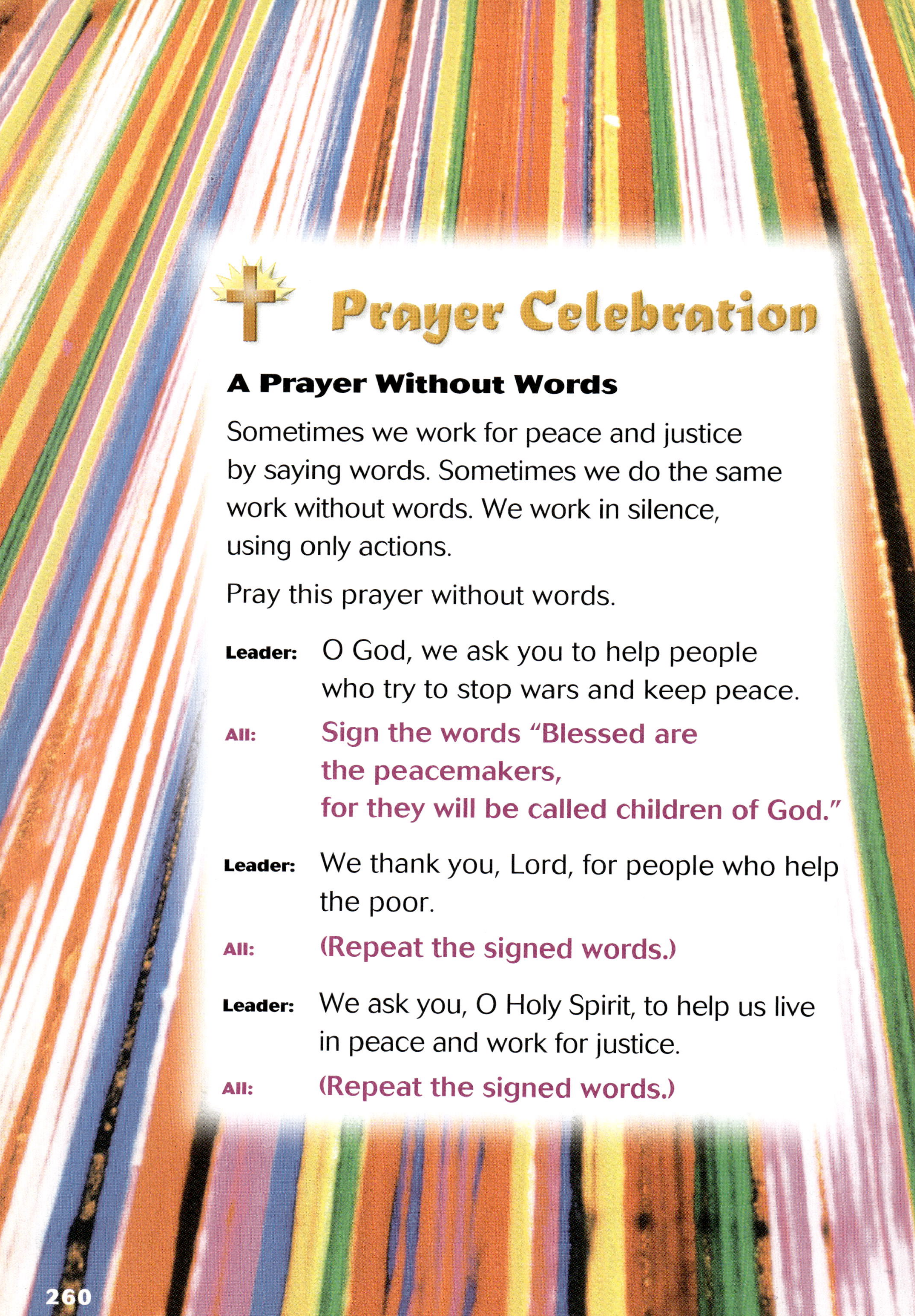

Prayer Celebration

A Prayer Without Words

Sometimes we work for peace and justice by saying words. Sometimes we do the same work without words. We work in silence, using only actions.

Pray this prayer without words.

Leader: O God, we ask you to help people who try to stop wars and keep peace.

All: **Sign the words "Blessed are the peacemakers, for they will be called children of God."**

Leader: We thank you, Lord, for people who help the poor.

All: **(Repeat the signed words.)**

Leader: We ask you, O Holy Spirit, to help us live in peace and work for justice.

All: **(Repeat the signed words.)**

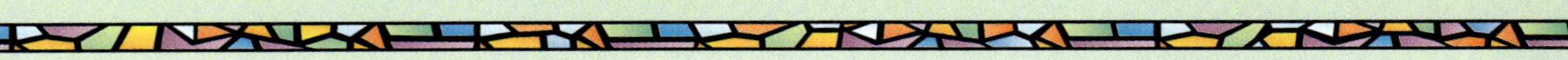

19 Chapter Review

A **Circle** the words that best complete the sentences.

1. Happy are those who are ____ with others.
   forgetful **fair** **unfair**
2. The first followers of Jesus shared what they had and tried to make ____.
   money **peace** **food**
3. ____ means getting along with others.
   Peace **Justice** **Healthy**
4. ____ means treating people as they deserve to be treated.
   Peace **Justice** **Stealing**
5. Christians share with people who have ____ than they do.
   less **more** **everything**

B **Find** four words hidden in the puzzle about peace and justice. Then use these words to make up four sentences.

A	S	D	F	G	H	J
F	A	I	R	L	Y	K
L	Z	X	I	C	P	O
V	B	N	G	M	E	Z
Q	W	E	H	R	A	H
J	U	S	T	I	C	E
T	Y	U	I	O	E	T
P	Q	A	Z	W	U	S

C **Put an X** next to the examples of peace and justice in the world today.

1. ____ Bradley steals a toy from the store.
2. ____ Angela protects women from people who want to hurt them.
3. ____ Jill peeks during a game.
4. ____ Doctor Johnston helps poor children by fixing their mouths.
5. ____ Sammy keeps peace in another country.

D **Write** your own prayer to God about a person who needs your love.

Dear God,

____

____

____

____

____

____

Your friend,

Getting ready for Chapter 20

A choice of things to do at home

We Go Forth in the Holy Spirit

Chapter 20 will highlight the virtue of peace and the beauty of blessings. Children will realize that blessings are signs of God's love, that we bless God when we praise and thank him, and that we can pray to God to bless others. They will recognize that the Holy Spirit guides us when we pray, and they will compose prayers of blessings.

Bedtime blessing

When your children go to bed this week, make a Sign of the Cross on each one's forehead and say, "Good night. God bless you." You will bring their day to a peaceful close.

Bless this mess

Some families have in their homes a sign that bears the motto "Bless this Mess." It invites God to be part of the family's life even though the house may not be perfectly neat and clean. With your child, make a sign that asks for God's blessing on the activities of your family.

Support peace

Some companies give a share of their profits to activities that promote peace and other good causes. Have your child help you look for a product your family would use made by a company that supports a good cause. Tell your family why you and your child selected the product.

A Prayer for the Week

O God, thank you
for the blessings you
give us. Bless others as you
have blessed us. Help us
go forth in peace.
Amen.

FAMILY TIME

Something to Do . . .

On Sunday

At the end of Mass when the priest says, "Go in peace to love and serve the Lord," think of one way to do that.

Through the Week

Think about the blessings you have, and take time to thank God. At dinner, take turns talking about your blessings.

Visit Our Web Site

www.blestarewe.com

Something to Think About . . .

The Peace of the Lord

The LORD bless you and keep you!
The LORD look upon you kindly and give you peace!

Numbers 6:24, 26

In the Scripture, God asks Moses to speak to his brother Aaron and to Aaron's sons to tell them how he wants them to bless others. God blesses us and gives us peace. In our lives we have moments when we experience real peace. We see the ocean or a sleeping child, and we have an experience that is free of worry, or plans, or anything but contentment. The peace of the Lord is like a continuation of that blessed moment. When we structure time in our home to allow for peace, we create an atmosphere for our family to receive the peace of Christ.

Something to Know About . . . Our Heritage in Architecture

In the place where Jesus spoke the Beatitudes to his followers, there is a church that is named after the famous blessings. The Church of the Beatitudes is located along the northern shore of the Sea of Galilee on the mount near Capernaum, home to five of Jesus' Twelve Apostles. Built in 1937, the church is octagonal in shape to represent the eight Beatitudes that Matthew describes in his Gospel (Matthew 5: 3–10). Inscribed on each church window are the beginning words of one of the Beatitudes. A dome of glittery gold mosaic covers the altar and rests on top of the building. Surrounding the entire outside of the church are columned cloisters. These provide a beautiful, panoramic view of the Sea of Galilee.

20 We Go Forth in the Holy Spirit

May God help us be strong in our faith.
May God bless us with peace.

Based on Psalm 29:11

Share

God's gifts are all around us. These gifts make us happy. We receive God's gifts through our five senses. Think about the good things that have happened to you this year. Write about them here.

Something beautiful I saw

____

Something wonderful I heard

____

Something nice I smelled

____

Something delicious I tasted

____

Something special I touched

____

How can we praise God and bless other people?

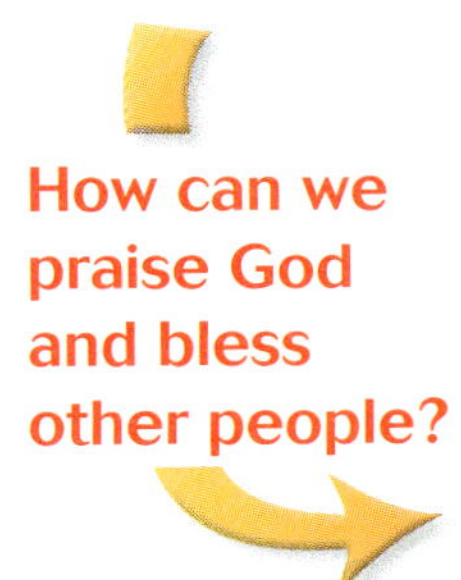

Hear & Believe

God's Grace and Blessing

One day God spoke to Moses. God said, "Moses, speak to your brother Aaron and to Aaron's sons. Tell them how I want them to **bless** others."

"All right," Moses answered. Then he told Aaron and his sons, "God wants you to bless other people. Pray for them and say, 'May God bless you and keep you safe! May God smile upon you. May he be generous with his love. May God look upon you kindly. May he always give you peace.'"

Based on Numbers 6:22–26

Signs of God's Love

A **blessing** is a sign of God's love for us. God told Moses how to give blessings to other people. The Holy Spirit helps us offer prayers of blessing to God. We bless God when we praise him and thank him for his gifts.

Faith Words

bless
Bless means to ask for God's good will toward someone.

blessing
A blessing asks for God's gifts for others or for ourselves.

Activity Complete the blessing prayer.

Dear God, I ask you to bless

____

____

forever. Amen.

What are more examples of blessings?

Hear & Believe

The New House

Jason was very excited. His family had just moved. Today Deacon Crawford was coming to bless their new house.

After the family and guests gathered, Deacon Crawford began. “Peace be with this house and with all who live here.”

Jason answered with everyone else, “And also with you.”

Jason’s sister read a gospel story. Everyone sang a hymn and prayed for the family’s needs.

Deacon Crawford stretched out his hands over Jason’s family as he prayed a blessing.

“Lord, be close to your servants who have moved into this home. Be their shelter when they are at home, their companion when they are away, and their welcome guest when they return.”

The deacon then went with them to each room in the house. He blessed each room and sprinkled it with holy water.

Then they all went to the back yard for a special party.

Based on the *Book of Blessings*

Our Church Teaches

When we bless God, we give him thanks and praise. When we ask God to bless others, we ask him to fill them with love and peace. When we ask God to bless ourselves, we ask for God's help through the Holy Spirit.

Activity Use the words below to complete the sentences.

peace	praise	blessing	bless

1. To ______________________ is to ask God's good will toward someone.
2. A ______________________ is a sign of God's love for us.
3. When we bless God, we give him thanks ______________________ and ______________________.
4. When we ask God to bless others, we ask him to fill them with love and ______________________.

We Believe

God gives everyone his blessing. We bless God with thanks and praise. We ask God to bless all people.

Respond

We Love and Serve

Each Mass ends with a blessing. The priest asks God to bless us. He reminds us to carry on the work of Jesus by helping, caring for, and serving others.

Priest: May almighty God bless you, the Father, and the Son, and the Holy Spirit.

All: Amen.

Priest: Go in peace to love and serve the Lord.

All: Thanks be to God.

The Order of Mass

WAYS TO LOVE AND SERVE OTHERS

We can be kind and patient.

We can cheerfully do chores and homework.

We can try to be helpful.

We can care for plants and animals.

We can share.

We can take part in parish activities.

We can ask God to bless others.

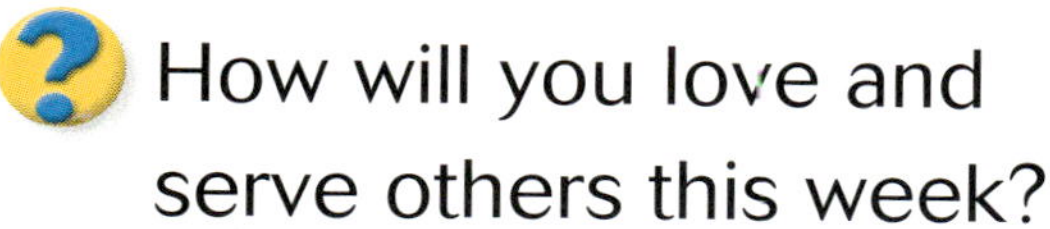

How will you love and serve others this week?

Activities

1. Read the blessing prayer of Moses again. Complete each sentence. Use the missing words to complete the puzzle.

    May God (3 down) you and keep you (5 across)!
    May God (6 across) upon you.
    May he be (1 down) with his love.
    May God look upon you (4 across).
    May he always give you (2 down).

1 g
2 p
3 b
4 i
5 s
6 s

2. Write your own prayer of blessing.

    ____
    May God bless you and ______________________
    ____
    ______________________.

How can we celebrate God's blessings?

Prayer Celebration

A Prayer of Blessing

Pray this prayer of blessing together.

Leader: Jesus, we thank you for your blessings. We ask you to listen to our prayers.

Reader 1: Protect us from danger and harm.

All: **Bless us, O Lord.**

Reader 2: Watch over our life and our health.

All: **Bless us, O Lord.**

Reader 3: Help us grow in wisdom and love.

All: **Bless us, O Lord.**

Reader 4: Care for all the children of the world.

All: **Bless us, O Lord.**

Reader 5: Bless our parents, our friends, and all who are kind to us.

All: **Bless us, O Lord.**

Based on the Order for the Blessing of Baptized Children

20 Chapter Review

A **Name** a part of God's creation that you enjoy through each of the senses.

1. Eyes ______________________

2. Ears ______________________

3. Nose ______________________

4. Mouth ______________________

5. Hands ______________________

B **Circle** the best answer.

1. Which word means "to ask for God's good will"?
   grace **bless** **generous**

2. What did God tell Moses to give to other people?
   gifts **maps** **blessings**

3. Who helps us to offer prayers of blessing to God?
   Moses **Thomas** **Holy Spirit**

4. To whom does God give his blessings?
   priests **pope** **everyone**

C **Complete** the sentences with words from the box.

God	love	praise	serve

1. When we ask God to bless others, we ask him to fill them with ______ and peace.
2. When we bless God, we give him thanks and ______.
3. At the end of Mass, the priest says, "Go in peace to love and ______ the Lord."
4. We answer, "Thanks be to ______."

D **Write** your own prayer of blessing for a friend, family member, or someone in your parish.

______

______

______

A Wise Law

Juan lives in a poor country called the Dominican Republic. His family is very poor. When Juan started school, he wore old, worn-out clothes. He did not have any shoes. Some children made fun of his clothes and his bare feet. They did not want to play with him. Juan did not like going to school.

Then a wise law was passed in Juan's country. All children had to wear school uniforms. The government helped poor families buy the uniforms. Everyone at school dressed alike. No one teased the poor children. All the children began to play together. Juan felt happy about going to school.

How did the wise law help the poor children?

Think About It

Some people choose their friends by the clothes they wear. Some people choose their friends by the color of their skin.

Circle your answer for each question.

Do you think these are fair ways to choose a friend?

yes **no**

What really matters about a person?

what is on the inside

how a person looks

Learn About It

Jesus teaches us how to love other people. He does not want his followers to be prejudiced. The word prejudice means "to judge ahead of time." It means judging people by how they look on the outside. It means not giving a person a fair chance.

Do Something About It

All over the world, people who seem different are treated badly. What could you do to make friends with someone who seems different? Add your ideas to the list.

Organizer

Connect the dots to find the picture.

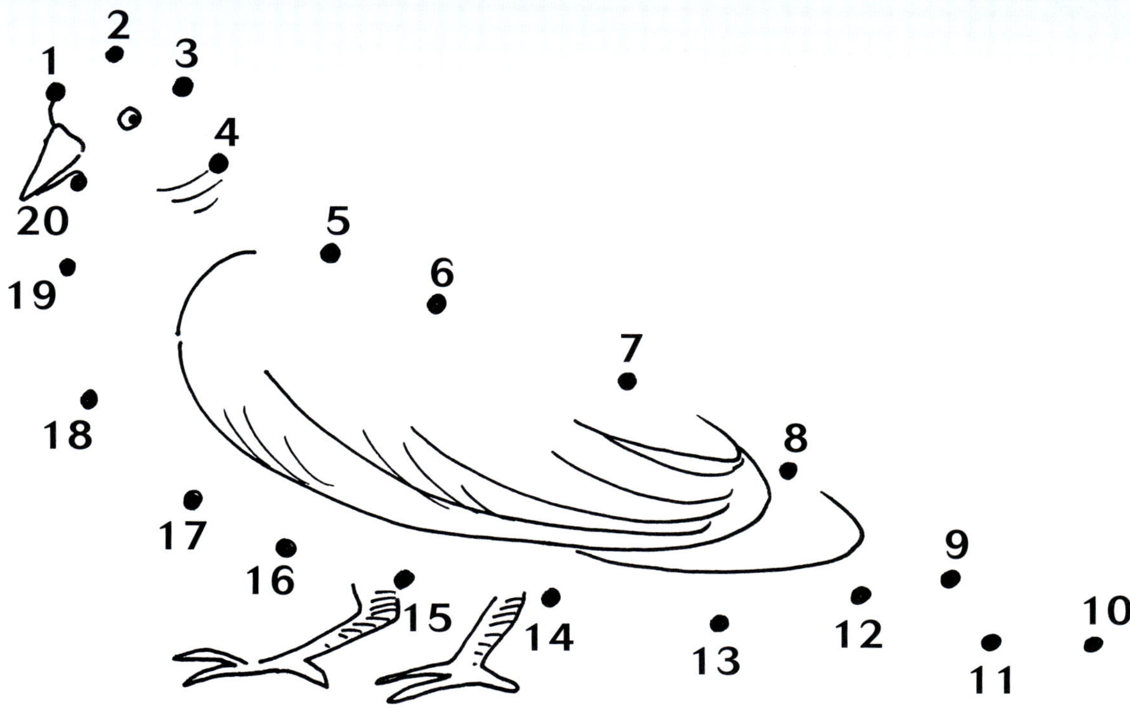

Use the chapter titles to complete the sentences.

1. God gives us the ________________ ____________________.

2. We celebrate ________________ and service.

3. We work for peace and ______________________.

4. We __________ ________________ in the Holy Spirit.

UNIT 5

Review

A Use the letters in the box to complete the sentences. It will help if you cross out the letters as you use them.

1. Spiritual gifts help us follow ____ e s u s.

2. The Holy Spirit is our h e l p e ____.

3. Some spiritual gifts are k n o w l e d ____ e,

   w i ____ d o m, h e ____ l i n g, and ____ a i t h.

B **Draw** a line to connect the parts of each sentence.

1. All members of the Catholic Church are called to •	• the sacrament of Holy Orders.
2. Baptized men and women •	• get along with everyone.
3. Deacons, priests, and bishops serve God through •	• live in peace and serve others.
4. The Sign of Peace reminds us that Jesus wants us to •	• may receive the sacrament of Matrimony.

UNIT 5

Review

C Complete the sentences with words from the box.

justice mind peace fair

1. The early Christians were all of one heart and one ______________.

2. The first followers of Jesus tried to be ______________ to everyone.

3. Jesus taught us to treat everyone with ______________.

4. When there is fighting, Christians try to make ______________.

D Write a blessing for your family or for a friend.

______________.

______________.

UNIT 5

Review

E Circle the word that best completes the sentence.

1. To bless means to ask for God's good ____ toward someone.

   acts   **will**   **grace**

2. A blessing asks for God's ____ for others or for ourselves.

   gifts   **prayers**   **justice**

3. ____ gifts help us follow Jesus.

   Prayerful   **Spiritual**   **Faithful**

4. Peace means getting along with ____.

   some people   **only my friends**   **everyone**

5. Justice means treating people as they ____ to be treated.

   deserve   **want**   **desire**

F Respond to the following questions.

1. What does the priest remind us to do at the end of every Mass?

   ____

   ____.

2. How do you carry out the work of Jesus?

   ____

   ____.

FEASTS AND SEASONS

Advent

Are you the one who is to come, or should we look for someone else?

Based on Matthew 11:3

The Season of Advent

Advent is the first season in the church liturgical year.

There are four Sundays in the season of Advent. The season ends with the celebration of the birth of Jesus on Christmas.

GO TO page 354 and locate the season of Advent

During Advent we prepare to remember the birth of Jesus. We get ready to celebrate his coming into our lives. We prepare our hearts for Jesus by being more loving and caring.

We show our love for members of our family.

We care for those in our school and church.

Activity

This Advent house has windows with messages written on them. Each message tells one way we can prepare our hearts to welcome Jesus.

For each week of Advent, choose one window and follow its message.

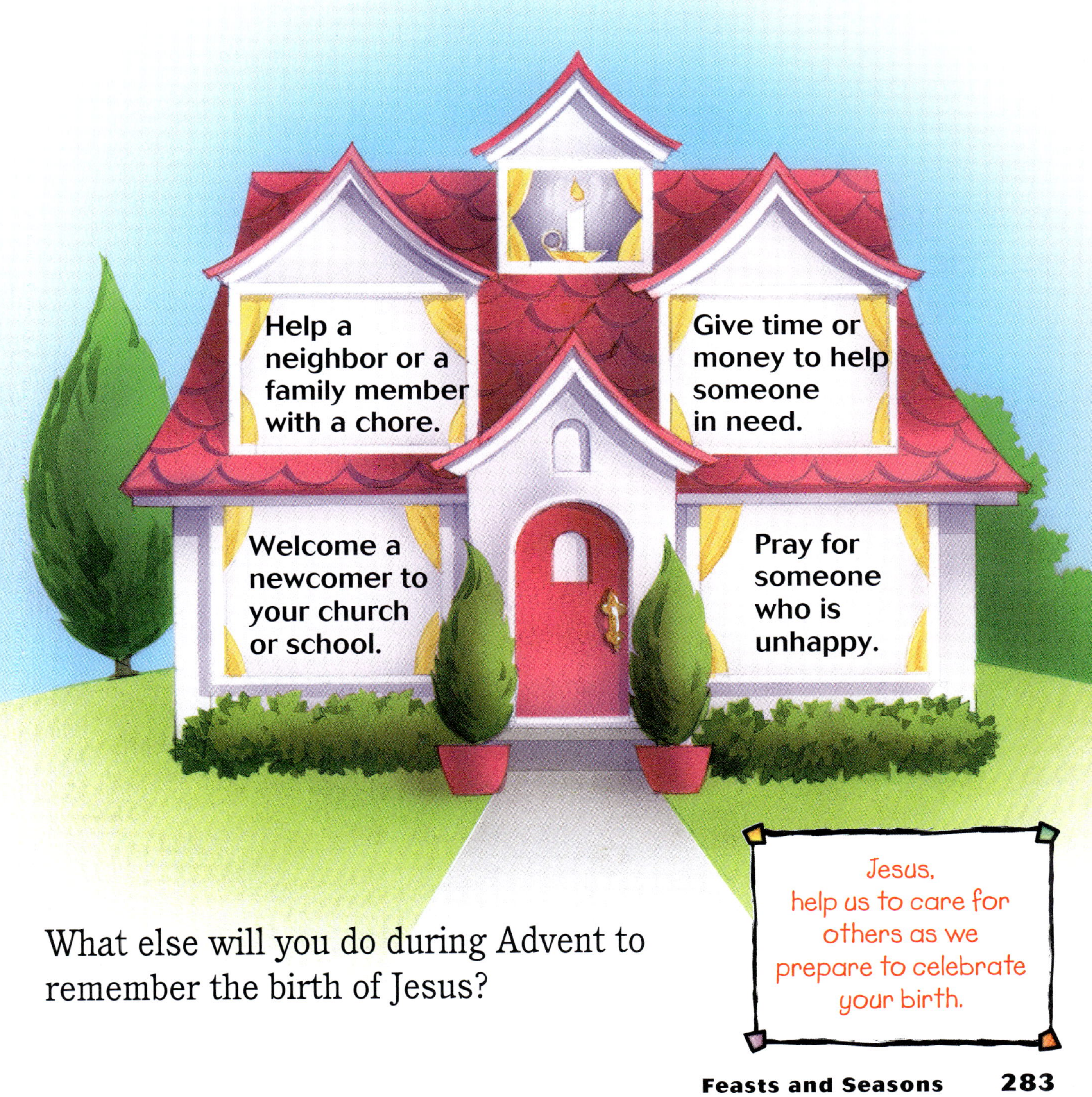

What else will you do during Advent to remember the birth of Jesus?

Jesus,
help us to care for others as we prepare to celebrate your birth.

Waiting for the Promised One

One Advent reading at Mass tells the story of John the Baptizer. He was an older cousin of Jesus. John went from town to town with a message. He said, "Make ready the way of the Lord." He wanted the people to prepare their hearts and minds for Jesus.

When Jesus began teaching, John sent a messenger to ask Jesus, "Are you the one for whom the people have been waiting for thousands of years?" Jesus answered, "Tell John that the blind see, the lame walk, the deaf hear, and the poor have heard the good news."

Based on Matthew 3:3; 11:2–5

Hearing these words, John knew that Jesus was the Lord. The time of waiting was over.

Activity

Find John the Baptizer's message. Circle all the letters that are not Z, X, or Q. Write the circled letters in order on the lines below.

Z	Z	M	A	Q
X	K	Q	E	Q
X	R	E	A	Z
X	Q	D	Q	y
T	H	Q	E	Z
Z	W	X	A	y
O	F	Z	Z	Q
Z	T	Z	H	E
X	X	L	O	Q
Z	R	X	D	Q

Lord Jesus, come and save our world today. You have done great things for us. We are filled with joy.

Saint Andrew the Apostle

During Advent we think about how we are following Jesus as his disciples. We can learn about following Jesus from the life of Saint Andrew the Apostle. We celebrate the feast of Saint Andrew the Apostle on November 30.

Andrew and his brother, Peter, fished for a living in the Sea of Galilee. Andrew was also a follower of John the Baptizer. He listened to the words of John about making ready the way of the Lord.

One day, John the Baptizer and Andrew saw Jesus walking nearby. John pointed to Jesus and said, "Behold the Lamb of God!" Andrew soon believed that Jesus was the Messiah, the one sent by God to save us.

Andrew began to follow Jesus. Andrew became one of the first disciples of Jesus. The excited Andrew brought his brother, Peter, to Jesus. Jesus welcomed both men as his disciples.

Based on John 1:35–42

Activity

Write the correct name under each sentence.

Andrew **Peter** **John the Baptizer** **Jesus**

1. During Advent we prepare to celebrate his birth.

2. He was one of the first disciples of Jesus.

3. When seeing Jesus, he said, "Behold the Lamb of God."

4. He was Andrew's brother. He also became a disciple of Jesus.

Jesus, help us this Advent to follow the example of Saint Andrew by placing our faith in you. Amen.

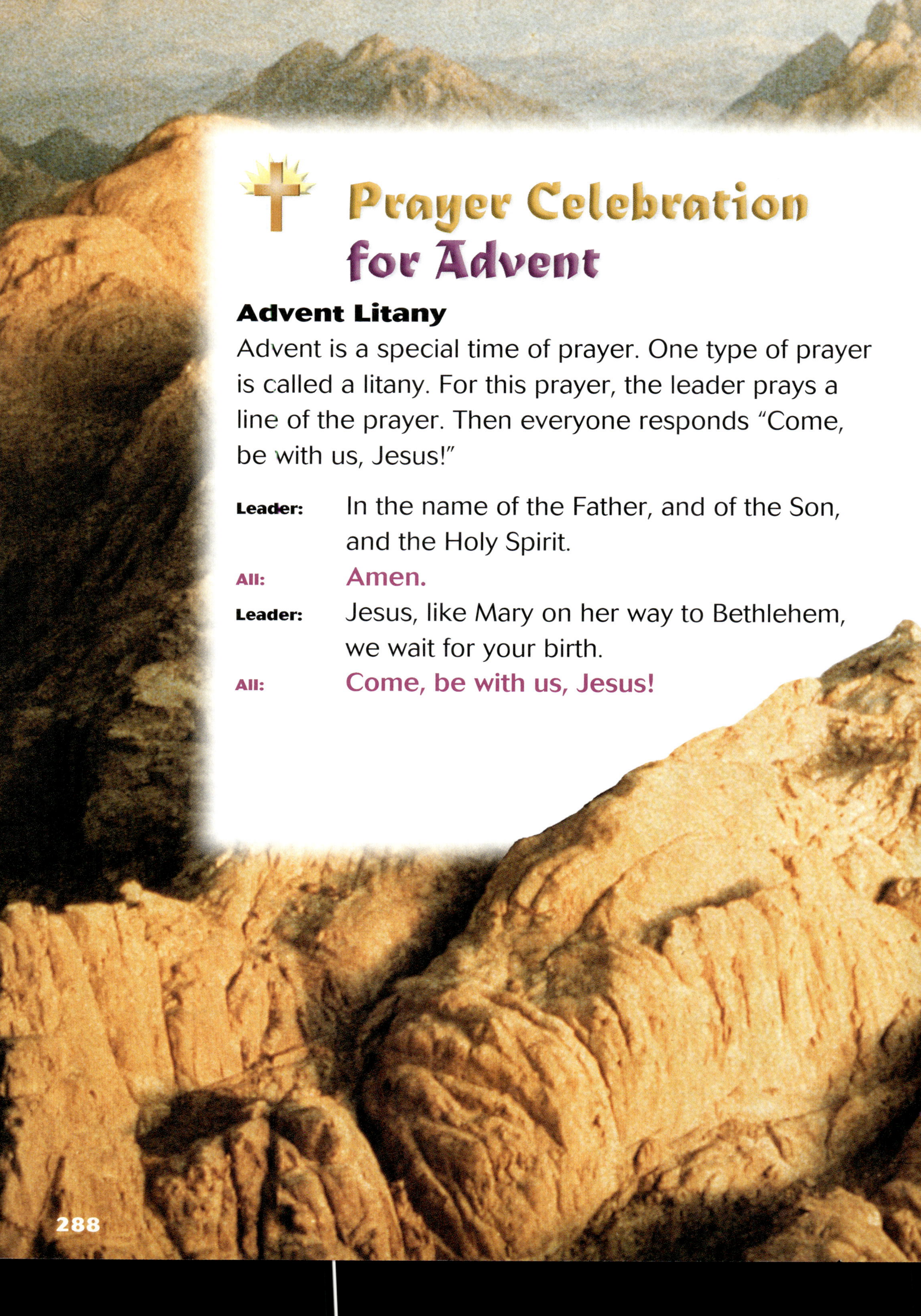

Prayer Celebration for Advent

Advent Litany

Advent is a special time of prayer. One type of prayer is called a litany. For this prayer, the leader prays a line of the prayer. Then everyone responds "Come, be with us, Jesus!"

Leader: In the name of the Father, and of the Son, and the Holy Spirit.

All: **Amen.**

Leader: Jesus, like Mary on her way to Bethlehem, we wait for your birth.

All: **Come, be with us, Jesus!**

Leader: Jesus, like John the Baptist praying in the desert, we prepare for your coming.

All: **Come, be with us, Jesus!**

Leader: Jesus, like Saint Andrew the Apostle, we choose to follow you.

All: **Come, be with us, Jesus!**

Leader: Help us keep our promises to be more loving and caring during Advent. (Pause)

All: **Come, be with us, Jesus!**

Christmas

The shepherds hurried to Bethlehem, where they found Mary and Joseph, and the infant Jesus.

Based on Luke 2:16

The Night Jesus Was Born

During the season of Christmas we celebrate the birth of Jesus. We remember that special night when Jesus was born.

Narrator: The night that Jesus was born, there were shepherds in the fields. An angel suddenly appeared to them. The shepherds were very frightened.

Angel: **Do not be afraid! I bring you good news. Today, in Bethlehem, a child has been born for you. He is the Savior. You will find him in a manger.**

Narrator: As the angel finished speaking, many angels appeared. They praised God.

Angels: Glory to God in the highest and peace to everyone on earth!

Narrator: The shepherds hurried to Bethlehem. They found Mary and Joseph and they saw the baby in the manger.

First Shepherd: We were watching our sheep when an angel came.

Second Shepherd: Your baby is so special! He has come for all people.

Third Shepherd: He is the Messiah, the Savior!

Narrator: The shepherds admired the baby. They left talking about the miracle that they had seen that night. Mary held Jesus and thought about all she had heard.

Based on Luke 2:8–20

God our Father,
thank you
for sending
your Son to us.

Telling the Christmas Story

Catholics love the Christmas story. We arrange figures into a lifelike display that retells the story. We call this display a crèche. This display is also called a nativity scene or a manger scene.

All during the Christmas season, we can visit the crèche in our church. When we do this, we think about the birth of Jesus. The figure of the baby Jesus is put in the crèche on Christmas Day.

Long ago Saint Francis set up the first crèche in Greccio, Italy. The crèche was in a cave with live animals in the manger scene. People came to pray at the crèche. By seeing the crèche, they learned the story of Jesus' birth in a way they would not forget.

Activity

Create a rebus or picture story about the birth of Jesus. Draw your own picture in each space to complete the sentence.

Long ago, [ ] and Joseph came into the town of Bethlehem. Mary rode on the back of a [ ]. They had to stay in a stable. There, [ ] was born. Some shepherds were watching their [ ]. An [ ] came to them. The angel told the shepherds about the special baby.

The shepherds went and found the baby Jesus in the [ ].

Share the story of the birth of Jesus with a young child. Read the rebus story together.

Today in a manger
is born
our Savior,
Jesus the Lord.

Prayer Celebration for Christmas

We Sing at Christmas

Christmas is the season when we celebrate the birth of Jesus. We sing Christmas songs to express our joy. Draw your own picture of the nativity scene. Then celebrate by singing "Away in a Manger."

Away in a Manger

Away in a manger, no crib for a bed,
The little Lord Jesus laid down his sweet head;
The stars in the bright sky looked down where he lay,
The little Lord Jesus asleep on the hay.

The cattle are lowing; the baby awakes,
But little Lord Jesus, no crying he makes;
I love you, Lord Jesus! Look down from the sky,
And stay by my cradle till morning is nigh.

Be near me, Lord Jesus;
I ask you to stay
Close by me forever,
and love me, I pray;
Bless all the dear children
in your tender care,
And fit us for heaven
to live with you there.

Lent

Guide me in your ways, O Lord. Your path leads to your truth.

Based on Psalm 25:4–5

Ash Wednesday

Ash Wednesday is the first day of Lent. On this day we gather in church and are marked with ashes. The priest or eucharistic minister dips a thumb into the ashes, then traces a cross on our foreheads. The cross of ashes means that you want to follow Jesus more closely.

The first time you were marked with the cross was at your Baptism. Your parents and godparents marked you with the Sign of the Cross. The priest or deacon anointed your head with holy oil in the Sign of the Cross. At Baptism, you became a member of Jesus' community, the Church.

The cross is an important symbol to Christians. Jesus died on a cross for our sins. We display the cross as a sign of our belief in Jesus as our Savior. During Lent we think about the meaning of the cross for our lives.

Activity

Decorate this cross with colored markers or crayons. Think about what it means to belong to Jesus.

Jesus, we are happy to belong to you. We are happy to be members of your community, the Church. Help us live each day as your followers. Amen.

The Forty Days of Lent

The season of Lent lasts for forty days. We spend this time getting ready for the great feast of Easter. On Easter we celebrate the resurrection of Jesus.

Lent is a time to ask questions. We could say that Lent is an "examination of conscience" for forty days. Am I acting the way a member of Jesus' community should act? Do I show care and kindness to other people? In what ways should I be more loving to others?

During Lent the readings at Mass tell stories about the life of Jesus. We hear about important things that Jesus taught to his followers.

During Lent we try to become better followers of Jesus. We try to show more love for other people. We do good works in the name of Jesus Christ. We pray that the Holy Spirit will help us make good choices. In doing all these things, we show our love for God and one another.

Activity

Fill in the correct word.

teachings **footsteps** **choices**

Lent lasts for forty days.

In this time there are many ways

____

to follow your ______________________________, Jesus.

Lent lasts for forty days.

In this time there are many ways

____

to make good ______________________________, Jesus.

Lent lasts for forty days.

In this time there are many ways

____

to walk in your ______________________________, Jesus.

What is one thing that you will do during Lent to follow Jesus?

____

____

____

Dear Jesus, help me to choose good things to do during Lent.

Time for Prayer

Sometimes Jesus needed time alone. He would walk out into the desert by himself. There Jesus found a quiet place to think and pray.

Once Jesus stayed in the desert for forty days and forty nights. During this time, he ate and drank very little. Jesus wanted to keep his mind on praying to God, his Father.

During the forty days of Lent, we remember this time of Jesus in the desert. We try to follow Jesus by fasting and praying. We give up some things we like. We ask ourselves how we can be more loving to other people. We pray as Jesus did.

Jesus calls us to think and pray as he did.

- We pray to **praise** God's goodness.
- We pray to **thank** God for our blessings.
- We pray to **ask** God to help us and others.

Activity

Think about how you will pray during Lent. Complete each sentence below.

I will ask God to help me

____

I will praise God for

____

I will thank God for

____

Dear Jesus,
help me to grow
closer to you
through my prayers.

Preparing for New Life

Sunday Mass was over. Seven-year-old Carlos and the rest of the Rodriquez family headed for their van for the ride home. Carlos' grandmother started asking him questions about the Mass.

"Carlos, do you remember what Father Andrew said in his homily?"

"I know he talked about Lent a lot," Carlos replied. "What is Lent anyway?"

"Lent is the time before Easter when we pray and fast as Jesus did," Grandma said.

"What does 'fast' mean?" Carlos asked.

"To fast means to do without food," Grandma answered. "Some people eat only one regular meal in a day. People also make other **sacrifices** during Lent."

"What is a sacrifice? Carlos asked.

"When we sacrifice, we give up something," Grandma said.

After thinking, Carlos said, "I will sacrifice by giving up TV. And I won't even pout about it!"

What will you give up for Lent?

Activity

Identify the correct word for each sentence. Then find the word in the puzzle and circle it.

1. During Lent we try to ________ people in need.

2. We also ________ for them.

3. To ________ is to choose to go without food.

4. Some children do not eat candy during ________.

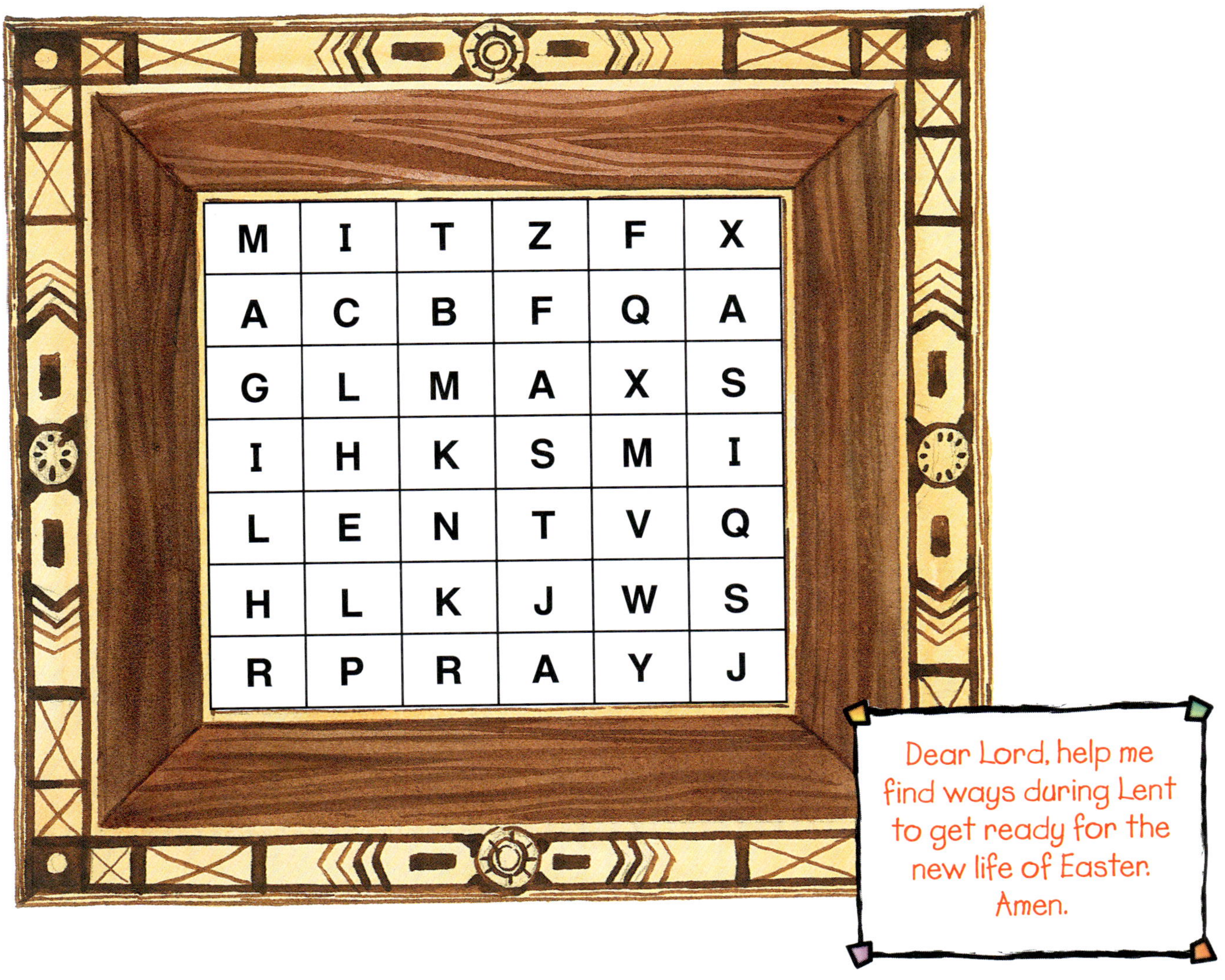

M	I	T	Z	F	X
A	C	B	F	Q	A
G	L	M	A	X	S
I	H	K	S	M	I
L	E	N	T	V	Q
H	L	K	J	W	S
R	P	R	A	Y	J

Dear Lord, help me find ways during Lent to get ready for the new life of Easter. Amen.

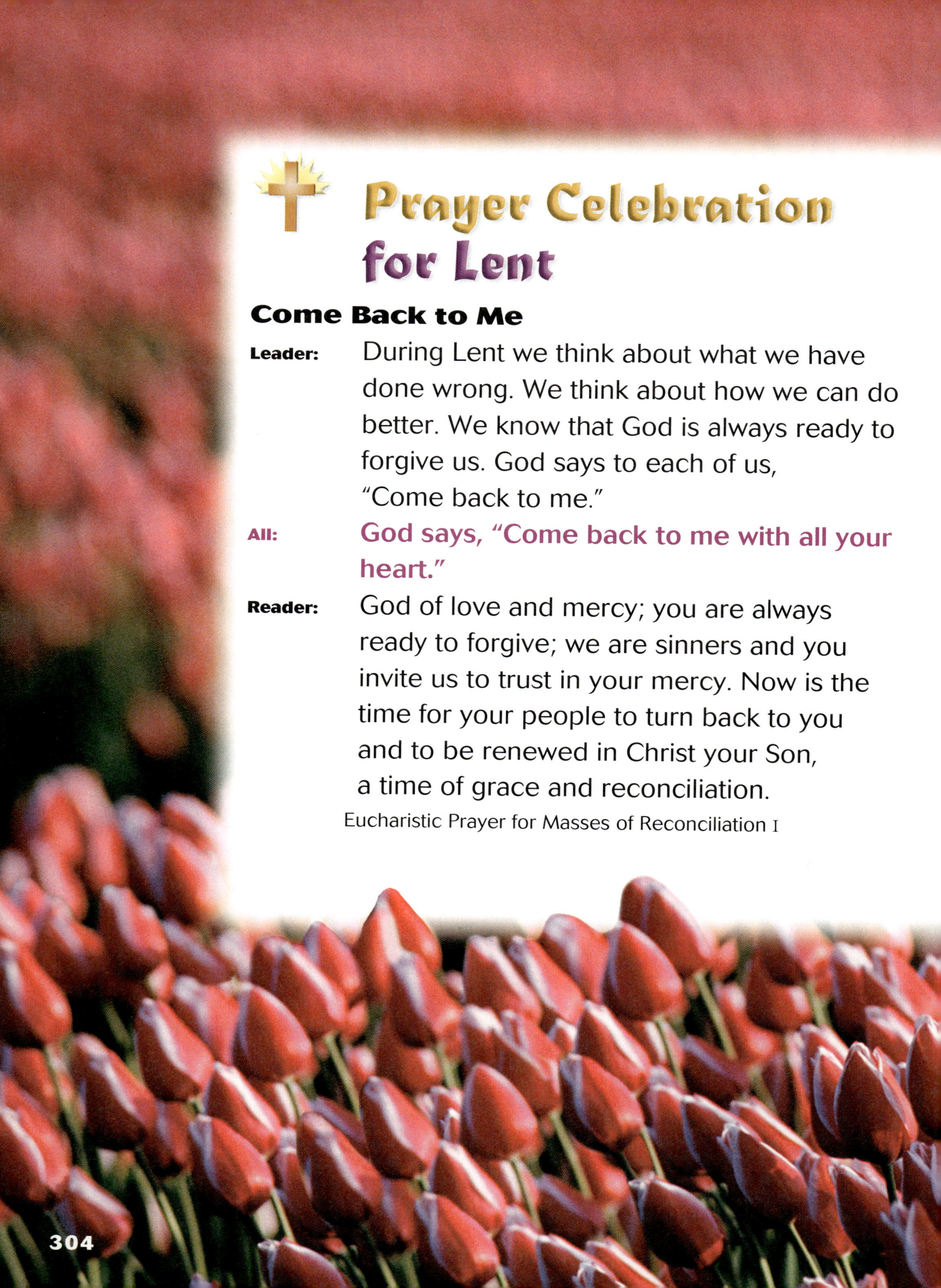

Prayer Celebration for Lent

Come Back to Me

Leader: During Lent we think about what we have done wrong. We think about how we can do better. We know that God is always ready to forgive us. God says to each of us, "Come back to me."

All: **God says, "Come back to me with all your heart."**

Reader: God of love and mercy; you are always ready to forgive; we are sinners and you invite us to trust in your mercy. Now is the time for your people to turn back to you and to be renewed in Christ your Son, a time of grace and reconciliation.

Eucharistic Prayer for Masses of Reconciliation I

Leader: When we chose to do wrong, we turn away from God.

All: **God says, "Come back to me with all your heart."**

Leader: When we hurt other people, we turn away from God.

All: **God says, "Come back to me with all your heart."**

Leader: When we do not live by God's laws or commandments, we turn away from God.

All: **God says, "Come back to me with all your heart."**

All: **We are sorry for our sins.**
We want to return our hearts to you,
O God. We know that you will forgive us.
Thank you, O God, for your goodness.
Amen.

Holy Week

Jesus said, "Take this bread and eat it. This is my Body. I give it to you."

Based on Matthew 26:26

The Three Days Before Easter

During Holy Week we celebrate three very holy days called the Easter Triduum. This is the most important time in the church year. The Triduum begins on Holy Thursday evening.

On Holy Thursday we remember the special meal that Jesus shared with his followers. This meal is called the Last Supper.

Read again Jesus' words at the top of this page. Jesus spoke these words at the Last Supper. Jesus gave his followers his Body and Blood in the Eucharist. He did this to show his love and concern for them.

Good Friday is another holy day of the Triduum. On Good Friday we remember the suffering and death of Jesus. We remember that Jesus died on the cross because of his love for us.

On the night of Holy Saturday we celebrate Jesus' rising to new life. We begin our Easter celebration and our new life in the Risen Christ.

Activities

1. Write the correct day under each sentence.

Holy Thursday **Good Friday** **Holy Saturday**

We remember the Last Supper.

____

We remember the day Jesus died on the cross.

____

We celebrate Jesus' rising to new life.

____

2. Think about the three days of the Easter Triduum. Choose one of the days and draw a symbol of the day. For example, a symbol of a cross could stand for Good Friday.

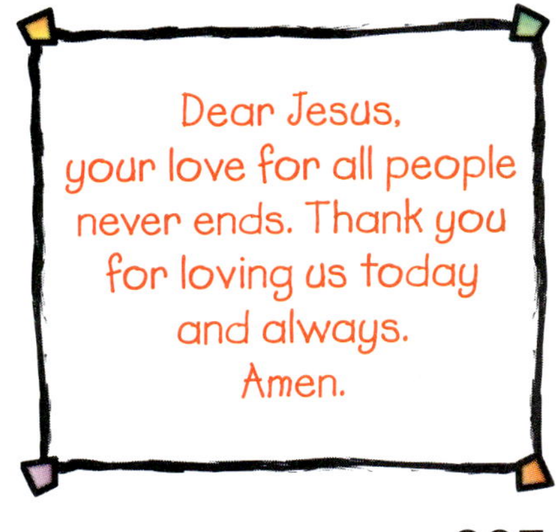

Holy Thursday

At the Last Supper, Jesus knew that he would soon die. He did not want to leave his followers alone. So Jesus took bread and wine and changed them into his Body and Blood. The Last Supper with his apostles was a special and holy meal.

Jesus shares the same holy meal with us at Mass. We call this meal the Eucharist, a word meaning "thanksgiving." We are thankful that God is with us always.

The bread and wine at Mass are changed into the Body and Blood of Jesus Christ. Jesus Christ is truly present in the bread and wine of Holy Communion. Jesus gives us himself each time we receive the Eucharist.

Activity

Identify the correct word for each sentence. Then fill in the words in the puzzle.

Across

1. At the Last Supper Jesus gave his apostles the ________.
3. Jesus gives himself to us in the Eucharist at each ______.
5. At Mass the ________ becomes the Body of Christ.
6. The Body and ________ of Jesus are truly present in the Eucharist.
7. On Holy Thursday we remember the _____ Supper.

Down

2. We receive Jesus in Holy ____________.
4. The Last Supper was a special ______ that Jesus shared with his followers.
5. At Mass the bread is changed into the ______ of Christ.

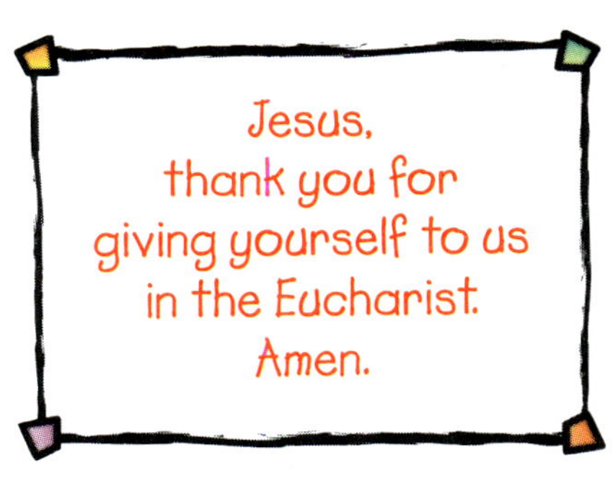

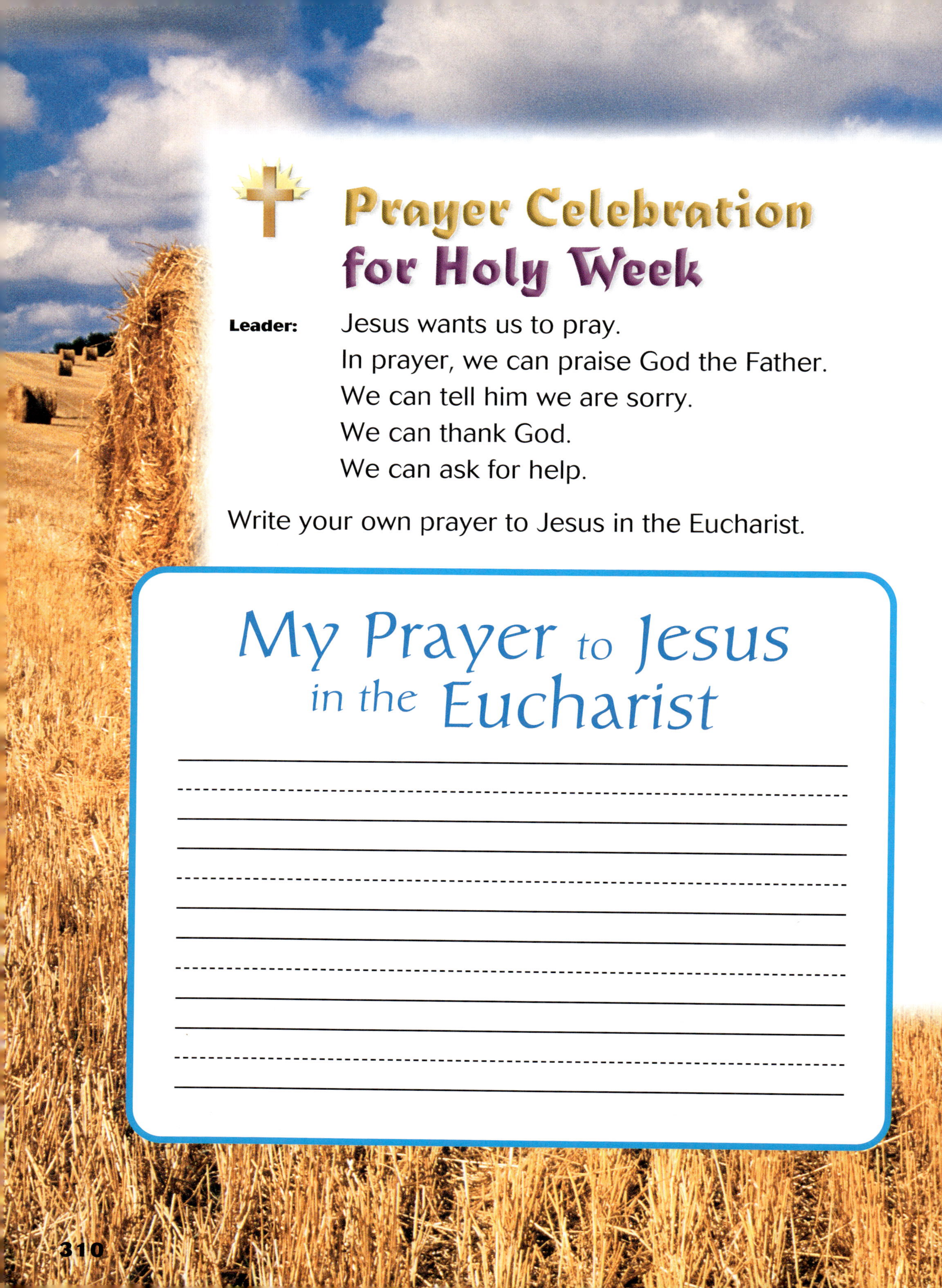

Prayer Celebration for Holy Week

Leader: Jesus wants us to pray.
In prayer, we can praise God the Father.
We can tell him we are sorry.
We can thank God.
We can ask for help.

Write your own prayer to Jesus in the Eucharist.

My Prayer to Jesus in the Eucharist

All: **In the name of the Father, and of the Son, and of the Holy Spirit. Amen.**

Leader: Let us offer our prayers to the Lord.

All: **We will offer our prayers with love.**

Leader: Jesus, on Holy Thursday you gave us yourself. You blessed the bread, saying "This is my Body." You blessed the wine, saying "This is my Blood."

All: **We now will offer our prayers with love.**

(Pause to share written prayers.)

Leader: Thank you, Jesus, for the gift of yourself in the Eucharist.

All: **Thank you, Jesus, for loving us so much.**

Easter

I have seen Jesus! He is alive!

Based on John 20:18

Alleluia! Jesus Is Risen!

On Holy Saturday night, it is dark and quiet in the church. This time before the great feast of Easter is called the Easter Vigil. It is the first celebration of Easter.

We light candles. Slowly, the whole church becomes filled with light. This is a sign of the Resurrection of Jesus from the dead. On Easter we celebrate the good news that Jesus is risen from the dead. He is alive and with us!

At every Easter Mass we sing songs filled with joy. We listen to readings from Scripture about the Resurrection of Jesus. We thank God for the new life he gave to Jesus and shares with us. We receive Holy Communion.

We say "Alleluia" to show how happy we are that Jesus has risen. During Lent, our church community did not sing "Alleluia." But now it is Easter, the most important feast of the church year. Jesus has been raised to new life! We pray and sing, "Alleluia," our Easter word of joy.

Activities

1. Answer the following questions.
   Why do we sing "Alleluia" at Mass during the Easter season?

   ____

   ____

   Why is Easter the greatest feast of the church year?

   ____

   ____

2. Circle the words below that you might use to show you are filled with joy.

Jesus,
you are risen
from the dead.
Alleluia! Alleluia!
Amen.

Yes!
Wow!
Alleluia! Alleluia!
Terrific!
Great!
OK!

Where Is Our Lord?

It was early morning, three days after Jesus died. Mary Magdalene walked to the tomb where Jesus had been buried. She knew a large stone covered the tomb's opening. When she got there, she was surprised. The stone had been moved!

Mary ran quickly to tell Jesus' followers. When she found them, she said, "They have taken the Lord from the tomb!"

The apostles Peter and John hurried to the tomb. They both ran, but John got there first. He looked in through the opening. There he saw the cloths that had been wrapped around Jesus' body. But there was no body!

Peter arrived and went inside the tomb. John followed. He looked at the cloths, and suddenly he understood. No one had taken Jesus' dead body away. Jesus had risen from the dead!

Based on John 20:1-8

At the Last Supper, Jesus had told his followers that he would die soon. But he also had told them that he would see them again. When John remembered this, he understood what had really happened. God had raised Jesus to new life!

How do you think Jesus' followers felt about this wonderful news?

Activity

Complete the prayer from Mass below. Use the code to write the missing words.

1 is for **a** **2** is for **d** **3** is for **e**

4 is for **g** **5** is for **i** **6** is for **n**

7 is for **r** **8** is for **s**

2, 5, 3, 2

Christ has ______________________.

7, 5, 8, 3, 6

Christ is ______________________.

1, 4, 1, 5, 6

Christ will come ______________________.

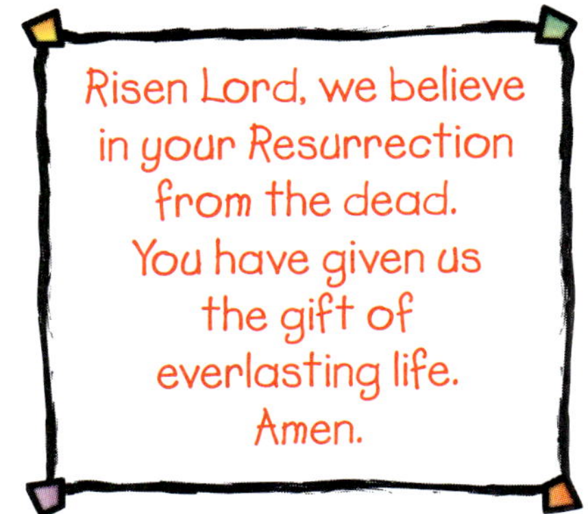

Come, Holy Spirit!

It was fifty days after Easter. Jesus' followers and his mother were together in a house. As they prayed together, a sound like a strong wind filled the house. Then, touching each person like a bit of fire, the Holy Spirit came to them. Filled with the Holy Spirit, they started telling people about Jesus. The number of Jesus' followers grew and grew.

Based on Acts 2:1–47

The members of the early Church taught more people about Jesus. They treated everyone with kindness and fairness. Those who had land and houses sold them. The money was divided to help everyone. There was no one in need. They loved each other, and they felt God's love.

Based on Acts 4:32–35

We celebrate the coming of the Holy Spirit to Jesus' followers on Pentecost Sunday. This feast of the Church is fifty days after Easter. On Pentecost we celebrate the birthday of the Church.

Activity

Cross out the letters **d**, **k**, and **m** in the puzzle.

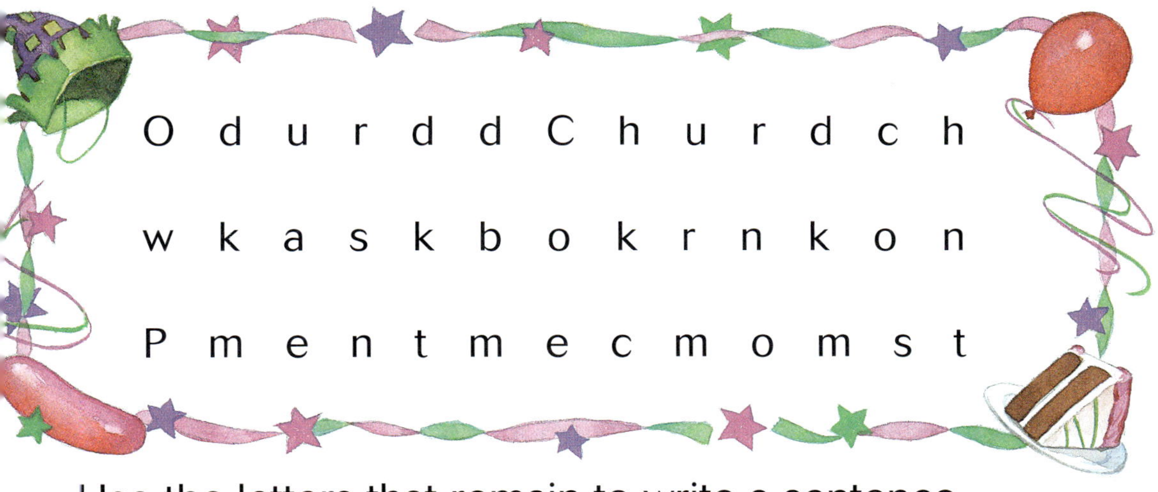

Use the letters that remain to write a sentence.

The liturgical color for Pentecost is red. Many people wear red to church on Pentecost Sunday.

Holy Spirit, you came to help and to guide Jesus' disciples. We ask you to help and guide us today. Amen.

Prayer Celebration for Easter

Alleluia!

We believe in Jesus Christ who was raised by God from the dead. We belong to his Church. We celebrate Easter with people around the world. We all celebrate the Risen Christ. We all shout "Alleluia!" with great joy.

Reader: God created the heavens and the earth.
God created the sun and the moon.
God created the land and the sea.
God created plants, animals and people.

Based on Genesis 1:1–27

All: **Thank you, God, for creating me.**

Reader: The Lord says, "Come to me when you are thirsty. Come to me when you are hungry."

Based on Isaiah 55:1–3

All: **God takes care of all his people.**
God takes care of me.

Reader: On Easter morning, the angel said, "Jesus was dead, but he is risen! God has given him new life."

Based on Matthew 28:5–7

All: **Alleluia! Alleluia!**
Jesus was raised from the dead!
Alleluia!

Holy Days

The Lord has made this day. Let us be happy and glad!

Based on Psalm 118:24

Mary, Mother of God

On January 1, the eighth day of the Season of Christmas, we celebrate the Solemnity of Mary, the Mother of God. This is a special feast to honor Mary as the Mother of God.

God gave Mary a special place. He chose her to be the mother of his Son, Jesus. Mary trusted God and agreed to be part of God's plan. Through Mary, Jesus was born into this world and became human like us.

On her feast day we remember Mary's strong faith in God. We remember her great love for Jesus.

The Gospel on the Solemnity of Mary, Mother of God, tells part of the Christmas story. We hear about the shepherds who came to see the newborn baby. The shepherds told about the angels who had brought them the good news of Jesus' birth. They told Mary and Joseph the words of the angels. "Today a savior has been born for you. He is the Lord."

Mary treasured in her heart all the things she was told about Jesus.

Based on Luke 2:16–20

Mary,
Mother of God,
help us to trust in God,
as you did.
Amen.

Activity

Think of what a mother does for her child. Write your ideas in a list. Compare your ideas with those of others in the class. Circle the things that you believe Mary did for Jesus.

The Baptism of Jesus

A few weeks after Christmas, we celebrate the Baptism of the Lord. Jesus was baptized just before he began his work of healing the sick and teaching about God's love.

In those days, John the Baptizer was baptizing people in the River Jordan. Jesus came to him to be baptized. So Jesus and John waded into the river together. Jesus went under the water. As he came up out of the water, the heavens opened up! The Spirit of God came to Jesus.

Then a voice came from heaven, saying, "This is my dearly loved Son. I am very pleased with him."

Based on Matthew 3:13–17

Activities

1. Complete the sentence in the picture. It tells what God said on the day Jesus, his Son, was baptized.

This is my dearly loved ______________.

I am very ______________

with him.

2. Go to the map on page 383. Locate the River Jordan on the map. This is the place where Jesus was baptized.

God the Father,
God the Son,
and God the Holy
Spirit, thank you for
hearing our prayers.
Amen.

Saint Valentine's Day

About 300 years after Jesus lived on earth, many people were becoming Christians. But there also were many people who did not like Christians. They often put Christians in jail. Many Christians died because they believed in Jesus.

A man named Valentine lived in this time. He was a good Christian, a priest, and a doctor. Because he followed Jesus, Valentine was used to helping people. He wrote letters to Christians in jail to help them feel brave. He signed his letters, "Your Valentine."

Then Valentine was put in jail himself. He still showed his love for other prisoners by writing to them. Like so many other Christians of that time, Valentine died in jail.

February 14 is Saint Valentine's feast day. On the next Saint Valentine's Day, remember the love Valentine had for Jesus and for other people!

Activity

Read the four sentences from Scripture below. Choose one to write in a valentine. Then decorate your Scripture valentine.

- The Lord looks into a person's heart.

  Based on 1 Samuel 16:7

- Create a clean heart for me, O God.

  Based on Psalm 51:12

- Blessed are those with pure hearts.

  Based on Matthew 5:8

- Your faith in God is in your heart.

  Based on Romans 10:8

Show us how to help others feel hopeful, strong, and loved. Amen.

The Feast of the Holy Trinity

Think about the words in the Sign of the Cross.

In the name of the Father,
and of the Son,
and of the Holy
Spirit.
Amen.

The words in this blessing name the Persons in the Holy Trinity. The word part "tri-" means the number three, as in tricycle and triplets. The word Trinity means that there are three Persons in one God. These Persons are the God the Father, God the Son, and God the Holy Spirit.

We cannot fully explain how three Persons can be in one God. We have faith in this mystery of God. Every time we pray the Sign of the Cross, we are saying that we believe in the Holy Trinity.

We celebrate our belief in the Holy Trinity on Trinity Sunday. Trinity Sunday is the Sunday after Pentecost. This special Sunday reminds us that Jesus sent the Holy Spirit to us. The Holy Spirit is with us each day.

Activity

Each time we pray the Sign of the Cross we name the Persons in the Holy Trinity. Fill in the correct name for each part of Sign of the Cross.

We offer praise and thanks to God the Father, God the Son, and God the Holy Spirit. Amen.

In the name of the ____________________

and of the ____________________

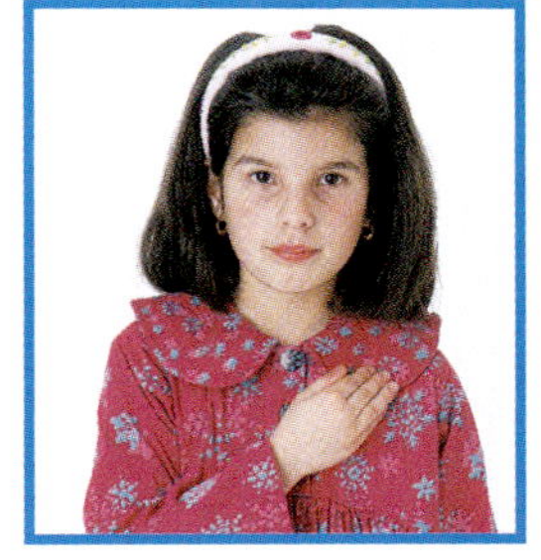

and of the ____________________

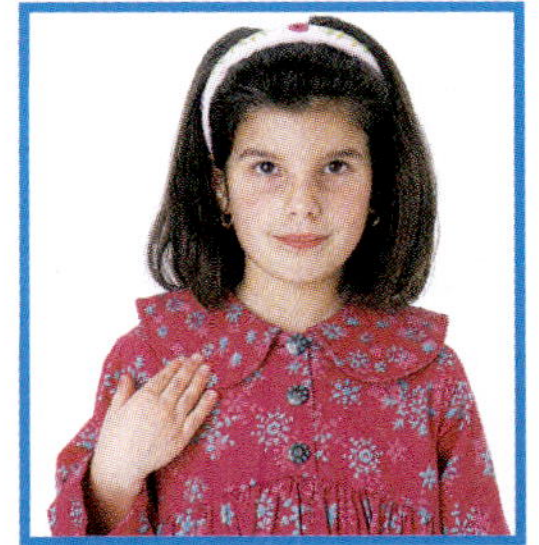

____________________________.

Amen.

Mary

Hail, Mary, full of grace. The Lord is with you.

Based on Luke 1:28

The Presentation of Mary

On November 21 of each year we celebrate the Feast of the Presentation of Mary. The Church has celebrated this feast day for hundreds of years. It is based on a very old story.

Mary's mother was named Anne and her father, Joachim. The story goes that after Mary's birth, Anne and Joachim took her to a very holy place called the Temple. There they presented their little one to God. They asked God to let them know his plans for their child.

We do not know much more about this event in Mary's life. We do know that she gave birth to Jesus, Our Lord, later in her life. We believe that from the beginning of her life she was dedicated to God. She loved God and served him all the days of her life.

Activities

1. Read the clues and complete the puzzle.

Down

1. a holy place
2. the Son of God
3. the month this feast is celebrated
4. the mother of Jesus
5. Mary served ____ always.

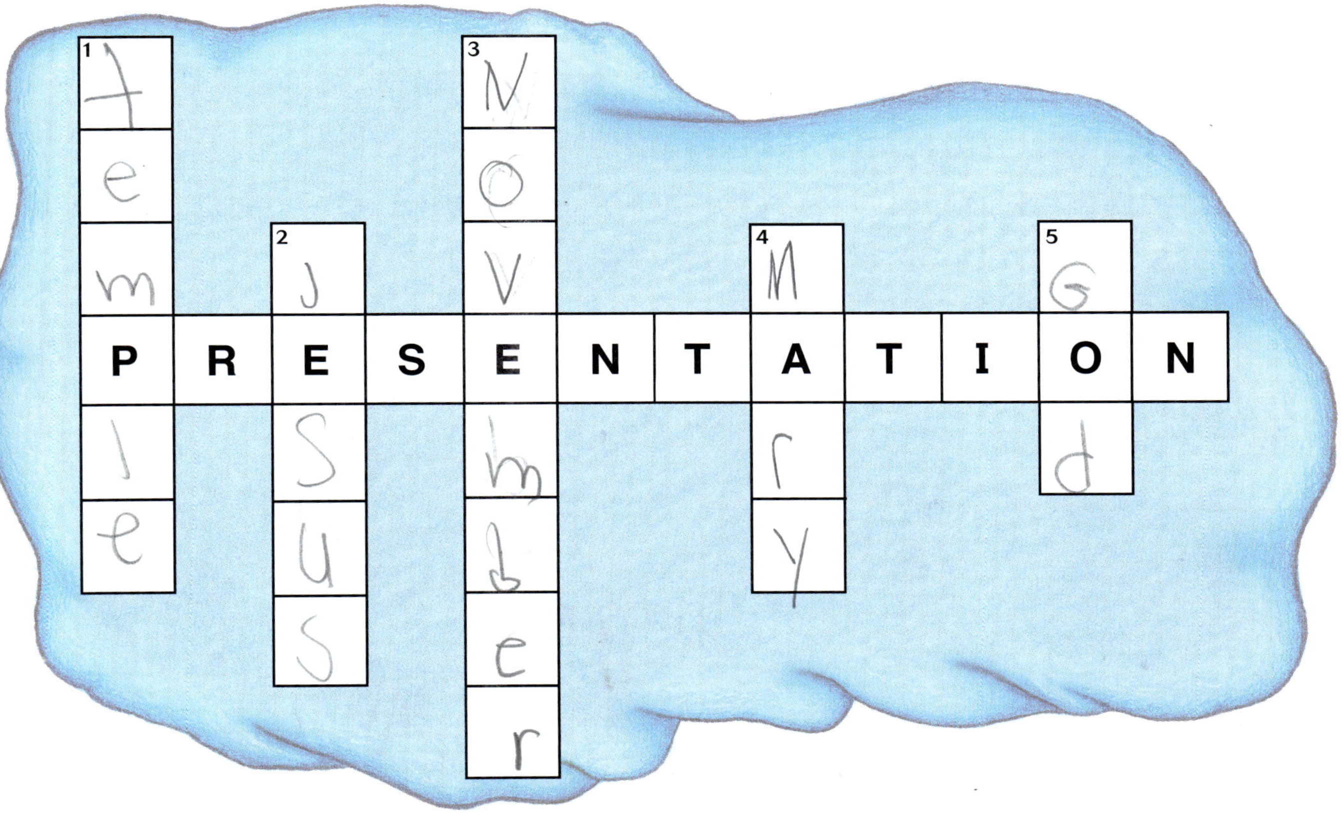
PRESENTATION

2. Write about one way you can serve God.

Being kind and sharing.

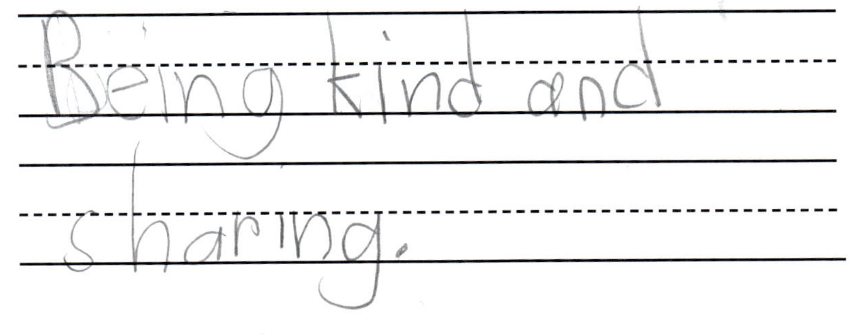

Dear Mary,
help us learn about
God and serve him
by sharing our gifts
and talents. Amen.

Our Lady of Knock

It was a rainy night a long time ago. In the village of Knock in Ireland, something wonderful happened. Mary, the Mother of Jesus, appeared outside the parish church. She stood with her husband, Saint Joseph, and with Saint John the Evangelist. Fifteen people of all ages—from five to seventy-five years old—saw them. It was a night to remember forever.

Each year more than a million and a half people journey to Knock in Ireland. These pilgrims give praise and thanks to God. They pray for help with their needs and problems. They pray to honor Mary, Our Lady of Knock.

Activity

Write a prayer to Mary. Ask for her help.

Dear Mary, help my grampa be blesed. And help my grama.

Amen.

Our Lady of Knock, pray for us. Help us each day to deal with the problems we face. Amen.

The Hail Mary

The angel Gabriel came to Mary and spoke these words. "Hail, Mary, full of grace. The Lord is with you!" Then the angel told Mary that she would give birth to God's own son. Mary loved and trusted God. She said "yes" with these words. "Behold, I am the handmaid of the Lord. May it be done to me according to your word." Then the angel disappeared.

Later Mary went to see Elizabeth, her cousin. Elizabeth called to Mary, "Blessed are you among women, and blessed is the fruit of your womb, Jesus."

Based on Luke 1:26–42

The words of the angel and of Elizabeth begin the Hail Mary. With this prayer we honor Mary, the Mother of God. We ask Mary to pray for us now. We ask her to pray for us always.

Our Church honors the saints with our prayers. Our greatest saint is Mary. The prayer we use most often as a church community to honor Mary is the Hail Mary.

Dear Mary,
pray that I always
want to love and trust
in God, as you did.
Amen.

Activity

Fill in the missing words of the Hail Mary.

Hail Mary, full of grace,
the Lord is with you.
Blessed are you among women,
and blessed is the fruit of your
womb, Jesus.
Holy Mary, mother of God,
pray for us sinners, now,
and at the hour of our death. Amen.

Our Lady of the Rosary

The Rosary is a special prayer that honors Mary. When we pray the Rosary, we remember important times in the lives of Jesus and Mary. These are called mysteries. Pope John Paul II in 2002 added five new mysteries to the Rosary. These are called the Luminous Mysteries.

In the months of May and October, we pay special honor to Mary. On October 7, the Church celebrates the Feast of Our Lady of the Rosary.

We can pray the Rosary alone. We can pray it with other people. We can pray the Rosary silently or aloud. No matter how we pray, Mary always takes our prayers to God.

The Mysteries of the Rosary

The Joyful Mysteries

1. The Annunciation
2. The Visitation
3. The Nativity
4. The Presentation of Jesus in the Temple
5. The Finding of Jesus in the Temple

The Sorrowful Mysteries

1. The Agony in the Garden
2. The Scourging at the Pillar
3. The Crowning with Thorns
4. The Carrying of the Cross
5. The Crucifixion

The Glorious Mysteries

1. The Resurrection
2. The Ascension
3. The Coming of the Holy Spirit
4. The Assumption
5. The Crowning of Mary as the Queen of Heaven

The Luminous Mysteries

1. The Baptism of Jesus
2. The Wedding at Cana
3. The Proclamation of the Kingdom
4. The Transfiguration
5. The Institution of the Eucharist at the Last Supper

Activities

1. Saint Margaret is a good example of a person who followed Jesus.

   She taught her children to love God.
   She read the Bible and prayed every day.
   She gave money to people who were poor.
   She spent time helping people in need.

   Do you know someone who follows Jesus in these ways? Write about the person here.

2. Saint Margaret wanted to live as Jesus lived.

   You can do that, too.
   You can pray every day
   You can share what you have with others.

   Think about ways to be a good follower of Jesus. Write one way here.

Saint Margaret of Scotland, pray with us for all those people who are in need today. Amen.

Saint Anthony of Padua

Anthony was born in Portugal. Because his family was very rich, Anthony could have lived a life of ease. But God had other plans for him. Anthony answered God's call and became a priest.

Anthony traveled far from home to do God's work. While he was away, he became very sick. He boarded a ship, heading for home. But God had a different plan! The wind blew the ship off course. Anthony landed in Italy instead of Portugal.

Anthony began teaching. He taught men who were training to be priests. He taught people who felt lost and confused. He helped people come to know Jesus.

In many famous paintings Saint Anthony is holding the child Jesus. The artists wanted to show how much people trusted Saint Anthony. People even trusted him to take care of the Son of God!

We celebrate the feast of Saint Anthony, a Christian hero, on June 13.

Saint Anthony was a member of the Franciscan Order. Today, many young men and women answer God's call by becoming Franciscan priests, brothers, and sisters. They teach and help the poor; they follow the example of Saint Francis of Assisi and Saint Anthony of Padua.

Activity

God calls each of us in different ways. Write about how God might call you. Finish the sentence.

God might call me to ______________________________

Dear Saint Anthony,
I pray that
I will always accept
God's plans for me,
as you did.
Amen.

Saints Elizabeth and Zechariah

Elizabeth was Mary's cousin. She and her husband, Zechariah, were good people who loved God. They had one great sadness in life. They had no children. Elizabeth and Zechariah grew old together.

One day the angel Gabriel appeared to Zechariah. Gabriel said, "Don't be afraid, Zechariah. Your prayer has been heard. Elizabeth will have a baby. Name him John. He will be filled with the Holy Spirit. John will bring many people back to God."

"But Elizabeth and I are too old to have a baby!" Zechariah said.

The angel Gabriel responded, "I came from God to bring you this good news. Since you don't believe, you will not be able to speak again until the baby is born."

Based on Luke 1:10–20

When John was born, Zechariah was able to speak again. The new parents were filled with joy. Their child would grow up to be the great John the Baptizer.

Based on Luke 1: 57–64

We celebrate the feast day of Saints Elizabeth and Zechariah on November 15 of each year.

Saints Elizabeth and Zechariah, you received an answer to your prayers. Help us to have the same faith that God will answer our prayers, too.

Activity

Complete the sentences below.

Elizabeth had no ____________________.

An ____________________ appeared to Zechariah.

Zechariah did not ____________________ the angel.

The new parents felt great ____________________.

Their son grew up to be John the ____________________.

Saint Angela Merici

Little Angela Merici had much sadness as a child. Her parents and sister had died. Then her best friend and her uncle who was raising her died as well. She could have grown up to live a sad life. But Angela grew up loving God. She lived simply and prayed often.

Angela saw that some people were sad. She noticed many poor children. They did not go to school. This upset Angela. She wanted to change this, so she began teaching. Soon many of her friends came to help her. Angela supported these women as they learned to be good teachers.

Angela believed that children and their families should learn to love God. Then these children could grow up to teach their own families about God's goodness.

The feast day of Saint Angela Merici is January 27.

Activity

Write your answers to the following questions.

1. Saint Angela worked to help families know and love God. What have you learned about God from your family?

____

____

____

____

2. Saint Angela said that children who love God grow up and teach their families. What would you like to teach your family about God?

____

____

____

____

Saint Angela,
help us know about
God's love.
Show us how to teach
others about God.
Amen.

Saint Vincent de Paul

Vincent de Paul lived in France more than four hundred years ago. At that time, there were many poor people in France. A good many rich people did not care that the poor were often hungry and sick. God called Vincent to help solve these problems.

Vincent found recipes for healthy food. He went to people who had little to do and said, "Come and cook with me. Help me feed people." Many did just that, helping to feed the many poor people who had no food.

Vincent helped people build hospitals. He urged others to take care of babies who had no homes. He set up clothing collections. Hundreds of years later, people are still carrying on Vincent de Paul's work.

Even though Saint Vincent was a very busy man, he always stayed close to God through prayer. We celebrate the feast day of Saint Vincent de Paul on September 27 of each year.

Activities

1. Catholic parishes continue the work of Saint Vincent de Paul. What does your parish do to carry on the work of Saint Vincent?

2. What will you do to help children who are poor?

Saint Vincent, pray with us that all the people in the world learn to share their blessings. Amen.

Holy People

See what love the Father has poured out on us. We are called God's children.

Based on 1 John 3:1

Dr. Martin Luther King, Jr.

Dr. Martin Luther King, Jr. grew up in the large city of Atlanta, Georgia. His father was a minister in a Baptist church. Martin studied hard at school and went to college. He became a minister, too.

When Martin was a child, he saw much unfairness. African-American people were not allowed to do what other people could do. They did not have the same rights.

When Martin grew up, he began his important work to change these conditions. He wanted everyone to be treated with respect and fairness.

Dr. King gave powerful speeches. He prayed. He preached the good news of Jesus. He planned and led marches of people in Atlanta and other cities. These marches helped people to realize the importance of treating everyone with fairness and justice. Dr. King became a strong leader, doing Jesus' work.

Not everyone liked what Dr. King was saying and doing. His words made some people feel angry with him. In 1968, Dr. King was killed because of the work he did. We honor this special follower of Jesus by celebrating his birthday in January of each year.

Activity

Dr. King gave important speeches about fairness and unfairness. He spoke of people treating each other with love and kindness.

If you were making a speech about fairness, what would you talk about?

Write a title for a speech you might give.

____

Dear Lord, thank you for the gift of Dr. King. Help us be like him, loving and fair. Amen.

Maria Montessori

Maria Montessori was born in 1870 in Ancona, Italy. In her day, very few women were educated as scientists. But Maria had other ideas. She went to medical school and became the first woman doctor in Italy.

Maria was ahead of her time in other ways. As a doctor, she met hundreds of children of all ages. Some of these children were handicapped. Many were the poorest of the poor. She loved these children and became interested in helping them to learn how to read and write.

Maria developed an approach to learning that would help even the youngest child. Her ideas on helping young children to learn are used by many teachers today. She taught teachers to have the greatest respect for children. She encouraged teachers to see every child as able to do great things.

Her loving approach treats children as Jesus did. Jesus said, "Let the children come to me and do not prevent them; for the kingdom of God belongs to such as these." (Luke 18:16) Jesus loved and accepted all children.

Maria Montessori died in 1952. Today, there are a large number of Montessori schools for young children. Besides her contribution in education, Maria Montessori also wrote books about the Catholic religion. She was a good Christian and a holy person.

Activities

Fill in the correct word in each sentence.

1. Maria Montessori was the first woman ______________________ in Italy.

2. She developed an approach to ______________________.

3. Her loving approach to children treats ______________________ them as ______________________ did.

Dear God, thank you for giving us the many people who teach us. May you bless their work and reward their efforts. Amen.

Blessed Andre Bessette

Andre was a not a strong child and he was often sick. Both of his parents died while he was young. When he was older, Andre needed to work. He tried to be a farm worker, a shoemaker, a baker, a blacksmith, and a factory worker. Because Andre was so weak, none of these jobs lasted very long.

Andre wanted to serve God. He joined a religious order of brothers. Since his health was so poor, Andre was given small jobs to do.

The sickly Brother Andre spent much time in prayer. After a while other sick people came to visit him. They asked Andre to pray for them. Soon thousands came, and many were healed.

Perhaps because his own father was a carpenter, Andre felt very close to Saint Joseph. In honor of this saint, Andre collected nickels and dimes to begin to build a church. It stands on Mount Royal, near the city of Montreal in Canada. Blessed Andre's feast day is on January 6.

Activities

1. Use the words in the box to complete these sentences about Brother Andre Bessette.

honor **jobs** **poor** **brother** **sick**

Andre had very ______ health.

He tried many different ______.

Then he became a religious ______.

People who were ______ asked for his prayers.

Andre wanted to ______ Saint Joseph.

2. Andre worked in small ways, but he served God well. Write a sentence about a way you are serving God.

______

______

Blessed Andre, pray that we may learn from Saint Joseph and you how to love Jesus. Amen.

School Sisters of Notre Dame

The School Sisters of Notre Dame is a religious community. It was started many years ago in Germany. At first the sisters taught girls who were poor and lived in small towns. Over 150 years ago, some of the sisters came to the United States to start new schools.

The School Sisters of Notre Dame believe that learning helps people to use their talents and live a good life. Learning makes it possible to do God's work.

The School Sisters of Notre Dame teach both girls and boys. They teach very young children, mothers, homeless children, and college students. They teach people who have just moved into the United States. They teach people things that will help them find a job. They teach people how to change things that are unfair. They teach as they know Jesus taught.

Activity

The lists of countries show where the School Sisters of Notre Dame work. Count the countries. In how many countries do the sisters work?

The School Sisters of Notre Dame work in ________ countries.

Dear Jesus,
you are our best teacher. Please bless the people who do your work in the world.
Amen.

Try to locate the countries on a classroom world map.

The Liturgical Year

Christmas Time
Holy Family
Epiphany
Baptism of the Lord

Ordinary Time

Ash Wednesday

Lent

Holy Week
Passion Sunday (Palm Sunday)
Holy Thursday
Good Friday
Holy Saturday
Easter Sunday

Easter Time
Ascension
Pentecost

Ordinary Time
Trinity Sunday
The Body and Blood of Christ
Christ the King

Advent

January
1 Mary, Mother of God
25 Conversion of St. Paul

February
2 The Presentation
22 Chair of St. Peter

March
17 St. Patrick
19 St. Joseph
25 The Annunciation

April

May
31 The Visitation

June
24 John the Baptizer

July

August
15 The Assumption

September

October
2 Guardian Angels
4 St. Francis of Assisi

November
1 All Saints' Day

December
8 Immaculate Conception
25 Christmas Day

OUR CATHOLIC HERITAGE

What Catholics Believe

How Catholics Worship

How Catholics Live

How Catholics Pray

What Catholics Believe

We can come to know and understand our faith in many ways.

About
The Bible

The Bible is the word of God. In the Bible there are many books written by different people. God especially chose each writer. And each writer tells stories about God's love for us.

The Bible is also called Scripture. Scripture means "holy writings."

The Bible has two parts—the Old Testament and the New Testament. At Mass there are readings from both parts of the Bible.

The Old Testament is about God's people who lived before Jesus was born.

The New Testament is about Jesus' life and his teachings. It includes important books and letters for the followers of Jesus.

The first four books in the New Testament are called Gospels. Gospel means "good news." The Gospels are named for four of Jesus' disciples—Matthew, Mark, Luke, and John. Each Gospel tells us good news about Jesus.

DO YOU KNOW THESE STORIES
FROM THE BIBLE?

ABOUT

THE TRINITY

There is only one God. There are three Persons in God—the Father, the Son, and the Holy Spirit.

We call the three Persons in God the Holy Trinity.

The Nicene Creed tells about the Holy Trinity. The words tell what we believe about God the Father, Son, and Holy Spirit.

God Our Father

God is our heavenly Father. Like a good father, God loves and cares for us. When Jesus taught us to pray, he told us to call God "Father." God is also our Creator. And God made everything in the world with love.

Jesus Christ

Jesus Christ is God's own Son. Jesus became a man and lived on the earth. God sent Jesus to teach us.

Jesus teaches us about God. He teaches us how to live as children of God. And he teaches us how to show love. When we do these things, we are followers of Jesus.

Jesus died on the cross and rose from the dead for us. Jesus is our Savior. He saves us from sin. And he saves us from death.

Jesus is alive. He shares new life with us.

The Holy Spirit

The Holy Spirit is God. The Holy Spirit is always with us. The Holy Spirit helps us follow Jesus.

We receive the Holy Spirit at Baptism. The Holy Spirit gives us gifts that help us live good lives. We can share these gifts with other people and with the Church. The Holy Spirit helps us live as Jesus teaches us to live.

ABOUT THE CATHOLIC CHURCH

We are Catholics. We are God's people. We call the Church the Body of Christ. We are followers of Jesus. We celebrate the sacraments. We pray to God. We can pray together or by ourselves. We care for and help others.

The Catholic Church is our faith community. Our church community shares the good news about Jesus.

ABOUT MARY

Mary is the mother of Jesus. She was chosen by God.

Mary loved and trusted God. Mary loved and cared for Jesus.

We call Mary "Mother," too. She is our mother in heaven. Like a good mother, Mary loves and cares for us. Mary hears our prayers.

Mary is our greatest saint. The saints are special people. Saints show us how to follow Jesus. We honor Mary and all the saints. We ask them to pray for us.

ABOUT NEW LIFE FOREVER

Jesus teaches us to act with love. When we act with love, we will be happy with God in heaven. Heaven is happiness with God forever.

HOW CATHOLICS WORSHIP

Worship is giving honor, thanks, and praise to God. We worship when we pray and when we celebrate the Eucharist. We worship when we celebrate all the sacraments.

ABOUT THE SACRAMENTS

The sacraments are celebrations of God's love for us. We celebrate that we belong to Jesus. We celebrate that we share in Jesus' new life. There are seven sacraments.

Baptism is a sacrament of welcome into the Church. At Baptism we receive the Holy Spirit. We are baptized with water. Water is a sign that Jesus shares his new life with us.

Confirmation is the sacrament of the Holy Spirit. In Confirmation we receive the Holy Spirit in a special way. The Holy Spirit helps us share the good news about Jesus.

Eucharist is the sacrament in which we share a special meal with Jesus. The Eucharist, a sacrifice, is God's gift to us.

When we celebrate the Eucharist at Mass, we remember that Jesus loves us. Jesus saves us from sin and gives us everlasting life. We thank God for giving us the Body and Blood of Jesus Christ to make us his people.

Reconciliation is the sacrament that celebrates the gift of God's forgiveness. It also celebrates the gift of God's love for us. We say we are sorry for our sins. We promise to turn away from sin. God always forgives us.

Anointing of the Sick is a sacrament of healing. It is the sacrament of Jesus' peace and forgiveness. People who are sick or elderly receive this sacrament.

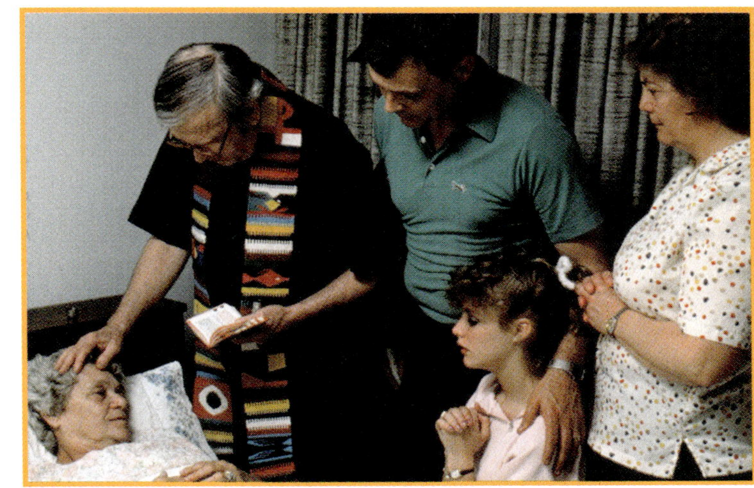

The sacrament of **Holy Orders** celebrates priests, deacons, and bishops. These people are called by God to do Jesus' work in the Church.

Matrimony is the sacrament that celebrates the love that a man and a woman have for each other. In marriage a husband and wife begin their own family. Together with their children they can be models for the whole community. They can show others what it means to follow Jesus.

ABOUT
THE MASS

1. Our celebration begins. The priest and the other ministers go to the altar. We stand and sing a welcome song.

2. We make the Sign of the Cross. The priest welcomes us with these words: "The Lord be with you." We answer, "And also with you."

3. We remember our sins. We ask God to forgive us.

4. We listen to God's word in two readings from the Bible. At the end of each reading we say, "Thanks be to God."

5. The priest or deacon reads the Gospel story. The word Gospel means "good news." We stand and listen to the good news of Jesus. We say, "Praise to you, Lord Jesus Christ."

6. The priest or deacon explains the readings to us in a special talk called the homily. We listen carefully.

7. We stand and pray the Prayer of the Faithful. We ask God to help the Church, our country, and all of God's people.

8. We bring the gifts of bread and wine to the altar for the special meal with Jesus. We remember that Jesus always loves us.

9. The priest offers our gifts of bread and wine to God.

10. We thank and praise God for all of our blessings. We especially thank God for the gift of Jesus.

11. The priest prays as Jesus did at the Last Supper. Our gifts of bread and wine become the Body and Blood of Jesus Christ.

12. The priest holds up the Body and Blood of Jesus. He says a prayer to praise God. We answer, "Amen." The word Amen means "Yes! We believe this is true."

13. We say the Lord's Prayer. This is the prayer that Jesus taught us to say.

14. We offer one another a Sign of Peace. This is a sign that reminds us to live as Jesus teaches us to live.

15. When we share Jesus' Body and Blood in the Eucharist, we promise to act like Jesus.

16. We receive God's blessing. We answer, "Amen." Together we sing a communion song that gives thanks and praise for the gift of Jesus in the Eucharist. We go in peace to love and serve all people.

About
Reconciliation

The sacrament of Reconciliation is a celebration of God's love and forgiveness. We can celebrate the sacrament of Reconciliation with others.

Introductory Rites We sing a song of praise. The priest welcomes us and prays with us.

The Word of God We listen to readings from the Bible. The priest or deacon helps us understand the readings.

Examination of Conscience We think about our words and actions. We ask the Holy Spirit to help us turn away from sin. We pray the Lord's Prayer together.

Rite of Reconciliation We pray a prayer of sorrow. Then each of us tells our sins to the priest. We talk about the words or actions for which we are sorry. Then we ask for forgiveness. The priest gives us absolution—the forgiveness of God.

Proclamation of Praise We praise and thank God. We are happy that God forgives us. We are happy that he loves us always and forever.

Concluding Prayer of Thanksgiving The priest offers a blessing for us. We sing a song of praise.

Steps to Reconciliation

When we receive the sacrament of Reconciliation, we follow these steps:

1. **Examination of Conscience**
   I examine my conscience. I ask myself some important questions. Have I hurt other people or myself? Have I done harmful things on purpose?

2. **Welcome** The priest offers a welcome. I make the Sign of the Cross and say, "In the name of the Father, and of the Son, and of the Holy Spirit. Amen."

3. **Reading** The priest may read a story from the Bible. The story is about God's love and forgiveness. God is always ready to forgive.

4. **Confession of Sins** The priest listens as I talk. I explain my sins. I tell the priest how I may have hurt myself or others.

5. **Penance** The priest asks me to say a prayer or do an act of goodness. This will help me make up for what I have done wrong.

6. Prayer of Sorrow I tell God I am sorry for my sins. I say a prayer of sorrow. This prayer is called the Act of Contrition.

My God,
I am sorry for my sins with all my heart.
In choosing to do wrong
and failing to do good,
I have sinned against you
whom I should love above all things.
I firmly intend, with your help,
to do penance,
to sin no more,
and to avoid whatever leads me to sin.
Amen.

7. Absolution The priest says a prayer in the name of the Church. Then the priest asks God to forgive my sins. The priest gives me absolution, which is the forgiveness of God.

The priest says, "I absolve you from your sins in the name of the Father, and of the Son, and of the Holy Spirit."

8. Prayer of Praise and Dismissal With the priest, I thank God for being forgiving. This is called the Prayer of Thanksgiving. Then the priest says, "Go in peace."

I answer, "Amen."

HOW CATHOLICS LIVE

Jesus teaches us how to live.
He gives us the Holy Spirit to help us.
He gives us the sacraments in the Church
to strengthen us in doing good.

ABOUT

THE GREAT COMMANDMENT

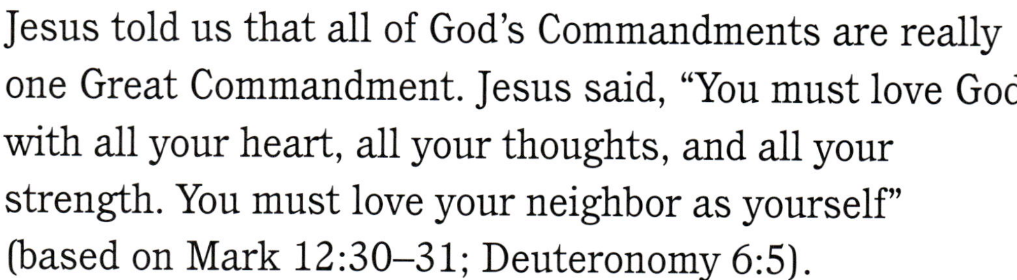

Jesus told us that all of God's Commandments are really one Great Commandment. Jesus said, "You must love God with all your heart, all your thoughts, and all your strength. You must love your neighbor as yourself" (based on Mark 12:30–31; Deuteronomy 6:5).

The Great Commandment tells us how to love God and other people.

ABOUT

THE NEW COMMANDMENT

Jesus gave us the New Commandment. He said, "Love one another as I have loved you." (based on John 13:34)

We can show our love by caring for all living things. We can be fair and kind to all people. We can be helpful. We can be forgiving. We can be peacemakers.

When we do not treat others with love, we sin. Sin is turning away from God and choosing to do what we know is wrong. God wants us to be sorry for our sins. God always forgives us. God wants us always to be loving people.

The Holy Spirit Helps Us

We can make the choice to love or to sin. The Holy Spirit helps us turn away from sin and choose what is good.

ABOUT

THE BEATITUDES

The Bible tells us a story of Jesus as a great teacher. The story is called "The Sermon on the Mount." This story tells us about the lesson that Jesus taught his followers. He taught them about the eight Beatitudes. The Beatitudes tell us how to live and how to treat others.

The Beatitudes	Living the Beatitudes
Happy are the poor in spirit. The reign of God is theirs.	We are poor in spirit when we know that we need God more than anything else.
Happy are the sorrowful. They will be comforted.	We try to help those who are in sorrow or those who are hurting. We know God will comfort them.
Happy are the gentle. They will receive all that God has promised.	We are gentle and patient with others. We believe we will share in God's promises.
Happy are those who hunger and thirst for justice. They will be satisfied.	We try to be fair and just toward others. We share what we have with those in need.
Happy are those who show mercy. They will receive mercy.	We forgive those who are unkind to us. We accept the forgiveness of others.
Happy are the pure of heart. They will see God.	We try to keep God first in our lives. We believe we will live forever with God.
Happy are the peacemakers. They will be called the children of God.	We try to bring God's peace to the world. When we live peacefully, we are known as God's children.
Happy are those who are treated unfairly for doing what is right. The kingdom of heaven will belong to them.	We try to do what is right even when we are teased or insulted. We believe we will be with God forever.

ABOUT
THE TEN COMMANDMENTS

We can find God's commandments in the Bible. The Ten Commandments tell us how God wants us to live. When we live by the commandments, we grow in holiness.

The Ten Commandments
We Live God's Laws

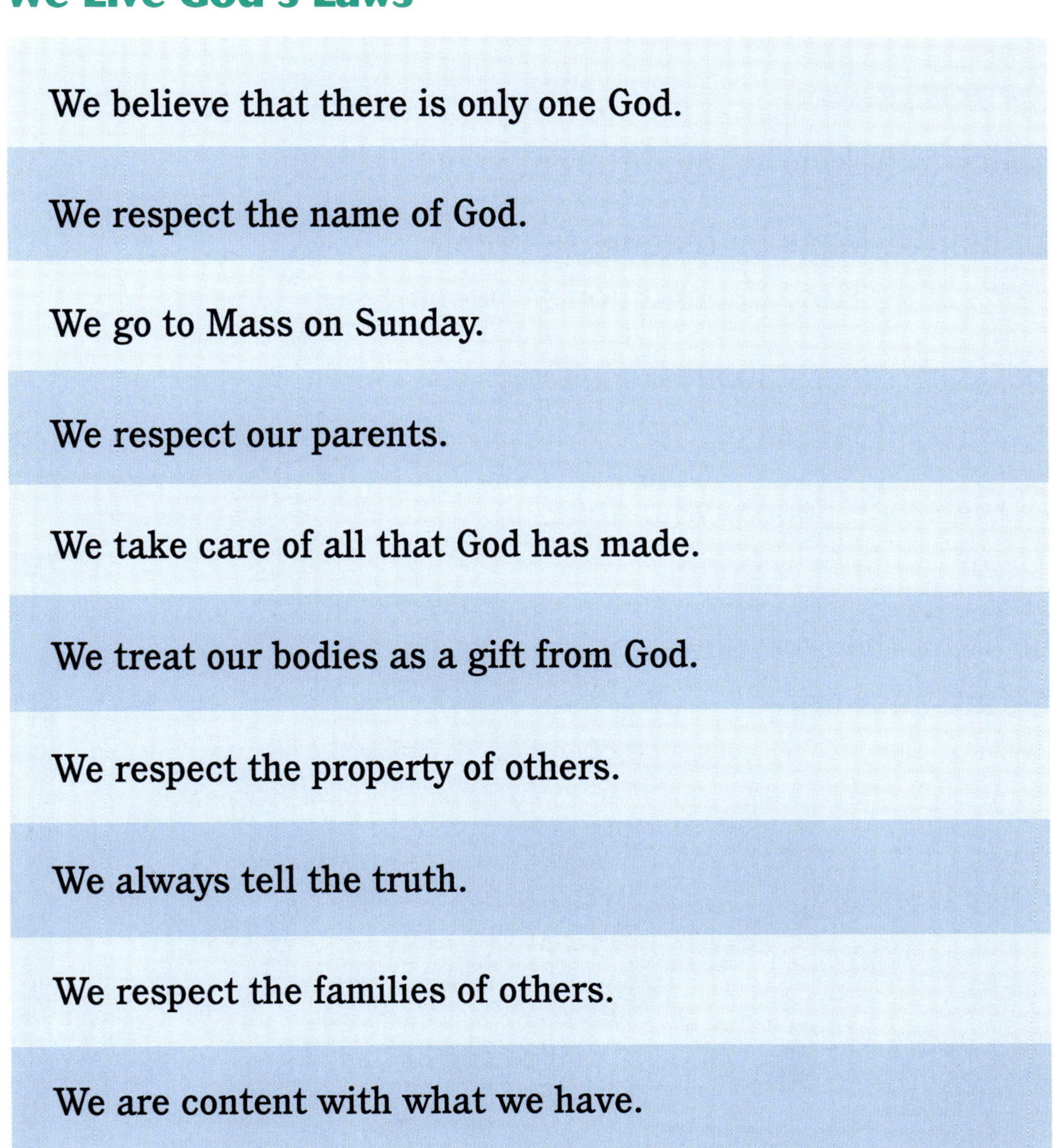

We believe that there is only one God.

We respect the name of God.

We go to Mass on Sunday.

We respect our parents.

We take care of all that God has made.

We treat our bodies as a gift from God.

We respect the property of others.

We always tell the truth.

We respect the families of others.

We are content with what we have.

ABOUT
VOCATIONS

When we were baptized, we became members of the Catholic community. God calls each of us to live our lives in a special way. This is called our vocation.

God calls some people to a religious vocation. This is a call to a special way of life in the Church. Priests, religious sisters, and other clergy have a religious vocation.

Many Ways of Helping

God calls Catholics to help in many different ways.

Catholics can help at Mass by reading the Bible, leading songs, or giving Holy Communion to people.

Catholics can teach others about God. They can teach Jesus' Gospel message.

Catholics can visit sick people who need help. Catholics can teach in schools.

Catholics who share the good news about Jesus' love are answering God's call.

God calls some people to help the Church in a special way. Priests do the work of Jesus by saying Mass, celebrating the sacraments, and leading the parish community.

Some religious sisters and brothers teach. Other religious sisters and brothers help the poor. Others serve as parish leaders.

Deacons help our priest in many ways. At Mass they can read the Gospel or give the homily. Deacons can celebrate the sacraments of Baptism and Matrimony. They also help people who are in need.

As you get older, God will call you to serve him in your Catholic community. You might read the Bible at Mass. You might be a teacher. Perhaps God will call you to a religious vocation.

ABOUT
RELIGIOUS SISTERS

Religious sisters have a special vocation. They belong to groups called communities. They spend their lives working for God and for all of God's people.

Some sisters teach in elementary schools, high schools, and colleges. Some sisters work among the poor, the sick, and the elderly. Still others are missioners. They bring the good news of the Gospel to people in countries all over the world.

Each religious sister makes important promises. She promises God that she will love him. She promises that she will live a simple life. She promises to be an example of what is good. She promises to be an example of a good Christian life.

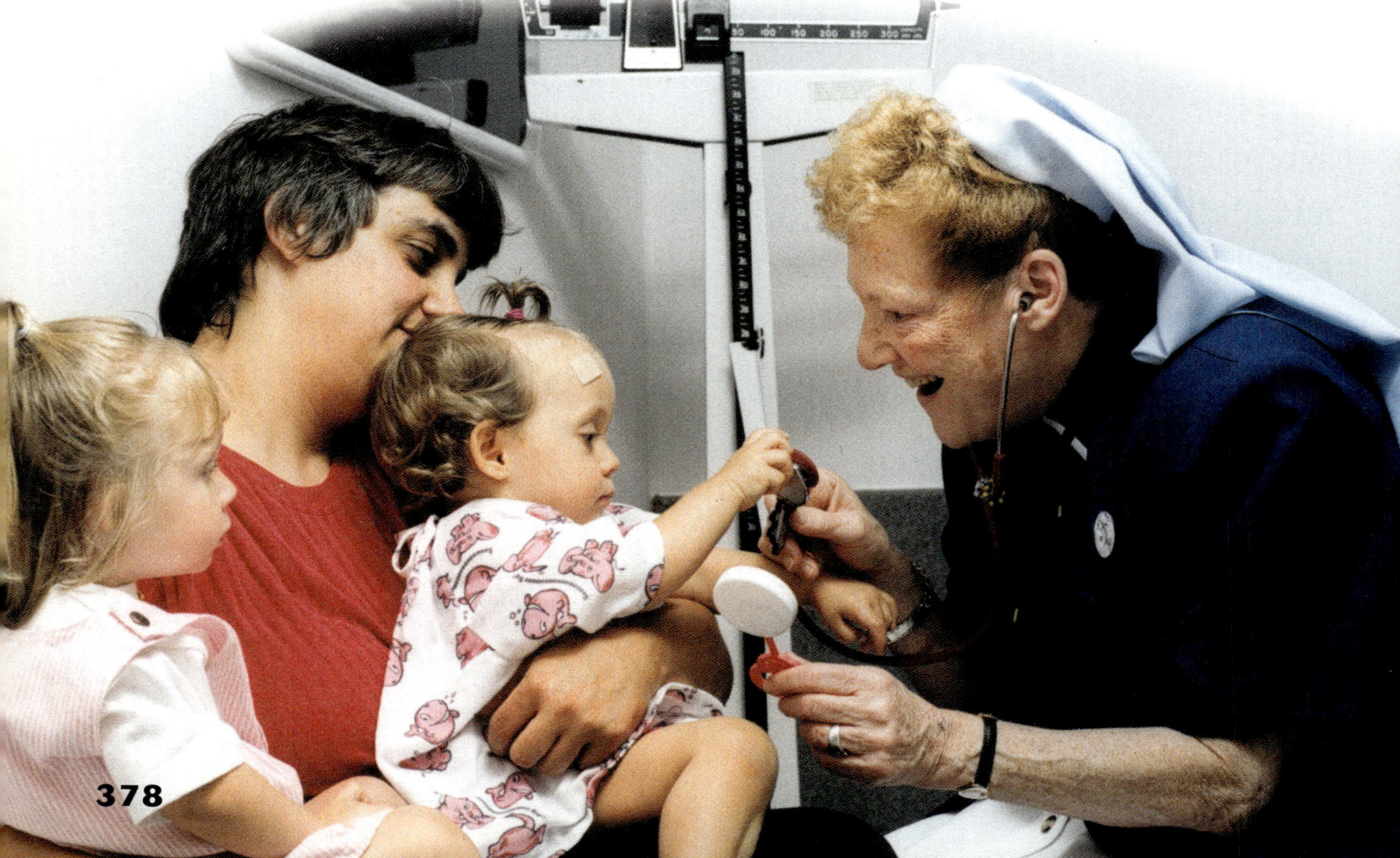

HOW CATHOLICS PRAY

Prayer is talking and listening to God. We can pray anywhere and at any time. God is everywhere. God always hears our prayers.

ABOUT
KINDS OF PRAYER

When we pray, we spend time with God. We need to pray every day.

Everyone can pray. There are many different reasons why we pray.

We can pray for someone we love. We can say a prayer to praise God. We can say a prayer of sorrow to God. We can pray just to share our thoughts with God. We can say, "I love you, God." We can pray to say, "Thank you, God."

We can pray with others, as we do at Mass. We can pray by saying a prayer quietly in our hearts. We can pray by sitting very still. We can just listen to the sounds around us.

A dance, a song, and a smile can all be a special prayer. If our hearts are filled with love, then our actions become special prayers.

ABOUT

THE LORD'S PRAYER

The Lord's Prayer is a very special prayer. Jesus taught us the words to say.

In this prayer Jesus teaches us to call God "Our Father." In this prayer we honor God. We pray that what God wants for us will be done. We ask God for what we need. We ask God to keep us safe. Then we say, "Amen."

The Lord's Prayer

Our Father, who art in heaven, hallowed be thy name;

God is our Father. We praise God.
We pray that everyone will say God's name with love.

thy kingdom come;

Jesus told us about God's kingdom. God's kingdom is happiness with God forever.
We pray that everyone in the world will know God's love.

thy will be done on earth as it is in heaven.

We pray that everyone will live in peace. We pray that everyone will follow God's word.

Give us this day our daily bread;

God is good. God cares for us. We pray for our needs and for the needs of others.

and forgive us our trespasses as we forgive those who trespass against us;

We ask God to forgive us when we sin. We remember that we must forgive others, too.

and lead us not into temptation,

We pray that God will help us make good choices.

but deliver us from evil.

We pray that God will protect us from things that may harm us.

Amen.

Our "Amen" says that Jesus' prayer is our prayer, too.

Map of Palestine in the Time of Jesus
N
W
E
S
Mediterranean Sea
GALILEE
Sea of Galilee
Nazareth
SAMARIA
River Jordan
Jerusalem
Bethlehem
Dead Sea
JUDEA

Write-In Glossary

absolution ______________________ is the forgiveness of God given through the priest in the sacrament of Reconciliation.

act of contrition An ______________________ is a prayer that tells God we are sorry for our sins. We make up our minds not to sin again.

Anointing of the Sick ______________________ **of the** ______________ is a sacrament that brings peace and the forgiveness of Christ to people who are sick or elderly.

Baptism In the sacrament of ______________________ the Church welcomes us as new members. Baptism takes away original sin and all other sin. The Holy Spirit comes to us in Baptism.

Bible The ______________________ is the word of God. It tells about the love God has for us. It is also called the Scriptures.

bless ______________ means to ask for God's good will toward someone.

blessing A ______________ is a prayer that praises God. A blessing asks for God's gifts for others or for ourselves.

Body of Christ The Catholic Church is the ______________ ______________

confession ______________ is telling our sins to a priest in the sacrament of Reconciliation.

Confirmation In the sacrament of ______________ we receive strength to follow Jesus.

conscience Our ______________ helps us know right from wrong.

contrition ______________ means to be sorry and to want to stay away from sin.

Eucharist The sacrament of ______________ is a sacrifice and a special meal of thanks. In the Eucharist, God gives us the Body and Blood of Christ.

forgive To ____________ means to excuse or to pardon. God is always ready to forgive us.

free choice ____________ is the freedom God gives us to choose between right and wrong.

Gospel The word ____________ means "good news." The four Gospels are books in the Bible that tell the good news of Jesus' life and teachings.

grace The gift of God's ____________ helps us stay away from sin. Grace is God's loving presence in our lives.

Great Commandment The ____________ ____________ is "You must love God with all your heart, all your thoughts, and all your strength. Love your neighbor as yourself."

hallowed ____________ is another word for "holy."

heaven ____________ is happiness with God forever.

holy To be ________ means to be like God. Holy people act like Jesus.

Holy Communion We receive the Body and Blood of Christ in ________________.

Holy Orders ________________ is a sacrament of service. God calls some men to serve the Church as deacons, priests, and bishops.

homily A ________________ is a talk given by a priest or deacon. It explains the Bible readings we have heard at Mass.

Intercessions ________________ are prayers to God for the needs of other people. We pray a prayer of intercession called the Prayer of the Faithful at each Mass.

justice ________________ means treating people as they deserve to be treated.

Liturgy of the Eucharist The ________ **of the** ________ begins as we prepare to share a special meal with Jesus.

Liturgy of the Word The ______________ **of the** ______________ is the part of Mass when we listen to readings from the Bible.

Lord's Prayer The ______________ is a special prayer that Jesus gave us. We remember that God is the Father of all people in this prayer.

Mass The ______________ is a special meal that Jesus shares with us. The Mass is both a sacrifice and a celebration.

Matrimony ______________ is a sacrament of service. God calls husbands and wives to love one another and form a Christian family.

mortal sin A ______________ is a serious sin that separates us from our friendship with God.

New Commandment The ______________ is "Love one another as I have loved you."

Nicene Creed Catholics tell what they believe when they pray the ______________ ______________ at Mass. The creed tells about God's love for us and about how Jesus saved us.

original sin ____________ is the sin of the first people on the earth. Because we are born with original sin, it is harder for us to do what is right.

peace ____________ is not fighting. It means getting along with others.

penance A ____________ is a prayer or kind act to make up for doing wrong.

Petitions ____________ are prayers in which we pray for our own needs.

praise ____________ is a joyful type of prayer. It celebrates God's goodness.

prayer ____________ is talking to and listening to God.

Prayer of the Faithful The ____________ **of the** ____________ is the last part of the Liturgy of the Word at Mass. During this prayer we pray for ourselves and for people everywhere.

priest A ____________ is a person called by God to lead the community in worship. The priest leads the celebration of the Eucharist..

Psalms ______________ are prayers from the Bible that are often sung. Psalms are often prayers of praise and thanksgiving to God.

Reconciliation ______________ is a sacrament of healing that celebrates God's love and forgiveness.

Resurrection ______________ is Jesus' being raised from the dead to new life.

sacrament A ______________ is a special celebration of the Church. The sacraments are signs that God is here with us now.

sacraments of initiation There are three ______________ ______________. In Baptism we become members of the Church. In Confirmation we receive strength to follow Jesus. In Eucharist we share a special meal with Jesus.

sacrifice A ______________ is a special gift that is given out of love.

saint A ____________ is a person who shows great love for other people and for God.

Savior A ____________ is someone who rescues others from danger. Jesus is our Savior. He saves us from sin and death.

Scripture The Bible is also called ____________. Scripture means "Holy Writings."

service ____________ means doing work that helps others.

sin We ____________ when we choose to hurt others and turn away from God.

Son of God ____________ is a special title for Jesus. Jesus is human, like us. Jesus is also God's Son.

spiritual gifts The ____________ help us follow Jesus. Some of these gifts are knowledge, wisdom, healing, and faith.

temptation A ____________ is a feeling of wanting to do something that is wrong.

Ten Commandments The ______________________ are God's laws. They teach us how to love God, others, and ourselves.

trespasses ______________________ are sins or wrongs we do on purpose. Trespasses separate us from God and other people.

venial sin A ______________________ is a less serious sin than a mortal sin. It weakens our friendship with God, but it does not take it away.

vocation A ______________________ is God's call to us to live our lives in a special way.

word of God The ______________________ is another name for the Bible.

works of mercy The ______________________ tell how Jesus wants us to help others.

Index

T

V

W

CELEBRATING CATHOLIC SCHOOLS

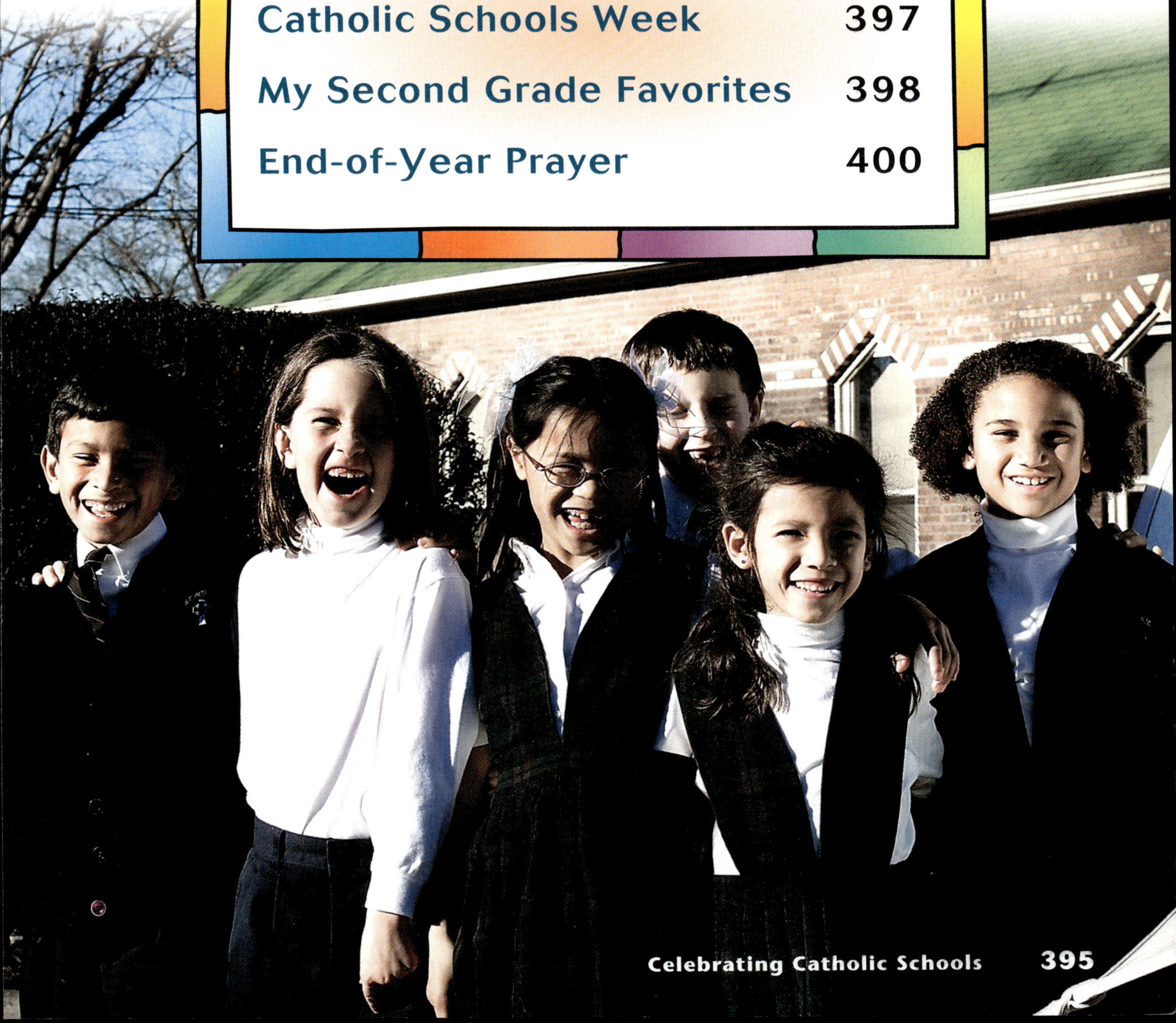

CATHOLIC SCHOOLS IN AMERICA

Archbishop John Carroll

Father of American Catholic Education

Pope Pius VI made John Carroll the first bishop in the United States in 1789. That same year, George Washington became our first president. The two men were close friends and true patriots.

About 25,000 Catholics lived in the United States at that time. They lived in places far from each other. Only about thirty priests were in the country. The Pope asked Bishop John Carroll to guide the growth of the Catholic Church in the new nation.

John Carroll believed in Catholic schools. In these schools children would learn about Jesus and about their religion. He worked with Mother Elizabeth Ann Seton to open Catholic schools in Baltimore. With his blessing, religious sisters began Visitation School. In 1791 Archbishop Carroll opened what is now Georgetown University.

Prayer Celebration for Catholic Schools Week

A Thank-You Prayer

All: In the name of the Father, and of the Son, and of the Holy Spirit. Amen.

Side 1: Let us thank God for our Catholic faith.

Side 2: We thank you, Lord.

Side 1: Let us thank God for our Catholic schools.

Side 2: We thank you, Lord.

Side 1: Let us thank God for our parents.

Side 2: We thank you, Lord.

Side 1: Let us thank God for our teachers.

Side 2: We thank you, Lord.

Side 1: Let us thank God for people in Catholic education.

Side 2: We thank you, Lord.

All: Dear God, send your Holy Spirit to us. Holy Spirit, help us to do our school work well. Jesus, our brother, help us to follow your example. Amen.

MY SECOND GRADE FAVORITES

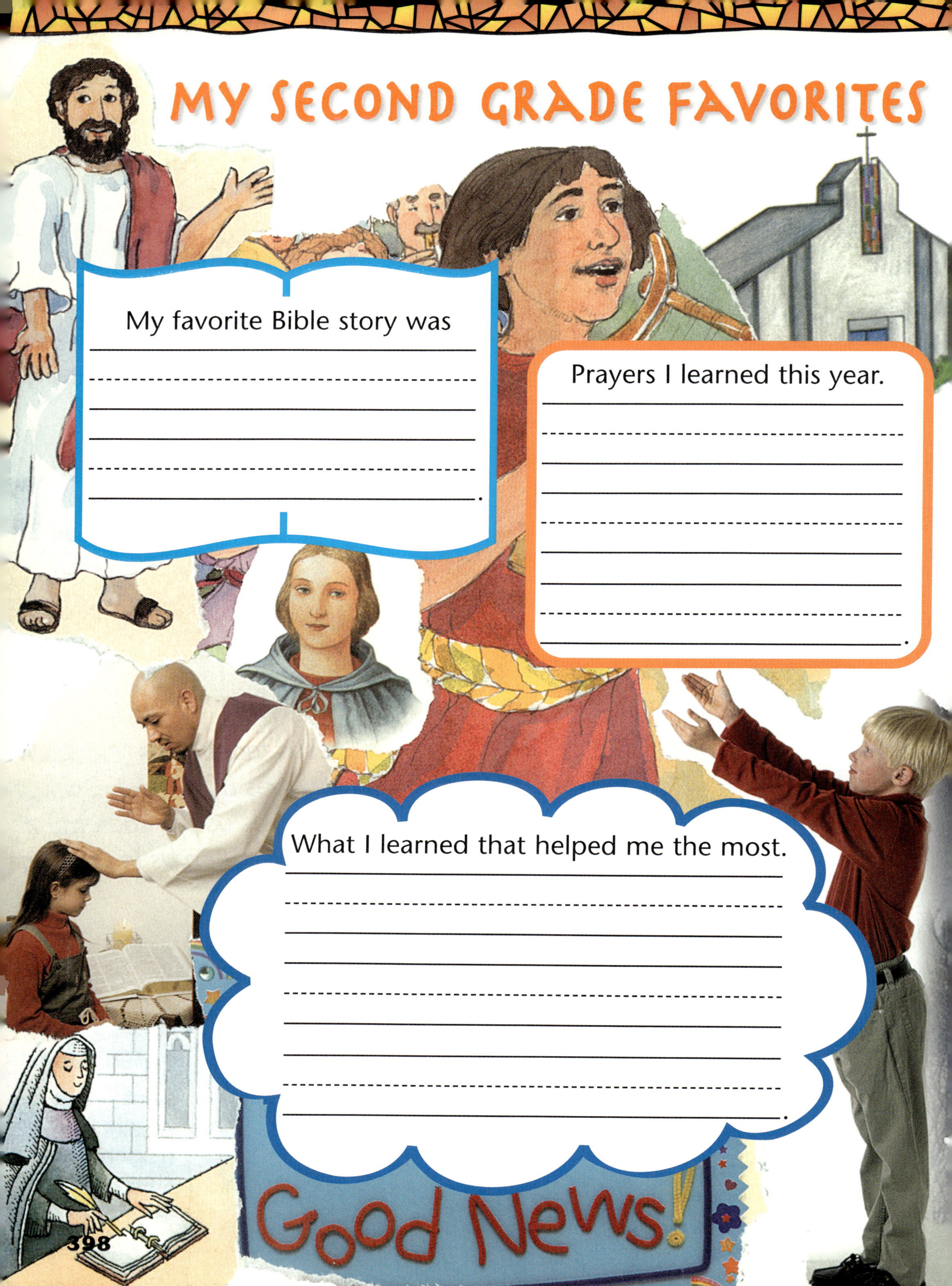

The best activity was on page

____________________.

Something I learned that I will always remember

____.

My favorite saint was on page

____________________.

My picture of me following Jesus.

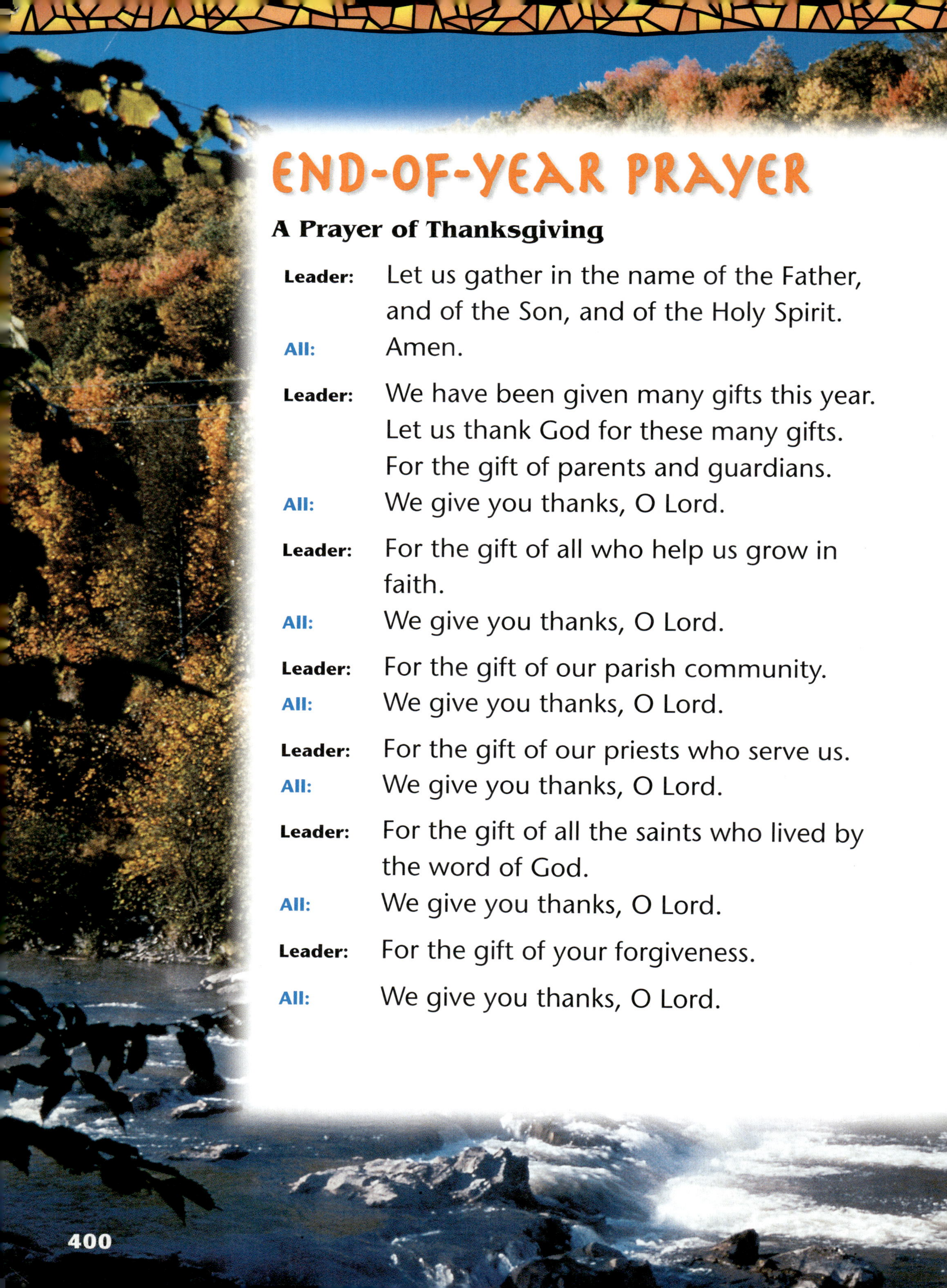

END-OF-YEAR PRAYER

A Prayer of Thanksgiving

Leader: Let us gather in the name of the Father, and of the Son, and of the Holy Spirit.

All: Amen.

Leader: We have been given many gifts this year. Let us thank God for these many gifts. For the gift of parents and guardians.

All: We give you thanks, O Lord.

Leader: For the gift of all who help us grow in faith.

All: We give you thanks, O Lord.

Leader: For the gift of our parish community.

All: We give you thanks, O Lord.

Leader: For the gift of our priests who serve us.

All: We give you thanks, O Lord.

Leader: For the gift of all the saints who lived by the word of God.

All: We give you thanks, O Lord.

Leader: For the gift of your forgiveness.

All: We give you thanks, O Lord.

Leader: For the gift of the Bible.

All: We give you thanks, O Lord.

Leader: For the gift of your commandments.

All: We give you thanks, O Lord.

Leader: For the gift of the works of mercy.

All: We give you thanks, O Lord.

Leader: For the wonderful gift of your presence in the Eucharist.

All: We give you thanks, O Lord.

Leader: For the invitation to share the Body and Blood of Christ at Mass.

All: We give you thanks, O Lord.

Leader: For the gift of one another.

All: We give you thanks, O Lord.

Leader: For these and all the gifts we have received this year, we thank you, God, our Father. Be with us and protect us this summer as we go forward to continue to be your disciples. We ask this in the name of Jesus, our brother, and the Holy Spirit.

All: Amen.

Credits

DESIGN: Pronk & Associates and Scott Foresman

COVER: Gene Plaisted, OSC/The Crosiers

SCRIPTURE ART: Diane Paterson

ILLUSTRATIONS: B Maria Jimenez; C Maria Jimenez; D Maria Jimenez; E Maria Jimenez; F Maria Jimenez; G Maria Jimenez; H Maria Jimenez; I Maria Jimenez; 6 Diane Paterson; 7 Craig Terlson; 11 Nan Brooks; 17 Diana Magnuson; 20 Diane Paterson; 21 Jack McMaster; 23 Heather Holbrook; 25 Lyn Martin; 30 Diane Paterson; 32 Diane Paterson; 33 Jackie Snider; 34 Masami Miyamoto; 35 Laura Huliska-Beith; 37 Laura Huliska-Beith; 40 Diane Paterson; 41 Melinda Levine; 42 Diane Paterson; 44 Cindy Rosenheim; 47 Lyn Martin; 49 Bernadette Lau; 50 Heather Holbrook; 53 Marion Eldridge; 61 George Ulrich; 62 Diane Paterson; 65 John Hovell; 66 Dorothy Stott; 70 Diane Paterson; 73 Randy Chewning; 76 Diane Paterson; 77 Barb Massey; 78 Morella Fuenmayor; 86 Diane Paterson; 91 Jean & Mou-Sien Tseng; 94 Beth Foster Wiggins; 98 Diane Paterson; 101 Paige Billin-Frye; 103 Laura Huliska-Beith; 109 Jean & Mou-Sien Tseng; 111 Shelley Dieterichs; 117 Judy Stead; 118 Diane Paterson; 121 Dirk Michiels; 123 Tom Sperling; 126 Teresa Berasi; 130 Diane Paterson; 138 Anne Stanley; 141 Barb Massey; 141 George Hamblin; 142 Diane Paterson; 143 Scott Cameron; 146 Dorothy Stott; 146 Roman Dunets; 147 Dorothy Stott; 149 Donna Perrone; 150 Julie Monks; 153 George Hamblin; 154 Diane Paterson; 157 Bernadette Lau; 159 Linda Howard Bittner; 164 Marcie Hawthorne; 165 Shelley Dieterichs; 174 Diane Paterson; 178 Anne Stanley; 182 Bernadette Lau; 185 Randy Chewning; 188 Diane Paterson; 191 David Austin Clar; 197 Randy Chewning; 198 Diane Paterson; 203 Lauren Cryan; 209 Randy Chewning; 210 Diane Paterson; 213 Amy Vangsgard; 215 Pat Hoggan; 220 Marcie Hawthorne; 221 Marion Eldridge; 230 Diane Paterson; 234 Jill Dubin; 241 Morella Fuenmayor; 243 Bernadette Lau; 244 Diane Paterson; 247 Gregg Valley; 251 Marion Eldridge; 253 Donna Perrone; 254 Diane Paterson; 257 Teresa Berasi; 259 Tom Sperling; 262 Donna Perrone; 265 Pat Hoggan; 266 Diane Paterson; 268 Heather Graham; 269 Bernadette Lau; 271 Sandy Rabinowitz; 276 Marcie Hawthorne; 277 Shelley Dieterichs; 283 Lyn Martin; 284 Linda Weller; 285 Lyn Martin; 286 Diane Paterson; 290 Bernadette Lau; 293 Dorothy Stott; 294 Bradley Clark; 296 Jack Kurtz; 297 Kathleen Kuchera; 298 Bernadette Lau; 299 Jackie Snider; 303 Bradley Clark; 306 Cindy Rosenheim; 307 Bernadette Lau; 313 Morella Fuenmayor; 314 Diane Paterson; 315 Barb Massey; 316 Diane Paterson; 317 Barb Massey; 322 Diane Paterson; 323 Bernadette Lau; 325 Bernadette Lau; 328 Diane Paterson; 329 Donna Perrone; 331 Cindy Rosenheim; 332 Diane Paterson; 336 Dorothy Stott; 337 Bernadette Lau; 341 Bernadette Lau; 342 Heather Graham; 343 Bernadette Lau; 345 Heather Holbrook; 354 Carol Lusignan; 357 Tom Sperling; 383 Elizabeth Wolf

PHOTOGRAPHS: Every effort has been made to secure permission and provide appropriate credit for photographic material. The publisher deeply regrets any omission and pledges to correct errors called to their attention in subsequent editions. Unless otherwise acknowledged, all photographs are the property of Scott Foresman, a division of Pearson Education.

1 © The Israel Museum, Jerusalem; 1 Jim Whitmer; 4 Gene Plaisted, OSC/The Crosiers; 5 Michael Newman/PhotoEdit; 9 (BL) © Michael Newman/PhotoEdit; 9 (CR) © Tony Freeman/PhotoEdit; 9 (CL) © Myrleen Ferguson Cate/PhotoEdit; 15 © W.P. Wittman; 16 National Gallery, London/Photograph by Erich Lessing/Art Resource, NY; 29 Vince Streano/Corbis; 29 Kwame Zikomo/SuperStock; 29 Myrleen Ferguson/PhotoEdit; 36 ©Donald Nausbaum/Stone; 48 Pablo Coral/Corbis; 57 Z. Radovan, Jerusalem; 60 Hermitage Museum, St. Petersburg, Russia/Bridgeman Art Library, London/SuperStock; 64 (R) Gene Plaisted, OSC/The Crosiers; 68 ©Tim Brown/Stone; 72 Corbis Sygma; 80 Fotopic/Omni-Photo Communications, Inc.; 84 Everett Collection, Inc.; 92 Adam Woolfitt/Woodfin Camp & Associates/PictureQuest; 96 Everett Collection, Inc.; 104 CLEO; 113 James L. Shaffer/Editorial Development Associates; 113 Barry Searle/©Sonia Halliday Photographs; 116 Newberry Library, Chicago/SuperStock; 120 (R) AKG London Ltd.; 122 Sisters of Providence White Violet Center for Eco Justice; 124 Robert Fried Photography; 128 Macduff Everton/Corbis; 129 ©Lawrence Migdale/Stone; 132 (BR) James L. Shaffer (c); 133 (CL) © H.Rogers/Art Directors & TRIP Photo Library; 133 (BL) James L. Shaffer (c); 134 Stephen McBrady/PhotoEdit; 136 Paul Conklin/PhotoEdit; 140 Catholic News Service; 144 (BR) © Photo Courtesy of Prudential Spirit of Community Awards 2000; 148 Bettmann/Corbis; 148 Danilo G. Donadoni/Bruce Coleman Inc.; 152 Gene Plaisted, OSC/The Crosiers; 156 (BR) Discalced Carmelite Nuns of Maryland, Inc.; 158 Index Stock Imagery; 158 Peterson/Liaison Agency; 163 Patrick Johns/Corbis; 164 Milt & Joan Mann/Cameramann International, Ltd.; 169 Z. Radovan, Jerusalem; 169 © Tony Freeman/PhotoEdit/PictureQue; 176 (BR) Gene Plaisted, OSC/The Crosiers; 180 Tony Freeman/PhotoEdit; 183 Felicia Martinez/PhotoEdit; 184 Bettmann/Corbis; 186 (R) Myrleen Ferguson Cate/PhotoEdit; 196 Catholic News Service; 200 (BR) Photo(s) by Jim Whitmer; 201 (B) © David Muench/Corbis; 204 Milt & Joan Mann/Cameramann International, Ltd.; 207 Milt & Joan Mann/Cameramann International, Ltd.; 208 Scala/Art Resource, NY; 214 (BR) © John Henley/Corbis; 216 John Gerlach/TOM STACK & ASSOCIATES; 216 C.P. George/Visuals Unlimited; 225 David Lees/Corbis; 225 Michael Newman/PhotoEdit; 228 Rasmussen/Sipa Press; 229 Catherine Karnow/Woodfin Camp & Associates; 232 (TR) The Granger Collection; 232 (BR) Giraudon; 234 Don Smetzer/Stone; 236 Peter Cade/Stone; 240 Courtesy, Little Sisters of the Poor; 242 (B) Gene Plaisted, OSC/The Crosiers; 246 Jane Robbins/Young Sparrow Press; 248 Michael Gadomski/Animals Animals/Earth Scenes; 252 Dick S. Ramsay Fund/Brooklyn Museum; 256 (BR) © Tony Freeman/PhotoEdit; 258 Lori Grinker/Contact Press Images; 258 Daemmrich Photography; 258 Charles Caratini/Corbis Sygma; 258 Lawrence Migdale/Stock, Boston/PictureQuest; 260 © David Tejada; 264 ©Richard T. Nowitz; 270 Robert Brenner/PhotoEdit; 270 Myrleen Cate/PhotoEdit; 275 Stuart Cohen/Image Works; 281 (CR) Ariel Skelley/Stock Market; 282 (BL) Roger Allyn Lee/SuperStock; 288 (Bkgd) © I. Genut/Art Directors & TRIP Photo Library; 291 (BR) The Granger Collection; 292 (BR) Ariel Skelley/Stock Market; 294 (Bkgd) Tim Brown/Getty Images; 295 (BR) International Stock/ImageState; 296 Jack Kurtz; 300 (B) Bridgeman Art Library; 304 (Bkgd) Photo(s) by Jim Whitmer; 308 (B) Réunion des Musées Nationaux/Art Resource, NY; 310 (TL) © Grandmaison Photography/AGStockUSA; 312 (BR) © H. Rogers/Art Directors & TRIP Photo Library; 317 (Bkgd) © Bill Wittman; 318 SuperStock; 320 (BR) Scala/Art Resource, NY; 321 (BL) Francisco Cruz/SuperStock; 324 (BR) Gene Plaisted, OSC/The Crosiers; 326 (CR) Houses of Parliament, Westminster, London, UK/Bridgeman Art Library International Ltd.; 330 (B) Tim Thompson/Corbis; 338 (BR) Gene Plaisted, OSC/The Crosiers; 339 (B) AP/Wide World Photos; 340 (BR) Scala/Art Resource, NY; 343 (B) Skjold Photographs; 344 (BR) Giraudon/Art Resource, NY; 345 (BC) Myrleen Ferguson Cate/PhotoEdit; 346 (B) Bettmann/Corbis; 347 (TR) Flip Schulke/Corbis; 348 (CR) Bettmann/Corbis; 349 (B) © OnRequest Images; 350 (BR) Jan Butchofsky-Houser/Corbis; 350 (TR) © Archives of the University of Notre Dame; 352 (B) Steve Liss/TimePix; 353 (C) Jennifer Thermes/Getty Images; 359 © W.P. Wittman; 361 © W.P. Wittman; 362 MacDonald Photography/Unicorn Stock Photos; 363 MacDonald Photography/Unicorn Stock Photos; 368 Gene Plaisted, OSC/The Crosiers; 372 Myrleen Ferguson/PhotoEdit; 372 The Pierpont Morgan Library/Art Resource, NY; 373 Jose L. Pelaez/Stock Market; 377 CLEO; 379 Myrleen Ferguson/PhotoEdit; 380 Bob Daemmrich/Stock, Boston/PictureQuest; 396 (TR) ©Collection of Georgetown University Library-Special Collections Division; 396 (TR) ©Collection of Georgetown University Library-Special Collections Division; 396 (BR) © Peter Cade/Getty Images; 397 (BR) © Comstock Inc.; 400 (Bkgd) SuperStock.